ADVANCE PRAISE

"Dr. Bill Cohen has done it again! In his latest book, *Peter Drucker's Way to the Top*, he managed to stomp on my complacency, grabbed my attention, and sat me down to learn some new lessons and to unlearn a few stale truths that were no longer working. Thanks for the new epiphanies and insights, and for reminding me of what's important."
Ariel Koropitzer, CEO, iSubTech Corp.

FROM OTHER DRUCKER BOOKS BY DR COHEN

"Peter F. Drucker helped me found the Peter F. Drucker Academy in China. It was a pleasure to see his concepts and what he instructed me brought together in one place and explained so that they could be applied by any executive. This is a valuable and useful book."
Minglo Shao, Chairman and CEO of the Bright China Group, Founder of the Peter F. Drucker Academy

"William Cohen's new book has brought the genius of Drucker to life for all of us. Easy to read, easy to understand and easy to use. The book should be in everybody's leadership toolbox."
Howard Behar, President, retired, Starbucks International

"Bill Cohen has done us a wonderful service by faithfully combing through Peter Drucker's vast writings and weaving together Peter's thoughts on marketing. This has never been done before. We owe it to Bill Cohen to have taken the various strands of Peter's observations on all aspects of marketing and put them together in the 25 chapters of this fine book. I highly recommend his work to you."
Philip Kotler, Distinguished Professor of Marketing, Kellogg School of Management, Northwestern University

"I am constantly amazed at how Bill Cohen is able to effectively and elegantly draw on his experience as Drucker's student and then tie it together with his own research. If you want to apply Drucker's theories and see how to do them in the real world, this book is definitely the place to start."
Jim Kouzes, Co-Author of the bestselling *The Leadership Challenge*, Dean's Executive Fellow of Leadership, Leavey School of Business, Santa Clara University

"*A Class with Drucker* is more than a book – it is a great gift, bringing Peter Drucker and his classroom alive for all of us who never had the privilege of a class with Drucker . . . Bill Cohen's journey with Drucker adds a new dimension to our understanding and appreciation and keeps the Drucker legacy vibrant and alive for future generations."
Frances Hesselbein, Chairman and Founding President,
Leader to Leader Institute

"Of the thousands of testaments written about a giant of our times – none can rival this. Only one person in the world could have written this book. Cohen has captured the essence of Drucker in every page of this marvelous book. Bravo, Bill – Peter would be proud!"
Bill Bartmann, Billionaire Business Coach and winner of the
National Entrepreneur Award from NASDAQ, USA Today,
Merrill Lynch and the Kauffman Foundation

"Cohen has written with clarity and authority about the major challenges facing leaders today. And Cohen, like Drucker, emphasizes *responsibility* and *integrity* in leadership, qualities so desperately needed today. I strongly recommend this book to you."
Joseph A. Maciariello, Horton Professor of Management Peter F. Drucker and Masatoshi Ito Graduate School of Management, Co-Author of *The Daily Drucker* by Peter F. Drucker and *Management* by Peter F. Drucker

"Peter F. Drucker helped me found the Peter F. Drucker Academy in China. It was a pleasure to see his concepts and what he instructed me brought together in one place and explained so that they could be applied by any executive. This is a valuable and useful book."
Minglo Shao, Chairman and CEO of the Bright China Group,
Founder of the Peter F. Drucker Academy

"Bill Cohen was a singularly stimulating and attractive student from whom my colleagues on the faculty and I learned at least as much as we could teach him."
Peter F. Drucker, 1983

PETER DRUCKER'S WAY *to the* TOP

LESSONS FOR REACHING YOUR LIFE'S GOALS

WILLIAM A. COHEN, PHD

LONDON   NEW YORK   SHANGHAI
MADRID   BARCELONA   BOGOTA
MEXICO CITY   MONTERREY   BUENOS AIRES

Published by
LID Publishing Limited
The Record Hall, Studio 204,
16-16a Baldwins Gardens,
London EC1N 7RJ, UK

524 Broadway, 11th Floor, Suite 08-120,
New York, NY 10012, US

info@lidpublishing.com
www.lidpublishing.com

A member of:

BPR
Business Publishers Roundtable

www.businesspublishersroundtable.com

Printed in Great Britain by TJ International
ISBN: 978-1-911498-75-9

Cover design: Matthew Renaudin
Page design: Caroline Li

CONTENTS

FOREWORD

When General William (Bill) Cohen asked me to write a foreword for his new book, *Peter Drucker's Way to the Top*, I was somewhat reluctant. As Dean of the Peter F. Drucker and Masatoshi Ito Graduate School of Management, I lead the Drucker School and protect the Drucker brand by making sure it remains well known and relevant to today's audiences, but I do not see myself as a Drucker scholar. That's not to say I don't know Drucker's work – I do, but I do not spend long periods of time studying what Drucker wrote. There are many others who have deeper knowledge of Drucker's work.

So, I sat down to read Bill's manuscript, not sure what I could add or say about his latest book.

I must say, I enjoyed reading the manuscript. It ultimately focuses on self-development but the book also provides a great overview of Drucker's work and includes many examples – both old and new – to illustrate the points being made. Personally, I enjoyed the summaries provided of Drucker's life and thought Bill covered the numerous topics on Drucker well.

The finished product is a well thought out and well-written book – an interesting read. Topics include entrepreneurship, leadership, ethics, integrity, and morality, and management by objectives, but Bill also provides an overview of the qualities of a leader and guidelines on how to develop these qualities.

I took many notes but I want to highlight two areas that caught my attention.

First, Drucker famously said: "Results are gained by exploiting opportunities, not by solving problems." (Bill uses this quote to open Chapter 19). I think of this quote a lot because I do feel that today's managers often spend an inordinate amount of time going from one fire to the next or implementing policies that address problems (even if the problem occurred just once). This is especially true of older-established firms in industries facing disruptive change – e.g. hotels (think: Airbnb), taxis (think: Uber or Lyft), education (think: online classes or MOOCs), or cable television (think: Netflix or YouTube).

As a manager, it is easy to allow the day to be filled with finding solutions to problems. Instead, and as Drucker advocated, a manager should switch his or her mindset to proactively identifying and exploiting opportunities. This simple shift of focus has a tremendous ripple down effect on organizational culture and employee engagement. I highly recommend it.

The second area that caught my attention was Chapter 5 on ethics. In this chapter, Bill opens with another Drucker quote: "Integrity may be difficult to define, but what constitutes lack of integrity is of such seriousness as to disqualify a person for a managerial position." And in Chapter 4, Bill reminds us of the well-known Drucker position on character: "Character is not something you can fool people about. The people with whom a person works, and especially subordinates, know in a few weeks whether he/she has integrity or not. They may forgive a person for a great deal: incompetence, ignorance, insecurity or bad manners, but they will not forgive a lack of integrity."

These quotes are powerful reminders that we find ourselves in an unusual environment today, one in which many world political and business leaders do, at times, demonstrate a lack of integrity.

As we look for guidance, Bill first offers definitions in Chapter 5: "Ethics is a code of values. Integrity speaks to adherence to this code of values. Morality is the quality of this adherence." He then reminds us that Drucker saw Confucius's principles as "the most successful and most durable [code of values] of them all", partly because Confucius focused on interdependence and the importance of mutual obligations between, for example, employers and employees.

My takeaway is a reminder that we have an obligation to lead with integrity and a responsibility to lead well-run, sustainable organizations that flourish and allow those connected to the organizations to also flourish. I am also reminded that we operate in a global and highly interconnected world where we have much to learn from people who have come from different histories and operate in different contexts.

I want to close by congratulating General William Cohen on his latest book, *Peter Drucker's Way to the Top*.

Professor Jenny Darroch
Henry Y. Hwang Dean, The Peter F. Drucker and
Masatoshi Ito Graduate School of Management

CHAPTER 1

HOW DRUCKER BECAME DRUCKER

*The most crucial and vital resource you have
as an executive and as a manager is yourself.*

– Peter F. Drucker

HOW PETER DRUCKER BECAME A GURU

Millions of managers worldwide have heard the name Peter Drucker. Even if you are not involved in management or business you may have heard that Drucker was the most famous management thinker over the last hundred years, and perhaps of all time.[1] Few know, though, that Drucker could easily have qualified as a self-help and motivational guru even though 'guru' was a term he did not agree with when describing himself. Drucker not only believed in and taught self-development, but he practised the methods he developed (which he called self-management) himself. As noted by Drucker researcher Bruce Rosenstein, self-development is a major theme throughout Drucker's writings and teachings.[2] Moreover, Drucker believed that every person was responsible for their own acquisition of learning and applying these principles in their practice of business to reach their personal best. And there was a real reason that this was important. "The most crucial and vital resource you have as an executive and as a manager is yourself; your organization is not going to do better than you do yourself,"[3] he said.

In an article in *Harvard Business Review* he wrote:

We live in an age of unprecedented opportunity. If you've got ambition, drive, and smarts, you can rise to the top of your chosen profession – regardless of where you started out. But with opportunity comes responsibility. Companies today aren't managing their knowledge workers' careers. Rather we must each be our own Chief Executive Officer.

Simply put, it's up to you to carve out your place in the world in of work and know when to change course.

It's up to you to keep yourself engaged and productive during a work life that may span 50 years.[4]

THE METHODS DRUCKER DEVELOPED TO REACH SUCCESS

I don't think that he intended it, but his own career and accomplishments confirmed his concepts. Drucker practised what he taught and wrote. And he reached even the loftiest of his goals and dreams. There are hundreds of great managers, and distinguished professors by the bunch, who could potentially claim the title that Drucker holds. Yet, if you input "The Father of Modern Management" into a search engine, you will see that it is his name which pops out – every time.

How did this inexperienced young man, born and raised in Austria early in the last century become a seer, predicting events decades into the future, an advisor of powerful chief executives and heads of state about what they should or should not do? How did he write books that, years after his death, are read by tens of thousands of executives worldwide seeking success, who often go on to intensely study, reflect on, and apply Drucker's wisdom to managing activities from corporations to politics to religion? It is only Drucker to whom Jack Welch, the legendary CEO of General Electric (*Fortune*'s "Manager of the Century"[5]), Rick Warren, Pastor of the famed Saddleback Church, and billionaire Chinese businessman Minglo Shao share common allegiance for success. And it is only for Drucker's thinking and teachings that managers and academics from around the world have formed formal societies to study his ideas.

DRUCKER'S LITTLE-KNOWN BIG SECRET

I became his student by accident. Before the internet, it was his university that, partly at his urging, hit on the idea of an executive working part-time to earn a PhD. With all my time as Drucker's student and my own considerable time in the military (I was a former Air Force major at the time and started my military service as a cadet at West Point), I never knew of Peter's knowledge or admiration of the Army's training, education, and methods to self-development until I attained my PhD from Drucker and our relationship changed from my being his student. It was partly from what I learned from Drucker that I became an Air Force general before I retired.

Years later, his wife Doris told me that I was his favourite student. I certainly never knew this at the time, nor that this may have been due at least partly to my military background. True, he had on rare occasions cited examples or statistics from the military in illustrating management points he wanted to make to the class. But he did this with many other subjects too, from religions to many other occupations. As his students, we assumed this was further evidence of his vast general knowledge and experience. Once, in class, he commented that the reason for the large losses and missteps in battle during World War I was that "too few generals were killed". This was an odd comment. Not only was Drucker not 'bloodthirsty', in any way, but he wasn't any kind of fire-eater promoting a big military or an enlarged defence budget. According to Drucker, for the first time in history, because of technology, generals were not up at the front where they shared the same dangers as those they commanded. This not only had consequences for leadership, but also for knowing what was happening, and resulted in numerous mistakes in decision-making as well as unnecessary casualties.

After graduation, we had many talks with regard to the military, several of which he initiated. His general knowledge of the profession's methods, training, strategy, and even logistics in the military amazed me. He knew a lot about my profession.

Some years after I studied with Drucker, I graduated from the year-long Industrial College of the Armed Forces in Washington, DC. I was asked if I could recommend a pro bono guest speaker who knew something about business. Of course, I recommended Peter although I cautioned the requester that he rarely travelled great distances to speak. He was already in his 90s and I doubted if Drucker would accept an invitation. I was wrong and was pleasantly surprised when I heard that he had accepted.

Then, in 2004, only a year before his death, his admiration for the military was confirmed in a testimonial he wrote for Frances Hesselbein and General Eric Shinseki's book *Be, Know, Do: Leadership the Army Way* (Jossey-Bass, 2004). "The Army trains and develops more leaders than all other institutions together and with a lower casualty rate," he wrote.

With this I knew Drucker's secret for his personal self-development that he had never divulged, nor previously put in print. Drucker admired the military and had read extensively about military practices and strategy, and as you will see in this book, he applied many of their ideas in his own career.

HOW AVOIDING COLLEGE LED TO GENIUS

Drucker claims to have developed his start because he was encouraged to participate in conversations with his father and his father's friends. This may be common for many fathers, yet one doesn't see their offspring being acknowledged as a genius, or becoming known as the founding father of anything except perhaps grandchildren. But clearly Drucker started with something somehow and his ideas grew to be powerful and effective. He learned from his mistakes and constantly refined his principles over his long lifetime of 96 years. Again, although a fair number of individuals live well into their 90s today they do not necessarily become acknowledged as the 'father of modern management'. Most tend to repeat the same types of mistakes in particular activities without any improvement at all. Such was not the case with Drucker.

As he grew older, Drucker did not at first want to attend a college, at least the way most students do. Instead he took an apprenticeship with a cotton-exporting company in Hamburg, Germany away from his parents. At that time, even more than today, an apprenticeship was mostly applied to the trades. The idea was very much like *The Sorcerer's Apprentice*. Whether the intent was to become a sorcerer or something else, the apprentices were expected to spend their time mastering the work to learn the position. During his apprenticeship, Drucker had been attending night school, studying law at Hamburg University, even though his parents had the money and wanted him to study full-time in a prestigious institution as a more conventional student. After just one year Drucker quit the apprenticeship but continued studying. Then he got his first job as a journalist afterwards writing for a regional newspaper, the Frankfurter *General-Anzeiger*. Moving to

Frankfurt after Hamburg, he again went to night school at the University of Frankfurt. He explained to us, his own PhD students, that he graduated in the easiest doctorate that he could attain; a practical PhD in international and public law.

Until I wrote these words, it never occurred to me that all of us, his students at the time, were or had been senior executives and that we too were studying and working towards a practical PhD in his new PhD programme at what was then Claremont Graduate School. Today it is the Peter F. Drucker and Masatoshi Ito Graduate School of Management, part of Claremont Graduate University. Like Peter, we mostly went to night classes. While we were required to take one or two courses in each discipline, we looked at no discipline in depth nor took a multitude of courses in a single chosen business speciality as most PhD students did then and now. Therefore, while we considered the work challenging, our professors felt, for the most part, that we were getting an easy doctorate, rather than in-depth studies that would help us do research in a single discipline after the acquisition of our doctorates. This must have been very much like Drucker's doctoral study in international and public law at the University of Frankfurt, a degree he completed in 1931. Drucker had designed this PhD, we had been told, to educate 'super managers' for the new challenges coming in the new century.

BEGINNING PUBLIC WORK WITH A PUBLIC HUMILIATION

As a journalist and a doctoral candidate in 1929, Drucker wrote an article which predicted a rosy future and a bullish stock market worldwide. He was forced to retract these words two weeks later in a major newspaper article about the stock market crash that began the world's great depression.[6] It was published in German in the Frankfurter *General-Anzeiger* and entitled "Panic on the New York Stock Exchange". On the bright side, it was early in his career and Drucker learned to be unafraid and to publicly acknowledge his grossly inaccurate prediction, even a major blunder ... but he learned not to make the same mistake twice.

I have seen many faulty predictions made by pundits on national TV over the last few years. Few acknowledge their mistakes and most continue committing similar errors in future predictions. Drucker didn't. He never made the same mistake by attempting to predict the stock market again.

HUMILIATION TURNS INTO APPLAUSE

Drucker continued to make predictions throughout his career. Most of them were years ahead of their time and almost every prediction was heralded as a major success because it was. These ranged from *The End of Economic Man* (the title of his first book) which earned a glowing recommendation in 1939 from one Winston Churchill, not yet prime minister; to the rise of the "knowledge worker" (a term he invented); to how the insurance industry would become a major factor dominating his adopted country (the United States) – published almost 40 years before it happened; to how the country would have to pay a terrible price for the actions of both top management and the unions – predicted decades earlier; to the rise of executive education on the internet; and a lot more. In fact, hardly a day passes that a reader cannot find something written by Drucker and noting his phenomenal ability to predict the future years before a major event occurs – a modern seer who rivals Nostradamus in the magnitude of his predictions but without the mysticism and ambiguity in interpretation! According to Drucker, unlike his failed prediction about the stock market, his much more accurate predictions came "by simply looking through the window" (Drucker's words) and noting events that had already happened. However, a key step that Drucker took, which others did not, was to ask himself what events were likely to mean for the future.

DRUCKER'S ACCOMPLISHMENTS – MORE THAN STAGGERING PREDICTIONS

Drucker did more than gaze into a crystal ball and write about what he saw. In the 1950s Drucker became one of the first to assert that workers should be treated on the asset side of the ledger instead of being listed as liabilities. Additionally, he was one of the first to say that marketing and selling were not the same, and the only one that I know of to claim that selling was not a subset of marketing but could be adversarial to it. It was Drucker who introduced the idea of decentralization, a concept adopted by almost every large organization in the world and the basis of many other management concepts. He promoted management by objectives, whereby performance evaluations are not based on generalities or appearances, but on objectives and goals agreed earlier by both supervisor and subordinate. He introduced the revolutionary idea that since there was no business without a customer, the purpose of a business was not profit after all, but the rather peculiar notion that it was to create a customer. This led to the rise of companies which focused primarily on the customer and thereby became immensely successful. How else do you explain a college dropout like Steve Jobs creating an entire high technology industry? Jobs himself explained: "If you keep your eye on the profit, you're going to skimp on the product. But if you focus on making really great products, then the profits will follow."[7]

Nor was Drucker afraid to point out what everybody knew was in fact wrong. Take Douglas McGregor's management concept of Theory X (authoritarian management) versus Theory Y (participative management) in which most people assumed that Theory Y should always be adopted over Theory X. Drucker pointed out that McGregor had meant only that the two approaches should be further investigated to determine when each was more appropriate for motivating employees, not to adopt one over the other automatically.

HOW DO WE KNOW DRUCKER HAD A METHOD?

Self-development was a major theme throughout Drucker's writings and teachings though it has been overlooked by almost all those who read and even those who to this day analyse Drucker's ideas. "What matters," he wrote, "is that the knowledge worker, by the time he reaches middle age, has developed and nourished a human being rather than a tax accountant or a hydraulic engineer."[8]

Drucker was not putting down tax accountants or hydraulic engineers, but rather trying to say that by his definition, to be a human being, one had to take the time to do more and even become highly proficient in more than one field. Not everyone knows that in addition to his management books Drucker was a professor of Japanese art while teaching at Claremont Graduate School and had co-authored a book on this subject. It was one of the key concepts that he practised to accomplish any goal and to be recognized as one of the best in numerous fields. Yes, Drucker thought that every individual had to become an expert, and be recognized as such, in more than one discipline. This was one of many concepts that he uncovered, developed, and practised to attain the incredible success that was to be his.

In his later years, he gave an interview where he explained that he used methods he had learned in the fourth grade to teach himself, and already by the age of 14 he had decided not to attend college, or at least not in the standard method of choosing a campus, leaving home, and embracing a full-time career as a student. This was the standard method known in Drucker's early 20th-century Austria and is still the regular method in the 21st century for most up-and-coming intellectuals in 21st-century America.[9]

RE-EXAMINING WHAT HAPPENED
WHEN DRUCKER LEFT HOME

For the initial seed that grew into the genius Drucker, we left him, according to his autobiographical description, being allowed to participate and discuss things, on an equal basis with his father and his father's friends. Is that all? Like many modern parents, Drucker's parents wanted to see him off to college. He declined. His own preference was for a different path and he began his apprenticeship. That's pretty weighty stuff when his father, Adolph, was an Austrian civil servant ranked highly enough to be awarded a medal and certificate of appreciation from the Austrian Emperor on his retirement. Drucker's apprenticeship must have been enough to get the attention of his conservative father, although he must have felt proud of his law degree.

His father was a lawyer. Maybe attending law school at night was part of the deal and a way to avoid his father's wrath?

However, studying at night for his law degree and then his PhD wasn't enough to occupy Drucker. He began a programme of reading both fiction and nonfiction books, in what he himself termed "every field". I do not know whether he truly read such a wide variety of books while both working and studying. In *The Practical Drucker* (AMACOM, 2013) I wrote that several years earlier his wife, Doris Drucker, was interviewed and was asked what management books Peter read by the Drucker School at Claremont. She divulged an important secret. Though he read business magazines and newspapers extensively, he only skimmed most management books. However, he did read many books on history, as he sought the lessons they offered that could be adapted to business management. In any case, we would have to write down training himself as one of the keys to how Drucker became the genius known today. Additionally, focus was an important principle that particularly interested him and was not a concept that Drucker ignored.

THE FINAL STEP

As noted, on completion of his apprenticeship and his law degree Drucker neither entered business nor practised law, but worked as a journalist and for a PhD at the same time. However, by then he was on to a system and he left Hamburg for Frankfurt on completion of his apprenticeship in 1929. He got a job as a journalist and at the same time accepted into what he claimed to his students, of which I was one, was the perceived easiest doctorate to get at that time, in international law. So, there he was again, writing and working simulta-neously. However, by then he had decided on a career as an academic. He contacted his uncle at the University of Cologne seeking help in attaining a teaching job.

However, before this could result in an academic position, Hitler came to power in 1933. Although Drucker and his parents were prac-tising Christians, they had direct Jewish ethnic lineage, and fortunately he had the foresight to draw clear conclusions about what was likely to happen to ethnic Jews, Christian or not by religion, under Hitler's rule. He immediately left the country.

Many of Drucker's contemporaries with similar ethnic backgrounds refused to accept what Hitler's rise meant. Drucker had read Hitler's autobiography *Mein Kampf* (*My Struggle*). He said that Hitler was the most dangerous man in Europe. Others said that Hitler was only transitory and would soon disappear. Others yet still refused to believe that anything could happen to the Jews in 'civilized' Germany. They stayed in place and waited for some normalcy to return. Most perished.

Drucker was still in his 20s, hoping for a promising career at the University of Cologne. Instead he dropped everything and left for England within days of Hitler's becoming German chancellor. Drucker may have already known that he himself had the brains and the internal strength to become all that he could be. Perhaps so, perhaps not. I once read that someone who was on the ship with him four years later when he sailed from England to America in 1937 claimed that Drucker, at the age of 28, had already mapped out his future including academia, writing, and consulting. In any case, Drucker did eventually attain these goals and went on to become world famous, although this was far from instantaneous. This book is not so much about what he did, but how he did it. It will show you how to adapt his techniques to your dreams, become whatever you want and reach your own unique goals, just as Drucker did. So, let's move on to Chapter 2 and see how you can do this.

1. Harris, Kathryn. "Peter Drucker, Considered Greatest Management Guru, Dies at Age 95". *Bloomberg.com*, 11 November 2005. https://bit.ly/2K1zW2m.
2. Rosenstein, Bruce. "Peter Drucker's Principles for a 'Total Life'<TNBS>", *The American Society of Mechanical Engineers*, March 2011. https://bit.ly/2mMzYSE.
3. Drucker, Peter F. "Drucker: Manage Yourself and Then Your Company". Lecture before IEDC, 1996. *DruckerAcademy.com*. https://bit.ly/2LCwX5D.
4. Drucker, Peter F. "Managing Oneself", *Harvard Business Review* 77, no. 2 (1999): 64-74.
5. See TimeWarner press release "FORTUNE selects Henry Ford Businessman of the Century; GE's Jack Welch Named Manager of the Century". 1 November 1999. https://bit.ly/2NZaopi.
6. Straub, Richard. "What Drucker Means Around the World", Perspectives. *People and Strategy* 32, no. 4 (2009): 4-5. *Peter Drucker Society of Austria*. "Peter Drucker as Journalist", Peter Drucker Society of Austria. https://bit.ly/2v994by.
7. Jobs, Steve. *Motivating Thoughts of Steve Jobs* (New Delhi: Prabhat Books, 2008).
8. Rosenstein, "Peter Drucker's Principles for a 'Total Life'<TNBS>".
9. Harris, "Peter Drucker, Considered Greatest Management Guru, Dies at Age 95".

CHAPTER 2

FOUR ENTREPRENEURSHIP STRATEGIES THAT DRUCKER USED TO BUILD HIS CAREER

The entrepreneur always searches for change,
responds to it, and exploits it as an opportunity.

– Peter F. Drucker

D rucker was known as the consummate "big company man" consulting major corporations until suddenly and surprisingly in 1985, he wrote a bestselling book called *Innovation and Entrepreneurship*.[1] In this book, Drucker demonstrated how small organizations could not only be successful over their regular competitors, but how these small 'David' companies could also best the 'Goliaths' they competed against. As it turned out, Drucker had the knowledge, passion, and credibility for such a book as he was one of the first to teach an academic course in entrepreneurship for New York University in the early 1950s.

Drucker recognized that small companies have important advantages over larger competitors and that these can be very effective if used properly. One enormous advantage is speed of decision-making and action. To assist 'buy-in' of their employees, large organizations take much longer to make decisions or to respond to a competitor's actions and initiatives. In addition, because of other simple facts of strategy, a smaller competitor could concentrate in markets less attractive to a large corporation where it was less worthwhile for a larger competitor to invest. For example, in the early days of computers a small 96-person, relatively unknown company, ICS, Inc., specializing in computers for education was able to take on mighty IBM head to head. In comparison to IBM, ICS, Inc. was minuscule, yet IBM withdrew from the marketplace. Sure, IBM could have rolled over ICS, Inc. But IBM had better things to do with its resources: other markets, where it could make more money, a lot easier if it abandoned this small and less important market to its tiny competitor.

Drucker set out to think through special strategies which small companies could put to good advantage. He organized his results into four systematic entrepreneurial approaches. They can work for larger organizations as well. In fact, they can work for any entity as a winning strategy under the right conditions.

Consider this: entrepreneurship requires application of specific skills which most organizations already have but frequently fail to take advantage of. These include the willingness to analyse the situation, access the risks, and then the courage to assume these risks when necessary in the implementation of the strategy. The successful practice of entrepreneurship also requires the moral courage to avoid procrastination, and to make decisions followed by action. Drucker certainly had this ability. However, moral courage and overcoming hesitation also require systematic actions. Drucker developed four such strategies and numerous substrategies that he applied in his own career as a management consultant. You can apply them too.

DRUCKER'S FOUR BASIC SYSTEMATIC STRATEGIES FOR ENTREPRENEURSHIP[2]

- Dominance of a new market or industry
- Development of a market which is currently unserved
- Finding and occupying a specialized niche
- Changing the financial calculations of the situation.

Drucker used all four in his own career. He pointed out that these strategies are not mutually exclusive and all four can be used simultaneously, just as he did himself.

DOMINANCE OF A NEW MARKET, NEW INDUSTRIES, OR UNSERVED MARKETS

The basic idea here is very simple. You enter and dominate a market or industry before anybody else does. While an unserved market may not be new, serving it properly or better may well be new and different.

Drucker began to write about business and management when he got involved in a major study for GE (General Electric) immediately after World War II. No doubt his analytical work, presented in an earlier book he had written on industrial markets, helped him to get this assignment. In this study and the resulting book, *Concept of the Corporation*,[3] he discovered that management was considered almost an accidental activity. One worked in finance, accounting, personnel, production, sales, etc. but there was no department of management and there still is not. The function of management is needed in all departments, although a few of these subfunctions were collected under what was then called the Personnel Department and more frequently today, Human Resources.

As a result, Drucker did think deeply about management as a specialized function that needed to be mastered across all departments.

When Drucker went to a bookstore to buy books on management to help him with this early research, the shelves, unlike today, bore only a couple volumes. Drucker decided to fill that space. After several years of study, practice, and analysis, he began to write his own books and soon dominated the market for books about management. In doing this, he reasoned, either consciously or unconsciously, that to really have an impact, his books had to supply something that was missing. He wrote books such as *The Practice of Management* and *The Effective Executive*.[4] His books essentially established the field of modern management and spawned many others to write books in this relatively unserved field. He developed a market which was not being served effectively.

CREATING A NEW MARKET BY SUPPLYING SOMETHING THAT IS MISSING

Drucker thought that there were two basic ways to supply any missing ingredient, whatever that missing ingredient was.

1. Imitate an established success, but to do so in a creative way that supplies what is missing. He called this "creative imitation", a term based on an original idea by marketing professor Theodore Leavitt, then at Harvard.
2. To find a product that already existed, but was currently unsuccessful. He gave this the rather imaginative term of "entrepreneurial judo".

It was always interesting to me that one of these strategies targeted a successful product, while the other targeted one that was not successful.

Drucker did this very effectively with his management consulting. His consulting was like no other. He asked questions of his clients and forced them to think the issue through to provide the right answer. Almost all consultants are asked questions by their clients and they assume it's their duty to provide the answers through the expertise they have gained through their studies and experiences. Drucker felt that asking the right question was the key for him. He took the view that the client was always in a better position to analyse their own situation and provide the right answer. After all, his client was the expert, with the experience in their business and industry. The consultant was not. How could he be? Was the consultant supposed to be an expert in all businesses and all industries? So, Drucker consulted, but he did so by adding the missing element of using the expertise of the client to solve the issue after he had identified the problem through his questions. As he famously asked *Fortune*'s 'Manager of the Century', Jack Welch, shortly after he became CEO of GE. "Are there businesses that GE would not be in if it were not already in them, and if so, what are you going to do about it?"

Drucker told his students that rather than bring his knowledge and experience to an industry in his consulting assignments, he brought his ignorance and lack of specific experience. This was clearly no bar to his effective consulting advice. He was able to charge as much as $10,000 for a few hours per day of using his "ignorance".

HOW IBM USED CREATIVE IMITATION TO STEAL APPLE'S MARKET

Life isn't fair, and neither is what goes on in business. IBM had opted out of even considering the personal computer market because of an error in assumptions made in its market research. It had assumed that a personal computer must be the size and cost of the huge industrial computers that it was already producing. So, IBM calculated that the size of the demand was only 1,000 computers a year. Steve Jobs at Apple, on the other hand, had made no such limits in his assumptions of demand. He recognized the need for personal computers, took the risks, somehow got together the resources that didn't exist and created the entire personal computer industry without having a PhD, with limited investment, and almost no resources. But mighty IBM was still mighty, and the mighty IBM empire struck back. It did this after Apple had proved the market by developing a computer operating system and a computer that became the standard in the industry for a sizable part of the market. Given IBM's challenge as a classroom problem, many students would have guessed that IBM would have created something of the nature of a technical breakthrough. However, the ingredient IBM added was not technical superiority. What IBM did was to create a reliable machine that worked well, and capitalized on the IBM name, and distribution system, and most importantly, it allowed anyone to write software for its system, something Apple didn't allow for its computers. With this strategy, IBM took over much of the market within two years. So, supplying the missing ingredient works, but so does creative imitation.

HOW CREATIVE IMITATION FREQUENTLY WORKS AGAINST INNOVATORS

Drucker thought entrepreneurial judo was a minimal risk strategy because innovators frequently make mistakes with the products that they themselves originally introduce. So sometimes it is relatively easy to take a market away from someone who actually got in the market first. One might argue that IBM's strategy combined elements of both creative imitation and entrepreneurial judo since Apple had erred in trying to control the software for their system. Could be. Understand that in the martial art of judo, the secret is to use your opponent's own strength against him. In Drucker's terms, this might mean that the innovator might even inadvertently ignore a product he invented.

The Japanese picked up the transistor and its radio application and ran with it this way. Even the term 'transistor' was coined by an American, John Pierce. It was invented by Bell Labs but was ignored because Bell Labs didn't think that the technology existed to really make it work in production, Sony did!

Some innovators are confident that they can do pretty much as they please without fear of competitive action. Innovators make this mistake all the time with price. They've come up with an excellent product but persist in charging 'whatever the market can bear' in the mistaken belief that no one else can get in the market. However, maintaining a very high price is almost certain to attract competitors, and the higher the price the more competitors are attracted.

The innovator may also mistake what constitutes value and quality for the buyer. It is always the user that determines what is or is not of value to them, not the supplier. Or, the supplier may try to maximize profits rather than optimize the product. That's what Henry Ford did after successfully innovating and producing the everyman's car in the Model T and famously (or infamously) maintaining that buyers could have any colour they desired so long as it was black. That rather arrogant statement typified the notion that cost Ford leadership of everyman's car for more than 40 years as General Motors (GM) introduced both many colours and options unavailable in the Model T, but at competitive prices also attractive to prospects seeking an economical automobile.

FINDING AND OCCUPYING A SPECIALIZED NICHE

The third of Drucker's entrepreneurial marketing approaches is essentially Philip Kotler's strategy of niche marketing. Drucker called it an "ecological niche". An ecological niche is the place or function of a given organism within its ecosystem. Drucker differentiates this approach by contrasting it as emphasizing positional occupation and control versus the previous strategies emphasizing grappling with competition. According to Drucker, occupying an ecological niche can make a marketer immune from competition altogether because the whole point is to be inconspicuous or to be in a market of what appears to be limited potential, despite the product's being essential, so that no one else is likely to compete until it's too late. The marketer places his offering or company in the optimum niche, in its very own ecosystem. I again refer to that little company, ICS, Inc., which once took on mighty IBM early in the computer wars and forced IBM to withdraw because it appeared that competing wasn't worth the effort. In effect occupying a specialized niche is a version of W. Chan Kim and Renée Mauborgne's popular book, *Blue Ocean Strategy*.[5]

Drucker saw three distinct ways for implementing this approach. First, he suggested gaining a tollgate position. In other words, you control an essential piece of something else needed by competitors such that would-be competitors cannot do business without what you supply. Sierra Engineering Company got itself into this position by being the only company that could manufacture a unique valve for oxygen breathing masks for aviators. If you wanted to sell oxygen breathing masks, you needed that valve.

The other two ways to occupy a specialized ecological niche was to either have a speciality skill, or to work in a speciality market. Life is so specialized today, that it is not so difficult to acquire a speciality in which few can compete in a specific market. Once a chiropractor was a chiropractor, just as a doctor of medicine was a doctor of medicine. This is no longer an accurate description of either of these professions. It's easy to mention oncologists or doctors that specialize in the treatment of cancer or how many physicians are not just surgeons but are cardiologists and how many of the latter perform heart transplants? If you want a board certified upper cervical chiropractor, there are fewer than 100 in all of the US. One man I know drives several hundred miles each way between two major cities several times a year to get these services. If you needed this specialized work, you would probably do the same. ICS, Inc. is as good an example as any of the specialized market. Sure, IBM could have forced ICS, Inc. out of the market had it wanted, but it had other fish to fry, and at that time chose to leave this market without much of a fight.

CHANGING THE FINANCIAL CHARACTERISTICS OF THE SITUATION

Drucker's final entrepreneurial marketing approach is the only one that does not require the introduction of an innovation. In this approach, the strategy *is* the innovation. These innovation strategies were of four distinct types, all having the ultimate objective of creating a customer, something Drucker had been maintaining since his first explorations into the practice of management. Drucker's four different strategy innovations involved:
- Creating utility
- Pricing in accordance with the customer's needs
- Adapting to the customer's social and economic reality
- Delivering what represents true value to the customer.

CREATING UTILS

Years ago, when I studied economics at the University of Chicago I learned that the measurement of utils was a shorthand measurement of utility, and that utility in turn was a representation of relative customer satisfaction. Drucker's first strategy with this approach involves changing the product or service to increase customer satisfaction. The ice cream cone might fall into this category. Although stories abound as to who came up with the idea first, the first patent was issued in 1903 to an Italian immigrant by the name of Italo Marchiony. He had come up with the idea as early as 1896 to solve the problem of his customers breaking or walking off accidently with the glassware that he and every other ice cream supplier used to serve ice cream. He increased the utils of the product by enabling customers to eat what they had formally taken with them. In this case, the marketer increased his own satisfaction as well, by saving the cost of glassware previously lost. The number of ways to increase utils are infinite. A manufacturer of exercise equipment uploaded exercises online for his equipment and made these available to his buyers. A restaurant added a free glass of wine with each meal, making the experience more enjoyable and romantic. Some cinemas add meals, wine, and reserved seats, and enhance the experience of simply going to the cinema and watching a film. The US Post Office made it easier to ship packages by providing free boxes of numerous sizes for priority shipping and convenience to the shipper and by charging a flat rate price for each box size instead of weight-based fees. Their utils were dramatized by the slogan, "If it fits, it ships" which considerably increased sales. Creating utils is easy. All you need to do is to ask yourself what would truly make things easier, or better for your customers from their point of view.

CHANGING HOW A PRODUCT OR SERVICE IS PRICED

Price has long been a tactic used by clever marketers. However, Drucker went further in entrepreneurial marketing. He said that pricing should be done in accordance with the needs of the customer and what the customer buys, not what the supplier sells. The personal photographic industry provides all sorts of good examples for this approach. Who would have thought that cameras would essentially be given to the customer along with the film? After all, neither is what customers really want. What they really want are the photos. And so, customers today can buy a throwaway camera, film, and developed photos at an economical price. Other companies had the idea to mail you free film. You shot the film and mailed the exposed rolls to the developer in protective envelopes along with a cheque covering the number and types of photos you wanted. When your order was fulfilled, you'd find two more rolls of free film. Of course, you needn't buy photo glossies nowadays. You can also get your pictures on CDs. With the advent of digital cameras and such along with cameras built into our mobile phones, the need now is primarily that of photo storage. Not to worry. Companies will store your digital photos and, in many cases, won't charge you anything. They even facilitate in building your photo albums and emailing these albums out to friends and family. Of course, pricing is calculated so that glossies, CDs, or printing your photos on cards, coffee mugs, or other items can all be accomplished, and that's where these companies profit. The Post Office's pricing by ability to fit your shipment in a particular size of box is also an example of changing the pricing. Notice how the pricing has changed from what the seller provides, camera, film, developing, etc. to what the buyer really wants. That's the key to this strategy.

ADAPTING TO THE CUSTOMER'S SOCIAL AND ECONOMIC REALITY

Many marketers speak of the 'irrational customer'. Drucker said that there was no such thing. He stated that the marketer must assume that the customer is always rational, even though this reality may be a far different rationality from the marketer's. Mary Kay Ash, the famed CEO of Mary Kay Ash Cosmetics who build a multibillion dollar company out of a $5,000 investment once told the story about saving the money to buy her first new car on her birthday. She did the financial analysis, looked at the various models from the various manufacturers, checked all the sticker prices, and selected the exact car she wanted. Believe it or not, she even had the money in cash in her purse ready to pay for the car! However, in those days most women didn't buy cars, and she was ignored by the only salesman present selling the car she wanted. Finally, she got his attention, but he was so condescending in his attitude that she asked to speak to the manager. She was told the manager was out to lunch for an hour. Having an hour to kill, she went to the showroom of a competitor nearby. Here the salesman treated her so well, even though she was a woman, that she ignored her previous decision and bought the car he showed her. She didn't return to talk with the manager at the first dealership. Irrational? Maybe, but not in her reality. Similarly, when considering tactical pricing, consider this. If you don't know the best from a selection of products and you need to make an immediate purchase, how do you know which is of the highest quality? Many potential customers go for the most expensive. Irrational? Not in their reality. Remember, it is the customer's reality that counts.

DELIVERING WHAT REPRESENTS TRUE VALUE TO THE CUSTOMER

True value, like quality, is up to the customer, not the marketer. This is critical because customers, or organizational buyers, don't purchase a product or service. They purchase satisfaction of a want or need. This means they purchase value.

Some companies spend millions providing additions that they think represent more value and are appreciated by the customer. Unfortunately, the customer may not think that these additions represent value. To teenagers, value might be defined primarily by fashion. That is, the fashion of what teenagers wear in their geographical area at that time. Even comfort might come in a poor second. To one teenager's parent, value may be represented by durability. To another parent, it might be price. That's why it's so important to do the research to find out who is using the product or service, who might influence the purchase decision, and who is putting out the money. It's about what the customer, and whoever might influence that customer (directly or indirectly), consider to be of value, not the supplier or marketer that is important. Some marketers consider this irrational, too. Value, however, is part of the customer's reality.

---

1. Drucker, Peter F. *Innovation and Entrepreneurship* (New York: Harper & Row, 1985).
2. Ibid., 209.
3. Drucker, Peter F. *Concept of the Corporation* (New York: John Day, 1946).
4. Drucker, Peter F. *The Practice of Management* (New York: Harper & Brothers, 1954) and *The Effective Executive* (New York: Harper & Row, 1967).
5. Kim, W. Chan and Renée Mauborgne. *Blue Ocean Strategy: How to Create Uncontested Market Space and Make the Competition Irrelevant* (Cambridge, MA: Harvard Business School, 2005).

CHAPTER 3

IF YOU DARE THE IMPOSSIBLE, YOU CAN ACHIEVE THE EXTRAORDINARY

For a new technology to replace old,
it must have ten times the benefit.

– Peter F. Drucker

Drucker wrote about what could be done and that included just about everything. His list of extraordinary leaders doing the impossible started in ancient times. His favourite book on leadership was Xenophon's *Anabasis*. *Anabasis* was written 2,300 years ago and Xenophon was a famous historian. But before he turned to writing history, Xenophon was a Greek general elected by soldiers after their former generals had been tricked into coming to a party weaponless and were killed by their enemies. The job Xenophon was elected to perform was to lead 10,000 leaderless Greeks, far from the sea, outnumbered, and in hostile territory over a thousand miles from the interior of Babylon to the coast of the Black Sea. This was a true 'mission impossible'. But Xenophon accomplished it successfully.

MORE OF DRUCKER'S FAVOURITE LEADERS DARED THE IMPOSSIBLE

Coming forward into modern times Drucker's favourite leaders included legendary CEO of GE Jack Welch, who increased GE's revenues by $130 billion; Frances Hesselbein, who became CEO of the Girl Scouts at its nadir, turned the organization completely around and was awarded the Presidential Medal of Freedom by President Clinton; and Rick Warren, who founded the fastest growing church in America, the Saddleback Church. From 200 people at church services Warren built the congregation to 20,000 and it became the eighth largest church in the US.

Extraordinary leaders dare the impossible and as a result they achieve the extraordinary. Challenges that average leaders would have never thought possible to achieve, they do every day. Dare the impossible and achieve the extraordinary aptly describes Drucker's concept of success for any organization.

I GET AN EARLY LESSON
IN ACHIEVING THE IMPOSSIBLE

As a young Air Force lieutenant, I was a member of the 11th Bomb Wing at Altus Air Force Base, Oklahoma. It had been one of the finest B-52 bombing wings in Strategic Air Command. This unit had been the only wing to win the coveted Fairchild Trophy three times for competition in bombing and navigational accuracy. It was also one of the few wings never to have failed an organizational readiness inspection (ORI) which was an important test of our flying and combat ready skills. Its aircrews were consistently rated superior in navigation, bombing, aerial refuelling, and other flying techniques that needed to be mastered in modern strategic air warfare. And these techniques were critical at this point in US history, and maybe the world's history, too. For these were the dark days of the Cold War when the two superpowers, the USA and the USSR, stood nose to nose, both armed with devastating nuclear weapons. The strategy on both sides was one of mutually assured destruction with peace dependent on the clear understanding that nuclear war would obliterate both countries. If one side was seen to be slipping, the other side might risk – just perhaps – a pre-emptive strike and attack.

A GOOD UNIT SLIPS
IN PERFORMANCE

Over a period of months, one unit, my wing, had begun to slip. We failed to complete some of our training requirements successfully. We were forced to make some late take-offs due to maintenance problems. Our sense of mission disappeared. We even failed an ORI. At one time, we had been ranked as one of the top three combat wings in Strategic Air Command. This was based on a system of points measuring everything from success at navigating only by the stars, to the distance from the target our bombs would hit measured electronically. On the same management control system, where we were once top-ranked, we were now ranked last.

On alert with my crew one evening, I received a hurried call from base operations. "There's a new commander on base. His name is Colonel William Kyes. Stay out of his way."

We couldn't stay out of his way, because Colonel Kyes visited us that night even while we were on alert on the runway with real nuclear weapons. He cancelled all leaves of absence. All free time of any sort that had been granted was rescinded until further notice. This included weekends and even crew rest after flight. Colonel Kyes moved commanders and staff he judged poor to positions of little or no responsibility on the spot. He encouraged others to retire. No individual's career was sacred. Our mission was clearly deemed more important.

Colonel Kyes met with each of the 1,500 officers and airmen reporting to him in the wing. He told each where we were going – back to the top position in Strategic Air Command – and he told us exactly how we were going to get there. He said we would brief every mission that was to be flown to him or his staff personally before we would fly it. Moreover, pilots had to know as much about the target as their bombardiers and navigators. And bombardiers and navigators had to be able to back up their pilots as well.

If you wanted a transfer out of the unit, Colonel Kyes would get you one. If you stayed in the wing, you were going to work pretty hard. And this was supposed to be peacetime and only a readiness for combat – we weren't actually fighting anybody.

At first, we hated Kyes. Our wives and girlfriends hated Kyes. Those whose careers he hurt especially hated him, and some did leave the Air Force. It was hard work without Colonel Kyes, but with him there it was much harder. Slowly our hard work began to show results. We improved. Our bombs were scored right on target. Maintenance problems began to disappear, and we took off exactly on time. The ground crews and maintenance personnel maintained our aircraft so that they flew better than they had ever flown before. Whether we were flying over oceans or the North Pole, our navigation based on use of a sextant and the suns or stars kept our aircraft always on course.

Flight crews, ground crews, and support personnel of all types worked together as a team, and they worked together well.

A couple of months after Colonel Kyes arrived, we had another surprise ORI. We not only passed but scored higher than we had ever done so in the past. We were now ranked number one and a strange thing began to happen. We felt pride in ourselves and pride in Colonel Kyes as our commander. Our hate turned to respect. Some months later when Colonel Kyes left the 11th Bomb Wing on his promotion to brigadier general, there was a genuine sense of loss. Our respect had by then turned to something approaching love.

Due to an untimely death caused by illness, Colonel Kyes was never promoted beyond brigadier general. But for this tragic event, I believe he would have been promoted on up and eventually attained the fourth star of a full general.

General Kyes' approach taught me some important lessons about leadership and the difference one individual can make in helping an organization to reach its goals, especially when this individual dared the impossible. Undoubtedly, it must have seemed impossible to take an organization which had fallen over several months of neglect, and to turn it around to reach the top. Yet I have seen this lesson accomplished repeatedly and Drucker saw it, too. I have seen it in large organizations and small, both in military organizations and civilian, and in formal organizations and informal ones. Drucker knew that one individual and his or her leadership makes all the difference between success and failure. In other words, you can win by leading others to dare the impossible. However, it wasn't just that one leader, that one man or woman doing this, but rather it was almost always a case of a group 'reaching for the stars' – daring the impossible. And it applies to all types of organizations, including sport.

DARE THE IMPOSSIBLE AND
CREATE A MIRACLE ON ICE

In the Winter Olympics of 1980, the Soviet team was the heavy favourite in hockey. It had won nearly every world championship and Olympic tournament since 1954 and had won the gold medal in the previous four Olympics. The Soviet team was led by players who were legendary in the sport. The American team wasn't even a close comparison. Their players weren't even on the same page. It even had only one returning player from the previous Olympic team, while the Soviet team included several players who were on full-time duty preparing for their Olympic roles while in the Red Army. They had the time and resources to get and stay in top form. The American team was made up of a mixture of amateur and collegiate players that had only recently been selected for their positions. They barely knew one another. There was even some hostility among the American players because of a bitter collegiate rivalry between two college teams that each had contributed several players. To pull this team together and win anything seemed an impossible assignment. Nevertheless, much to everyone's surprise, the American coach, Herb Brooks, brought the team together, dared the impossible, and achieved the extraordinary as his team defeated all international competitors and went on to both defeat the mighty Soviet team and to win the Olympic gold medal.

VINCE LOMBARDI AND
THE GREEN BAY PACKERS

No doubt you've heard of the great American football coach, Vince Lombardi. He was supposed to have said, "Winning isn't everything, it's the only thing." I'm told that what he really said was, "Winning isn't everything, but not expecting to win is." Lombardi took over as head coach of the professional Green Bay Packers team when even its very existence was uncertain. The team's record the year before Lombardi took the job was just one win, one tie, and ten losses. It was the worst year in the team's history. In Lombardi's first year as head coach the Packers had seven wins. Many said that this was impossible before it happened. Many observers called it a "unique, one time, miracle". Despite these comments Lombardi was named Coach of the Year. Surprise, surprise, with almost all the same players, the year following his arrival, Green Bay won the NFL regional championship and just missed winning the overall NFL title by a few yards on the final play. The third year Lombardi's Packers won the NFL championship title, too. These were the same players that were losers before Lombardi came. Lombardi went on to lead the team to three straight league championships without a loss and five total league championships altogether in seven years, including winning the first two Super Bowls ever played following the 1966 and 1967 NFL seasons. Want to be like hockey coach Herb Brooks or an NFL football coach Vince Lombardi? Dare the impossible!

THE MAN WHO DID THE IMPOSSIBLE IN ACADEMIA

You probably haven't heard the name Professor Richard Roberto. I didn't hear much about him, and I was on his home turf of California State University Los Angeles (CSULA) at the time. Professor Roberto was an engineering professor. He was also the chief faculty advisor to students who competed in a special competition, which concerned designing, building, and racing a solar car.

In 1990, with no prior experience in solar vehicle technology, his students, mostly undergraduates, designed and built the CSULA's first solar-powered electric car and entered the 1,600 mile Sunrayce from Orlando, Florida to Warren, Michigan. CSULA has a relatively small engineering school. It has some smart students, but it doesn't necessarily collect the engineering geniuses found in some of the top engineering schools. Rather, it has one of the highest percentages of students who are first in their family to go to college, most with very modest family incomes. Since CSULA was competing with students from top national graduate schools, everyone knew it had virtually no chance of winning.

THE SURPRISING RESULTS

Amazingly, the CSULA students came in fourth place nationally. But CSULA did more. It accomplished the extraordinary. It was number one in California, besting such well-known schools as the University of California and Stanford University. As Drucker frequently said, "What everybody knows is usually wrong."

A fluke? Maybe. Except that in 1993, they held the second national solar race with new designs, new cars, and mostly new students. CSULA did the same thing all over again with a new car, Solar Eagle II. This time, the CSULA team came in third nationally racing from Dallas, Texas to Minneapolis, Minnesota. Again, CSULA beat much better funded, much better researched universities to finish number one among other top-tier California universities in the race. Experts at the top schools in California were floored. They had the top students, they also had the resources in money, facilities, and alumni volunteers from top engineering firms. They had everything. How could this possibly happen?

Four years later, Roberto's students built Solar Eagle III to enter Sunrayce 97. This time CSULA raced from Indianapolis, Indiana to Colorado Springs, Colorado. It was 1,250 miles, and it took nine days, the competition was stiffer than ever before. There were 36 top-flight entries such as MIT, Yale, and even my own alma mater, West Point, the first engineering school in the USA. In California things were even tougher. Combined teams from Stanford University and the University of California at Berkeley vowed to overwhelm this state-school upstart.

Would CSULA prevail again in California? The Stanford/UC Berkeley teams came in third and second among California teams. But, CSULA was number one again in California. There were also some interesting national results. MIT came in second nationally. But CSULA was first in the USA. Roberto had dared the impossible three times, and not only succeeded every time, but crowned it all by winning the national award number one.

The *Los Angeles Times* quoted CSULA spokeswoman, Carol Selkin, "In the past, the winners were big-name schools with four-year research institutions and big money. We're a state university with no research arm. These other schools had people clamoring to support their team, doctors and lawyers. We just didn't have that."

What CSULA had was a leader who was willing to go after and achieve the impossible. In interviewing Roberto, I discovered something that hadn't come out in the press coverage. Ninety per cent of Roberto's students on the solar team were undergraduates. Their competitors, MIT, Stanford, Berkeley have a huge number of students in engineering many of whom are graduate students. The students at CSULA hadn't even received academic credit for their work. Many had to work part time jobs just to go to school. "About 50% of the students had family incomes of less than $20,000," Roberto told me. And only about 5% of CSULA students wanted careers in engineering compared to a national average of better than 7%.

"How did you do it?" I wanted to know. Roberto told me that the secret was reliability. "Our car just didn't break down, not once," he said.

But I knew there was more to it. At first, he was evasive. Finally, he told me his secret. "I'm like an unknown basketball coach," he said. "And that suits me fine. It is how it should be for the good of the team. The press wants to talk to our winning players, our drivers, those who had their hands on building the car. I stay in the background. Outsiders don't need to know me or know my name. The less I am in the forefront, the better for the team. This way, our team members get the publicity, and they get the job offers. They work hard for it, and they deserve it. I always refer questions to the students or to public relations. I'm proud to be their coach." Professor Roberto was a leader who rejoiced in the successes of those he led. Unfortunately for CSULA, Professor Roberto retired before the next race. CSULA never won another race. In fact, CSULA never entered another race. Perhaps they just couldn't find another leader like Professor Roberto who would dare the impossible and achieve the extraordinary.

YOU CAN LEAD BEFORE YOU ARE
MADE A PAID SUPERVISOR

There are numerous situations in which leaders are required, and in every one you can dare the impossible, whether it is organizing a company picnic, coaching a volleyball team, or being in charge of an annual savings bond drive. Frances Hesselbein, started as a volunteer and went on to became CEO of the Girl Scouts. She was so good that she was promoted to paid positions and finally to the CEO position. During this time, the Girl Scouts had been on a continual decline for many years. She turned this around and did such a great job against the most impossible odds, that she was awarded the Presidential Medal of Freedom by President Clinton. A friend of Peter Drucker, she founded what became the Frances Hesselbein Leadership Institute that promotes non-profit leadership following his concepts. She accepted the first Chair of Leadership at West Point, and I'm proud to say that she sits on the advisory board of my non-profit graduate university.

THE MOST IMPORTANT DECISION
YOU NEED TO MAKE

Why don't more leaders dare the impossible to achieve the extraordinary? There is a very important decision that these leaders we've talked about made before they dared the impossible. Peter Drucker told us that the first and most important decision is to become the kind of leader that would do this. Like much of Drucker's advice, this pronouncement sounds self-evident, overly simplified, and maybe even a trifle absurd. The truth is that it is profoundly true and important. For someone who has never dared the impossible, acceptance of these responsibilities may be challenging. Those who have not had the responsibility and authority of leadership at this level of importance fear both of these, the responsibility and the authority. They fear something going wrong, they fear being blamed for actions which may not be fully under their control, they fear that followers will not follow and they fear making the wrong decision. Many would-be leaders are afraid of the embarrassment and penalties of failure. Some individuals who have the capability to become great leaders never accept the challenge because they are afraid of failure. They go through life with a fear that limits the success they could achieve and the contributions they might make by helping others, if they could only overcome this fear. If you can act on this knowledge and make this decision, Drucker's wisdom can help you and will have a major impact on your life.

DARING THE IMPOSSIBLE REQUIRES PREPARATION

Mary Kay Ash built the billion-dollar Mary Kay Cosmetics corporation, beginning with only $5,000. She hired her first group of saleswomen and planned on living on her husband's salary until she started making money. Two weeks before she was going to open her doors her husband died of a heart attack. Experts told her that her situation was impossible and advised her to quit before she even started. She didn't. She had learned how to dare the impossible as a child.

When she was only three years old her father was invalided with tuberculosis and couldn't take care of himself. Her mother went to work to support the family. Mary Kay accepted the responsibilities for cleaning, cooking and caring for her father. I think she was nine years old at the time. She totally ran the household during the day. She made the decision to be the kind of leader who dared the impossible before she even knew what leadership was. The lessons she learned helped to develop her self-confidence, she learned to disregard well-intentioned, but bad advice and to persevere to success in an age when women were supposed to stay at home and let the men have professional lives.

If you haven't yet made the decision to dare the impossible, you can develop the trait of doing so by:

- Learning to take risks – just decide what's the worst that can happen and press on!
- Building your self-confidence by always raising your hand to offer your leadership – even if you fail, and sometimes you will, you'll learn important lessons.

- There is a first time for everything. Someone has to be first. Why not you? Many told Obama he was wasting his time running for president. They told Trump the same thing. Someone probably told Meghan Markle that there was no way she could marry Prince Harry. Oh yeah?

To achieve the extraordinary, you need to follow Drucker's way and go for the impossible.

CHAPTER 4

DRUCKER'S INSIGHTS INTO THE ESSENCE OF LEADERSHIP AND SUCCESS

*Above all, today's manager and career professional
has a responsibility to develop himself.
It is a responsibility he has towards his institution
as well as toward himself.*

– Peter F. Drucker

A bout 30 years ago I initiated a special study called the Combat Leadership Study. This grew out of my search to find the most challenging leadership situation and leaders who were successful in such situations as well as in management functions in business. There are many challenging conditions for leadership, of course. I felt that most likely this might be in life-and-death situations: the hospital room, unexpected situations on the street, emergencies at sea, a shark attack or a near drowning, an emergency in the air, an automobile accident, or a heart attack. But for an environment of leadership that might encompass any or all of those mentioned, it's hard to beat the almost daily leadership challenges of combat on the battlefield. Here there are daily settings that are not only routinely dangerous and life-threatening, but usually neither leaders nor those led would prefer to be involved if they had the freedom of choice. The payoff for the leader and those led is also usually higher than any other situation even if life and death were considered secondary to the main issue of defeat of an enemy.

Drucker focused on success in a very different way. He noted that many in the North American business culture experience confusion and sometimes even disgust with the very concept of success. He suggested replacing the word 'success' with a completely different word: 'contribution' when discussing one's own vocation or fulfilment of responsibility. He pointed out that contribution leads to prosperity.[1] Although use of the word 'contribution' may sound a bit strange when used in this context, it is appropriate to many fields of human endeavour. This confirms what we noted earlier. Success on the battlefield requires major effort and sacrifice. It presents a major challenge.

BATTLEFIELD LEADERSHIP PRESENTS THE GREATEST CHALLENGE

"Give me liberty, or give me death!" exclaimed Patrick Henry, who served as the fourth and sixth post-colonial governor of Virginia in a speech before the Virginia Convention on 23 March 1775 at St John's Church in Richmond, Virginia. His speech convinced the Virginians to commit the troops which helped the colonists win independence during the Revolutionary War. This underscores the important outcome of many battlefield successes or failures: "liberty or death".

Leadership in a battle probably represents the greatest challenge for any leader. In combat, conditions are frequently severe. Even weather can play an important role and may cause the cancellation of planned operations, and it may create particular problems such as when air or other support had been planned. There are of course, other terrible hazards besides weather. There is greater uncertainty than in other type of human activity. Moreover, the competition is not just trying to beat you or those you lead, but by necessity may seek to take your life to accomplish their own goals.

As Drucker pointed out to me once, "In no other type of leadership must the leader make decisions based on less or less reliable information." Workers of the type we refer to as soldiers may need to perform their duties with little food and irregular sleep. They must all take great risks. No wonder most followers and leaders alike would prefer to be somewhere else and doing something else.

While there are true military geniuses in battle, the clear majority, in most organizations, are ordinary men and women. In many battles, not all may be professionals. One side or the other may not even be trained properly or thoroughly, while not all are suited to their jobs or assignments. Professional or amateur, all are stressed far more than in any other situation or occupation. Moreover, leaders must not only carry out the mission, but do their best to protect the lives of those they lead at the same time. So, battle probably represents a worst-case condition. No wonder even traditional motivators such as high pay, good benefits, and job security may not be as effective as in other human endeavours. Moreover, there is no 'business as usual' on the battlefield. While there may be a normal routine, every day presents new and different challenges.

In battle leadership, leaders help their followers to reach very difficult goals and complete very arduous tasks despite everything. Leadership in battle can be the worst conditions any leader may encounter, and for this reason instead of managing workers in a battle it is important to lead them. In leading under terrible conditions, good battle leaders build and lead organizations which get things done ethically, honestly, and for the most part under the circumstances, humanely.

UNDERLYING LESSONS THAT ARE STILL THE BASIS OF ALL LEADERSHIP SUCCESS

I wondered whether there were underlying principles or lessons from this type of 'worst condition leadership' which were at the root of all leadership success. Thus, the motivation for my study.

To do this study, I sought subjects who had not only led in battle, but also had gone on to demonstrate successful civilian careers in leading non-military activities as well. The foundation of my research was a survey sent to more than 200 former combat leaders and conversations with hundreds more. All had become successful in the corporate world or in other non-military organizations after leaving the armed forces. Among the responses I received in the initial phase, 62 were from generals and admirals. I asked these former combat leaders what they had learned from leadership in battle. I asked about the tactics they used, about the importance of their style and the most important actions a leader must take. I asked about adapting these lessons in their civilian careers.

I found that while there were successful leaders practising assorted styles of leadership, there were universal principles or concepts that successful leaders followed to dramatically boost productivity and achieve extraordinary success in all types of organizations. The Emperor Napoleon, one of history's pre-eminent military leaders, developed and published 115 maxims on the conduct of war. How many hundreds of leadership principles would I uncover after analysing and tabulating the input from so many respondents?

Surprisingly, I discovered that approximately 95% of the responses I received boiled down to only eight principles. However, each of these leaders had seen one or more of these eight principles help them to achieve extraordinary results in their careers. More than a few wrote special notes or letters to express their support for my project.

It was as if they had seen extreme physical payment for what they had learned. They knew its value, and they didn't want to see it wasted.

In a latter phase of my research, I interviewed other successful senior business leaders and reviewed dozens of corporate situations and the actions taken by these corporations' senior leaders. Some also had combat experience in the armed forces. Most did not. Some allowed me to use their real names and companies. Some preferred to remain anonymous. Some had developed their own lists of principles of leadership over the years. While their lists differed from each other, they invariably included some version of the eight responses I had developed from my surveys. I also looked at 7,000 years of recorded history to confirm or to disprove these concepts in different settings.

I decided that these were far more than principles, they were Universal Laws of Leadership. There are hundreds of excellent techniques and rules that people may follow as guidance in leading others. But these eight are essential. I believe they are the very essence of all leadership. These eight laws are simple, but even one of these laws can make an important impact in any project on the results achieved. This is because you can make a lot of mistakes and still succeed as a leader. But if you violate one of these universal laws, it will have a measurable negative impact, even if you are ultimately successful. Of course, no one can guarantee success, because there are other factors which might override anything a leader may be able to do. But, there is no question that if you follow the universal laws, your chances of success increase greatly. I believe that these laws are powerful and that the consequences of following them or not can be the determining factor for success for most leaders in most situations. These are the eight laws that I uncovered:

1. Maintain Absolute Integrity
2. Know Your Stuff
3. Declare Your Expectations
4. Show Uncommon Commitment
5. Expect Positive Results
6. Take Care of Your People
7. Put Duty Before Self
8. Get Out in Front.

This work resulted in several books which discussed or incorporated the eight universal laws. As I became president of an accredited non-profit graduate school, I took note of these laws up close and saw that most who practised them were not only successful leaders, but that they were also highly successful in their careers. General Ronald Fogleman became Chief of Staff of the Air Force and was gracious enough to write the foreword to my first book explaining the eight universal laws. Many successful leaders wrote testimonials including General H. Norman Schwarzkopf who had recently led and been successful in the Gulf War and retired General and later Secretary of State Alexander Haig Jr, as well as astronaut Colonel Frank Borman and former marine Robert Lutz who was then vice chairman of the Chrysler Corporation and Bill Bartmann, who made and lost several fortunes and authored the book, *Bouncing Back*, and who was once listed as the 25th wealthiest man in America, right ahead of Ross Perot, in a survey published in *Forbes* magazine. Years later, I asked both General Fogleman and Bill to join the board of trustees of the graduate school that I co-founded.

I had a lengthy discussion about each law with Peter Drucker, these discussions were published first in my book *Drucker on Leadership*.[2] We had gone to what was Drucker's favourite Italian restaurant in Claremont near where he taught, and over a spaghetti lunch I discussed my research in some detail. Here is each law followed by Drucker's response to my inclusion on the list:

1. MAINTAIN ABSOLUTE INTEGRITY

"You are entirely right and absolutely correct in listing this as your first law. A leader can be well-liked and popular and even competent and that's all well and good, but if he lacks integrity of character he is not fit to be a leader."

Drucker had written in one of his books: "Character is not something you can fool people about. The people with whom a person works, and especially subordinates, know in a few weeks whether he/she has integrity or not. They may forgive a person for a great deal: incompetence, ignorance, insecurity or bad manners, but they will not forgive a lack of integrity."[3]

2. KNOW YOUR STUFF

"This seems obvious, but some managers do try to cut corners rather than mastering the knowledge that they must have and that is essential to the quality of their performance."

Drucker wrote: "leadership rests on being able to do something others cannot do at all or find difficult to do."[4]

3. DECLARE YOUR EXPECTATIONS

"I'm uncertain what you mean by this. If you mean that a leader should declare his objectives, his mission – by all means."

4. SHOW UNCOMMON COMMITMENT

"The failure of many is because they show no commitment, or commitment to the wrong goals. This gets back to your third law. Commitment comes from a worthy mission and then strong commitment."

Drucker wrote (referring to what non-profits could teach business): "non-profit directors tend to have a personal commitment to the organization's cause. Few people sit on a church vestry or a school board unless they deeply care about the religion or education."[5]

5. EXPECT POSITIVE RESULTS

"There is a cautionary tale. One must not be a 'Pollyanna'. Still the central thought is correct. One cannot be negative and succeed in anything."

Drucker wrote: "Whenever you see a successful business, someone once made a courageous decision."[6]

6. TAKE CARE OF YOUR PEOPLE

"Many managers are failing to do this, and it will catch up with them."

Drucker wrote: "A leader has responsibility to his subordinates, to his associates."[7]

7. DUTY BEFORE SELF

This point requires some further explanation. What I meant by this is that the leader had a duty to accomplish the mission and a duty to take care of those for whom he or she was responsible. The leader's own needs must come only after fulfilling these duties.

"This should be the basis of all leadership. The leader cannot act in one's own interests. It must be in the interests of the customer and the worker. This is the great weakness of American management today."

Drucker wrote: "Douglas MacArthur ... built a team second to none because he put the task first ... He was also unbelievably vain, with a tremendous contempt for humanity, because he was certain that no one came close to him in intelligence. Nevertheless, he forced himself in every single staff conference to start the presentation with the most junior officer. He did not allow anybody to interrupt."[8]

8. GET OUT IN FRONT

"Very true whether junior leader or the CEO the leader must be where the work is the most challenging. During World War I, the deaths among higher ranking officers was rare compared with those they caused by their incompetence. Too few generals were killed."

Drucker wrote: "the human being himself determines what he contributes."[9]

Peter was enthusiastic about the eight Universal Laws of Leadership, and for more than 25 years I have taught the laws to individuals and corporations all over the world.

THE ESSENCE OF SUCCESS

However, one day I was looking at what Bill Bartmann had written in endorsing my first book on this subject. Bartmann's endorsement was as follows: "You have discovered the essence of success. It will be mandatory reading for all of our managers because it will not only help them to become better leaders, but also enjoy a more successful life." I realized that Bill was right. The real authors of the eight Universal Laws of Leadership, those who I had surveyed and interviewed, had used them to become successful as leaders, but they were more than laws of success in leadership: they were as Bill had said, the essence of success in anything.

I recalled an incident that had occurred when promoting the book. I had arrived early at a radio station. In those days, I had the laws printed on business cards and I had handed one of these to the host of the radio show. He looked them over while we awaited the start of his show. Suddenly he exclaimed in amazement: "These laws are exactly what I have been looking for! I have had problems with my oldest son. These laws tell me exactly what I can do to overcome my problems with him." I encouraged him and told him that as a parent he was a leader, and that the laws would help him with leading his son towards better behaviour. All this was true, but what I didn't realize at the time is that the eight Universal Laws of Leadership were actually the eight universal laws of success in any endeavour. I realized that Bill Bartmann, the 25th wealthiest man in America at the time had been using them and recognized them for what they were, while Drucker and I were focusing on leadership. Drucker, too, had been using them unconsciously to attain his own success, and I found supporting evidence of this in his writings outside of the discipline of leadership. Of course, I had been using them as well.

1. Lee, Joshua Henry. "The Future of Economic Man: How Management Can Maximize Institutional Potential, Increase Human Prosperity and Create a Functioning Society". A manuscript awarded a top-15 place by the Drucker Forum, in the Global Drucker Challenge, Managers/Entrepreneurs Category, 2017. https://bit.ly/2mCyI7l.
2. Cohen, William A. *Drucker on Leadership: New Lessons from the Father of Modern Management* (San Francisco: Jossey-Bass, 2009).
3. Drucker, Peter F. *Management: Tasks, Responsibilities, Practices* (New York: Harper & Row, 1974), 462.
4. Drucker, Peter F. *On the Profession of Management* (Boston, MA: Harvard Business Review Books, 1998), 92.
5. Drucker, Peter F. *Managing for the Future* (New York: Truman Talley Books, Dutton, 1992), 209.
6. Drucker, Peter F., quoted in Barry Popik, "Entry from 8 May 2016". The Big Apple. https://bit.ly/2voW9SU.
7. Drucker, Peter F. *Managing the Nonprofit Organization: Practices and Principles* (New York: Harper Collins, 1990), 27.
8. Ibid., 23.
9. Drucker, Peter F. *The Practice of Management* (New York: Collins, 1986), 13.

CHAPTER 5

DRUCKER'S VIEWS ON INTEGRITY, ETHICS, HONOUR, AND DOING THE RIGHT THING

Integrity may be difficult to define, but what constitutes lack of integrity is of such seriousness as to disqualify a person for a managerial position.

– Peter F. Drucker

I didn't become good friends with Doris Drucker, Peter's widow, until several years after his death. I knew who she was of course, and I had met her formerly, but we didn't know each other well or socially. What had happened is that my first book on Drucker, *A Class with Drucker*[1] had been scheduled for publication in November of 2007. The first global symposium of Drucker Societies was held the same year at the Peter F. Drucker and Masatoshi Ito Graduate School of Management where Drucker had taught. Ira Jackson, then Dean of the Drucker School, who had written the foreword for my book had asked me to speak about the book and Drucker. Of course, I was honoured to accept his invitation. Normally at the Drucker School I was introduced as "Doctor Cohen" since I had been the first PhD graduate of the then new programme for practising managers which Drucker and Dean Paul Albrecht had developed. However, on this occasion Dean Jackson introduced me as "General Cohen", a title I normally use only when I am with the military. Doris was in the audience.

During the lunch break Doris sought me out. She said, "Bill, we have known each other for years, but until Ira introduced you as a general, I really didn't know who you were. Peter spoke about you all the time. You were his favourite student." Without even thinking about it I put my hand over my heart. Her words were a great and unexpected honour, and this led to a friendship which lasted until she passed away some years later at the age of 103. In the intervening years, we attended many meetings at Claremont where she was called upon to say a few words about her husband. I don't remember her ever speaking about his genius, his many accomplishments, or their personal life together although she may have done so. It was not what she emphasized primarily in her speaking about him. What I do remember is her speaking of his ethics and core values, and about his integrity. Integrity, ethics, and honour were all extremely important to him and these, not his genius or accomplishments, were what she said she most admired in him. Drucker was not fanatical about these issues, but he was certain and his students knew where he stood and what he believed.

NO SUCH THING AS BUSINESS ETHICS

He resented lawmakers punishing American executives who were victimized for paying kickbacks, with politicians stating that these executives lacked business ethics. Drucker maintained that there was no such thing as 'business ethics', and that one was either ethical or was not. Business was not a special case. He had struggled long and hard to analyse, think through, and come to this conclusion.

To Drucker, ethics and integrity were the bedrock of all business and personal practices. However, he recognized that there were differences in cultures and many challenges in operating from this bedrock. So, he used his talents to investigate all manner of ethics and integrity, so to identify an acceptable solution for resolving this issue. He told clients from all organizations that they could make lots of mistakes and still succeed, so long as they maintained their integrity. The clients who were able to resolve the apparent conflict between ethics and integrity and their private and business lives tended to be more successful than those who paid lip service to someone's lofty, but maybe less attainable pronouncements and recommendations. Drucker is rightly credited with distinguishing ethics and integrity from morality and the law. He said whether hiring call girls to entertain customers was ethical or not was the wrong question. According to Drucker, this was not a question of ethics, but rather aesthetics. To wit, "Do I want to see a pimp when I look at myself in the mirror while shaving?"[2]

TO GET STARTED WE NEED TO DEFINE THESE ISSUES

The concepts of integrity, ethics, morality, obedience to the law, and even honour are closely related in many instances, but they are not the same. Drucker spoke about the need for integrity. He raised issues regarding business ethics. It is important to distinguish among these and other connected concepts. I know that I've overly simplified these here, but it is necessary for an understanding of Drucker's views. *Ethics* is a code of values. *Integrity* speaks of adherence to this code of values. *Morality* is the quality and manner of this adherence. Drucker defined *honour* as demonstrable integrity and honesty, adding also that an honourable man stood by his principles.

Drucker's writing contained evidence of considerable concern with these concepts. What makes them particularly difficult to understand is that the unique interpretation of each concept determines what is right and good, and what is not. Drucker was acutely aware of the pronouncement often attributed to the 17th-century physicist mathematician, and philosopher Blaise Pascal's pronouncement that "There are truths on this side of the Pyrenees which are falsehoods on the other."

Drucker recognized that what one culture might find acceptable or even a requirement for ethical behaviour might be totally different for another and even considered unethical. An example he used in class was the custom for corporations in Japan to reward underpaid government officials after their retirement if the corporations had benefited from the actions of these officials when they were in office. In the US, this was considered unethical and corrupt. In Japan, this was both ethical and the right thing to do.

In brief, Drucker explained why the actions of a Japanese CEO which might be considered corruption and unlawful in the US could be regarded as an ethical duty and neither unethical nor unlawful in Japan. "In Japan," Drucker told us, "government officials are paid very little. They could live on what they receive in retirement only with great difficulty. It is therefore expected that when they retire, companies that have benefited from their actions during their tenure will assist them, financially and otherwise. Since they could barely get by on their retirement pay, this is considered the only right and ethical thing to do."

Yet Drucker did not agree with so-called 'situational ethics' and warned against them. In other words, one did not behave one way in private life and another way in business or professional life. He also believed social responsibility to be a part of an individual's and an organization's ethical behaviour. But here, too, he gave examples of corporations that, seeking to do good, had caused harm to customers, the organization, and to society. He cautioned that, under certain conditions, what might normally be considered a corporation's social responsibility should not be undertaken and could even be considered unethical behaviour from an unintended result or society's view. Drucker's positions on ethics and integrity might be argued, but they should be understood, for they form the basis of his ideas in dealing with customers and competitors, and in the application of all his management concepts.

DRUCKER'S STRUGGLES

Drucker took his examination of ethics seriously. He looked at the determination of right and wrong in questions of conduct and conscience by analysing cases that illustrated general ethical rules. This might be called cost-benefit ethics or ethics for the greater good. Essentially it means that those in power – CEOs, kings, presidents – have a higher duty if their behaviour can be argued to confer benefits on others. In other words, though it is wrong to lie, in the interests of 'the country' or 'the organization', it sometimes might be deemed acceptable according to one way of thinking. This approach carries the name of 'casuistry'. Drucker called it "the ethics of social responsibility" and it had to do with his dislike of the term 'business ethics'.

During the Cold War, and 20 years after the Japanese surprise attack on Pearl Harbor, the US was determined not to be caught short by a potential enemy again. With the U-2 reconnaissance aircraft, the Soviet Union could be overflown, and sensitive nuclear sites photographed from an altitude at which the aircraft was thought to be invulnerable. However, after several years of operations, a U-2 aircraft piloted by Francis Gary Powers was shot down from its extreme altitude by an anti-aircraft missile. Before it was known that Powers had survived and had been captured, President Eisenhower publicly lied about the fact that Powers was on a spy mission. However, in a widely published Soviet trial, Powers himself appeared and confessed that this was in fact the case. Yet, I don't think that President Eisenhower's ethics were ever challenged on this issue. He had lied for the greater good, a higher responsibility and so most thought this acceptable. This is casuistry.[3]

For the greater good, sounds very high-minded, but Drucker maintained that it was a dangerous concept to be considered, including in business, because it could easily become a tool for politicians and business leaders to justify clearly unethical behaviour. Adolf Hitler, the German dictator, had done this very thing by claiming Poland had attacked German territory when he invaded Poland, beginning World War II.

THE ETHICS OF PRUDENCE

After casuistry Drucker looked at prudence. To be prudent means to be careful or cautious. It has benefits, but also serious defects. When I first became an Air Force general, we were sent to complete a special two-week orientation programme. The unofficial name given to this programme by attendees was 'charm school'. During charm school, we were given lectures and advice by senior military and civilian leaders around the country. One lecturer gave us pretty good advice in saying, "Never do anything you wouldn't want seen on the front page of the *Air Force Times*."

Drucker gave a somewhat similar example. He said that Harry Truman, as a US senator in the early 1940s, advised senior army witnesses in the years before he became vice president to President Roosevelt that, "Generals should never do anything that needs to be explained to a Senate Committee – there is nothing one can explain to a Senate Committee."[4]

Now, the ethics of prudence may be pretty good advice for staying out of trouble, but it is not much of a basis for ethical decision-making. It doesn't say anything about the right kind of behaviour or actions that should be taken. Also, there are sometimes decisions that a leader must take that are risky and may be difficult, or even impossible, to explain but not necessarily unethical, especially if things go wrong after the decision is made. No serving Air Force general would like to see a controversial action coupled with his or her name on the front page of the *Air Force Times*, or something requiring his or her appearance before a Senate subcommittee. However, military decisions, and political ones too, are frequently controversial and high risk. Nevertheless, these may be the correct decisions even if results are sometimes not fully as desired. Drucker saw no basis for recommending this approach as the generalized way to come up with ethical decisions, but only noted it as a possible safeguard that his students should bear in mind.

THE ETHICS OF PROFIT

Drucker also thought through an approach that he called the "Ethics of Profit". This is not what you may think. Drucker was not talking about limiting profits. Much to the contrary, Drucker wrote that it would be socially irresponsible and most certainly unethical if a business did not show a profit at least equal to the cost of capital, because failing to do so would be wasting society's resources.[5] Nor should it seek to limit its profits to a certain formula. Since decisions are inherently risky there must be a margin of additional profitability to cover losses for those that go wrong. There were other reasons, too.

Drucker believed that the only logical rationale for the justification for profit was that it was a cost. He exhorted business leaders as follows: "Check to see if you are earning enough profit to cover the cost of capital and provide for innovation. If not, what are you going to do about it?"[6]

Drucker stated that profit as an ethical measurement rested on very weak moral grounds as an incentive and could only be justified if it were a genuine cost and especially if it were the only way to maintain jobs and to grow new ones.[7]

It is interesting that the rise in petrol (gas) prices in the US (prior to their dramatic fall) a few years ago prompted the following response by one refining company CEO when challenged by a Congressional investigating committee: "There is no 'profit'. Every dollar goes into exploration or research and development and is needed to sustain this business." If a truthful statement, Drucker would have certainly agreed with the CEO, although this would have probably been extremely difficult for someone not in the oil or petrol business, or any business for that matter, to understand or accept. It probably did not satisfy the Congressional committee, confirming Truman's advice to testifying generals.

CONFUCIUS WAS A GENIUS, TOO, BUT...

Drucker felt that Confucian ethics were the most successful and most durable of them all[77] although he came short of recommending Confucian ethics as the solution to all ethical issues. In Confucian ethics, the rules are the same for all, but there are different rules that vary according to five basic relationships, all based on interdependence. These five relationships are superior and subordinate; parents and child; husband and wife; oldest and youngest siblings; and friend and friend. The right behaviour in each case differs to optimize the benefits to both parties in each relationship.

Confucian ethics demand equality of obligations on both sides, of parents to children and vice versa, and of bosses to subordinates and vice versa, for example. All have mutual obligations. Drucker pointed out that this is not always the case and is not compatible with what is considered business ethics in many countries, including the US, where one side has obligations and the other side has rights or entitlements. Though he clearly admired Confucian ethics, which he called "the ethics of interdependence", they cannot universally be applied as business ethics, because this system deals with issues between individuals, not groups. According to Confucian ethics, only the law can handle the rights and disagreements of groups.[8]

DRUCKER'S EXCEPTIONS TO LYING

Through his stories and examples, Drucker taught his students, readers, audiences, and consulting clients what he had learned only after intensive study, analysis, and thought. However, he was sometimes criticized for the examples he used. Stories that he told occasionally misstated facts in illustrating his concepts. This was true, and if challenged, he did not deny the charge. His response invariably was,

"I'm not a historian; I'm trying to make a point." His argument was one of literary licence. It may be that his creditability suffered because of this, but he felt that these were in the same class as 'white lies', told for the benefit of the recipient to make the point and not the teller.

ETHICS DECISIONS ARE FREQUENTLY BASED ON DOING THE RIGHT THING

With ethics and the like, Drucker found an antagonist he could not easily overcome. Ethical challenges are pervasive and significant. A corporate client may pay for consulting. Does this client have a right to encourage the consultant to omit, de-emphasize, or 'spin' conclusions in a report and recommendations? Where does the difference between positive thinking about the future of a product, service, or business differ enough from the facts to make a statement a lie, rather than it being positive thinking in the face of adversity? Drucker's belief seemed to be that if the speaker was forthright about the challenges faced and put his money where his mouth was by buying an appropriate amount of additional stock in the company himself or some such, then he was right to give the situation a positive interpretation. However, if he presented a bright future when faced with a threatening circumstance and then secretly unloaded his stock, that's not only unlawful but immoral, and demonstrates a lack of integrity. How realistic or how optimistic to be gets back to doing the right thing and Drucker believed that this had to be left to individual judgement about what is and what is not the right thing.

DISTINCTIONS AMONG WHAT IS LEGAL AND WHAT IS RIGHT, MORAL, OR ETHICAL

Drucker made an important distinction: law may have very little to do with ethics or integrity. He made it clear that law and ethics are not the same and gave examples. Here's one. Until the 1860s, slavery was legal in some states in the US, illegal in others. Moreover, in the Dred Scott Decision of the late 1850s, the Supreme Court ruled that no African-Americans, not even free African-Americans, could ever become citizens of the USA. According to the law, the Declaration of Independence did not apply to them, nor did the US Constitution offer them any protection. Supporting these laws did not make you unethical, and going to jail and being punished for trying to subvert these laws did not make you unethical either. So, right and wrong must be separate from the law. Support for slavery could be a legal issue, as in the Dred Scott Decision, or it could be a moral issue. Slavery was despicable, but it was not an ethical issue by most definitions of the time.

DRUCKER VIEWED EXTORTION AND BRIBERY AS HE DID A ROBBERY

Drucker noted that bribery was certainly undesirable from the viewpoint of the victim, from whom a bribe was extorted. The payment of bribes overseas had recently been made illegal in the US by an Act of Congress, The Foreign Corrupt Practices Act in 1977. This penalized the victim, not the perpetrator. Drucker pointed out that if someone was robbed at gunpoint, the law did not punish the victim. Not long after the law was passed, an American company, Lockheed Aircraft, was charged with bribery as a violation of the law as well as violating 'business ethics'.

Senior Lockheed executives had paid bribes to members of the Japanese government when money was demanded in exchange for subsidizing the purchase of the L-1011 passenger jet for All Nippon Airways. In 1976, when the bribe was discovered, Lockheed chairman Daniel Haughton, and vice chairman and president Carl Kotchian were forced to resign in disgrace although they escaped jail.[9] "Lockheed has become the scapegoat for 300 companies that the S.E.C. said were doing the same thing, and Naughton [Daniel J. Naughton, who was forced to resign as chairman] and I are the scapegoats for the scapegoat," he said.[10] Yet these executives gained nothing personally from the sales of the L-1011. Why then did these two Lockheed executives commit such a stupid act?

In the years 1972–1973, 25,000 Lockheed employees had faced a significant threat of unemployment after cutbacks in the US government order of military aircraft and missiles. Because of delays due to difficulty with the foreign supplier of the L-1011's engines, airlines had cancelled orders for the planes. Unless a major contract to buy the L-1011 could be obtained, many jobs at Lockheed would be lost. The two executives gained not a cent in monetary or any other advantage from their submission to this act of bribery; their violation of the new law was committed to help workers keep their jobs and, one could say, in the interests of social responsibility. Stock analysts determined that had Lockheed simply abandoned the L-1011 instead of paying the bribe, company earnings, stock price, bonuses, and stock options for these two Lockheed executives would have substantially increased.

Almost everyone understood that because of the engine delays the L-1011 aircraft was a financial loser and nothing could be done about that. It simply could no longer make money. And, in fact, the project never made any money despite the bribe and other sales without it.

Drucker was very clear on this: he thought it stupid for the two Lockheed executives to pay these bribes. He thought that the decision to give in to the demand and to pay them was a very poor management decision. The L-1011 project should have simply been abandoned out of good management practice. But was this a violation of business ethics as was claimed?[11] Drucker noted again that the two Lockheed executives had nothing to gain and everything to lose by agreeing to pay bribes. They were victims. One doesn't punish the victims of a robbery or any other crime. Why is this done in bribery? And why was the decision to pay the bribe considered a reflection on the executives' business ethics rather than simply a bad management decision and a violation of the law which had been passed by Congress?

Most countries have laws against bribery. Yet it is a fact that bribery, as we define it, is frequently routine and expected in some countries. Many would perceive that the promise, or at least the understanding, of the Japanese CEO mentioned in Drucker's first example is that the act of his rewarding government officials who had helped his company while they were in office was a form of bribery. But managers and government officials in Japan understand the difference, and that the CEO in the case mentioned just wanted to do what was considered an ethical duty. Other countries that expect 'baksheesh' as the traditional way of doing business frequently ignore any laws that may have been enacted as 'window-dressing' for countries that do not have this as part of their culture, such as the US. One marketing executive from a major Western country (not the US), told me once that the company routinely paid bribes to secure business in many situations and that, in one case, they had to pay twice when the official they paid the first time had been deposed. The alternative was that a competitor from another country got the business. They considered paying bribes a cost of doing business.

Drucker also noted that a private citizen who was extorted to pay a bribe to a criminal, say for 'protection', would be considered a helpless victim of intimidation. Certainly, extortion privately or corporately is never desirable. But he felt that this was not an ethical issue on the part of the individual forced to pay. Of course, the law is the law and we would be well-advised to follow it whether we agree or not. Drucker did, despite his occasional disagreement such as that there is no such thing as business ethics, in which actions were acceptable that would not be ethical in private life.

Drucker did not think that a corporation should be viewed differently, and he strongly objected to this 'new business ethics', which asserted that acts that are not immoral or illegal if done by private citizens became immoral or illegal if done in the context of a business organization. They might be stupid, they might be illegal, and they might be the wrong things to do; however, corporations forced to pay bribes were not violating 'business ethics'. He predicted that that law was a feelgood law that would not be rigorously enforced. It was an attempt to punish the victim for something demanded by the perpetrator and in some cases in which the perpetrator was acting in accordance with what was considered ethical in that country. Although this was not the case with All Nippon Airlines, other practices in Japan may be ethical, such as showing understanding and appreciation for lowly paid government employees after their retirement.

I looked at the result of this law to see if it was effective in reducing bribery. Scholars have found that the act discourages US firms from investing in foreign markets. There have been other amendments to allow for other criticisms and to loosen the law. The amendments provided certain defences against finding violations of the act. For example, when is the bribe considered a gift and is therefore acceptable? The law now reads when the gift is lawful under the laws of the foreign country and that the gift is a bona fide and reasonable expenditure or for the performance or execution of a contract with the foreign government.[12]

Of course, Drucker had no sympathy for business executives who misled, deceived, or cheated customers, stockholders, the government or employees. He didn't think they had bad business ethics, however. He just didn't think that they had any ethics at all.

WHAT EXACTLY DID DRUCKER BELIEVE?

Ethics is a code of values which might differ in different societies and cultures "on the other side of the Pyrenees". According to Drucker, a differing codes should be respected so long as they did not violate one's own code of ethics or morality in the course of its practice. So, a Japanese executive might reward a government employee in thanks for something his company received after the government employee's retirement in Japan, but not for his company's operations in another country. However, if the other country's customs, practices, or laws were so abhorrent to his own ethics, he could not do business there or would suffer a lack of integrity.

Integrity speaks to adherence to this code of values. One must practise it with consistency. That is, there can be no situational ethics, no codification for special purposes, and therefore no special business ethics or situational ethics.

If ever business ethics were to be codified, Drucker thought they ought to be based on Confucian ethics, focusing on the right behaviour rather than misbehaviour or wrongdoing.

Drucker felt that managers should incorporate the following when they practise their personal philosophy of ethics:

- The ethics of personal responsibility from the physician Hippocrates: *primum non nocere*, which translates from the Latin to, "above all (or first) do no harm".[13,14]
- The mirror test: what kind of person do I want to see when I look into the mirror every morning?[15]

---

1. Cohen, William A. *A Class with Drucker* (New York: AMACOM, 2008).
2. Drucker, Peter F. *Management: Tasks, Responsibilities, Practices* (New York: Harper & Row, 1973), 367.
3. Drucker, Peter F. *The Changing World of the Executive* (New York: Truman Talley Books, 1982), 245
4. Ibid.
5. Drucker, Peter F. and Joseph A. Maciariello. *The Daily Drucker* (New York: Harper Collins, 2004), 126.
6. Ibid.
7. Ibid., 86
77. Drucker, Peter F. *The Changing World of the Executive* (New York: Time Books, 1982) p, 256.
8. Ibid. 248-254.
9. "Lockheed Bribery Scandals". *Wikipedia*, https://bit.ly/1O9rLSc, accessed 26 August 2017.
10. Galbraith, Kate. "A. Carl Kotchian, Lockheed Executive, Dies at 94". *The New York Times*, 22 December 2008. https://nyti.ms/2LQviKv; and Robert Lindsay, "Kotchian Calls Himself a Scapegoat". *New York Times*, 3 July 1977. https://bit.ly/2AFr96U.
11. Drucker, *The Changing World of the Executive*, 242.
12. Seitzinger, Michael V. "Summary." *Foreign Corrupt Practices Act (FCPA): Congressional Interest and Executive Enforcement, In Brief.* 15 March 2016. https://bit.ly/2LWMY6l. Accessed 28 August 2017.
13. Drucker, *The Changing World of the Executive*, 366-375.
14. Although Drucker, and others, declare *primum non nocere* to be part of the Hippocratic Oath, this is not true. See "Primum non nocere". *Wikipedia*, https://bit.ly/1F3eczW, accessed 2 March 2018
15. Drucker, Peter F. *Management Challenges for the 21st Century* (New York: Harper Business, 1999), 175-176

CHAPTER 6

WHAT YOU NEED TO KNOW ABOUT KNOWING YOUR STUFF

It takes far more energy and work to improve from incompetence to mediocrity than it takes to improve from first-rate performance to excellence.

– Peter F. Drucker

I t seems basic, but Drucker thought far too many managers spent more time on office politics than they did on knowing what they were supposed to know. I don't think that he intended that managers needed to be like the television character Doc Martin, who got ahead based on sheer ability, ignoring completely how he treated or interacted with his patients, or bedside manner.

Of course, one can go too far in the other direction. David Hackworth started his career as a private and was commissioned in combat from the ranks during the Korean War. He wrote several books on his military experiences and was especially known for his outspoken opinions about how the Army should operate. He maintained that an effective combat officer shouldn't put on the airs of 'a perfumed prince'. This was an opinion shared by many and probably would have been approved by Drucker. Hackworth also thought that the stresses of combat needed a controlled release and believed that the Army should sponsor a legal brothel for combat soldiers for this purpose, ignoring individual religious or moralistic beliefs, to fulfil what he perceived to be his soldiers' needs, while lessening the danger of disease. Would Drucker have agreed? This is such a major moral issue that could lead to such huge abuses that I think Drucker would have believed that the resulting problems and controversy would have outweighed any advantages of such a solution.

Drucker thought that extremes of any kind were bad. The real behaviour which top individuals of any profession should practise is that they know and understand what they are doing. General Groves built the Pentagon, an office building with 17 miles of corridors, and then the atomic bomb during World War II, without office politics, or being a 'perfumed prince', or establishing brothels. Although he had no experience in leading either project when he got the assignment, he took the time and made the effort to learn what was required to succeed. Experienced or not, he learned and knew his stuff without going to extremes and though most subordinates in the latter case were PhDs in physics, while he held no graduate degrees, he mastered enough to isolate the isotopes and not only complete the project successfully and develop the weapon but to participate in target selection.

THERE IS NO SUBSTITUTE
FOR VICTORY OR FOR SUCCESS

During World War II, the US Army conducted a study to find out what soldiers thought about their leaders. It was the first time any army had ever done this to such an extent, with several million subjects surveyed. The best and the brightest did this research, including professors from Harvard, Princeton, and the University of Chicago. They asked: "What are the most crucial factors associated with good leadership?" The most frequent answer these researchers received was: "That the leader knows his stuff."[1]

Why is it important that a general knows his stuff? Because without knowing, he can't be successful. Moreover, this injunction worked for those in other professions too. It will attract others to you. Everybody wants to be in an organization that is successful and is winning. Perhaps General of the Army Douglas MacArthur said it best: "There is no substitute for victory."

During World War II, someone on the other side, a German combat leader, said something similar. In 1943, Captain Wolfgang Luth spoke to a graduating class of naval cadets. Captain Luth was one of the most successful submarine commanders in the German Navy.

During World War II, 39,000 officers and men served in Germany's U-boat force. Only 7,000 survived. If you saw the award-winning movie *Das Boot*, you know under what difficult conditions these men, and our own, lived and fought. Just surviving a U-boat patrol was a severe challenge for any submarine crew. Yet, beyond mere survival, during three years of war Luth led 12 patrols and sank close to 250,000 gross tons of allied shipping. He was 600 days at sea in his submarine during which he set a record for 203 days at sea on one patrol. Not surprisingly, this amazing submarine captain held Germany's highest decorations for valour.

Luth's topic for these future naval officers at this graduating class was leadership on a U-boat. Captain Luth covered many areas in his lecture: the dos and don'ts, the life of the submariner, discipline. At times, he indicated that the captain's actions were matters of judgement – that another commander might have acted differently and still been successful. On one aspect of leadership, however, he said there was only one right answer.

"Crews will always prefer the successful commander, even though he may be a fathead, to the one who is consideration itself, but sinks no ships," he stated.[2] Like the conclusion from the US Army study, Captain Luth found a single characteristic that any leader of any organization must have. A leader has to know his stuff. This and not being a perfumed prince, or any form of posturing, or office politics can lead to success. Only knowing one's stuff. There is no other way.

British Field Marshall Montgomery, one of the leading English generals during World War II, and the man who defeated the famous German General Erwin Rommel in North Africa and won for himself the title of "Montgomery of Alamein", says the same. "The morale of the soldier is the greatest single factor in war and the best way to achieve a high morale in war-time is by success in battle. The good general is the one who wins his battles with the fewest possible casualties; but morale will remain high even after considerable casualties, provided the battle has been won and the men know it was not wastefully conducted."[3]

KNOWING YOUR STUFF IS AS IMPORTANT IN BUSINESS AS IN BATTLE

You'd think that knowing your stuff would be obvious in either military or civilian life. Yet, unfortunately some don't 'know their stuff' to the extent that they should, and don't seem to care. Drucker recognized this. It is true because their emphasis is less on becoming an expert, learning their trade, than on getting ahead. This leads to a focus on office politics and other aspects of the management scene rather than office expertise. It is equally true that several management books fall into this same trap in advising their readers. They fail to emphasize that a leader becomes the real leader of his organization when everyone in the organization recognizes that the leader knows what to do, not because the leader knew how to be promoted to the job.

Few follow leaders because they are good at office politics. They follow leaders because they are good at what they do. There is no substitute for a leader investing his or her time into becoming an expert. As an article in *Fortune* proclaimed: "Forget about fighting over titles and turf – it's what you know (and how you use it) that really counts."[4]

In 1994, Gordon M. Bethune took over as CEO of an ailing Continental Airlines that had twice filed for bankruptcy. In a little over a year, he built a $650 million cash reserve, and took Continental's position from last place on-time take-off performance to number two of all airlines. That's an important part of customer satisfaction. When he was younger Bethune had attended night school to graduate from high school. Bethune knew his stuff and how to use what he knew. He attended five colleges and finally got his bachelor's degree from Abilene Christian University. Starting out as a mechanic in the Navy, by the time he became CEO of Continental, he was both a licensed pilot and a mechanic. In fact, he was licensed to fly multi-engine jet planes. Few airline presidents, if any, could say that. He sometimes took delivery of the company's jet aircraft from Seattle and flew them to Houston where Continental was headquartered. No other airline president was able to do this. Continental needed such a leader. When Bethune took over as President of Continental Airlines the troubled airline was headed towards bankruptcy for the third time.

Bethune knew something that his predecessors had missed, and that Drucker knew well. It's not what the supplier believes is the most important value, but the customer's belief. Cost per available seat mile is an important metric for profit in the airline industry, but if the customer isn't satisfied with the product or service, this metric is almost irrelevant.

Bethune was elected chairman of the board of directors only two years after his hiring. Continental went from being ranked last in every measurable performance category to winning more awards for customer satisfaction than any other airline in the world. *Business Week* magazine named Bethune as one of the top 25 global managers. Under his leadership Continental's stock price rose more than 2,000%. Other accolades: *Fortune* magazine named Continental among the 100 Best Companies to Work for in America for six consecutive years and Most Admired Global Airline five times.[5]

THE FOUR ASPECTS OF KNOWING YOUR STUFF

Drucker knew that there were four main aspects to knowing your stuff. These are:

1. Know your people
2. Become an expert at what you do
3. Learn from every experience, whether successful or a failure
4. Never stop learning.

KNOWING YOUR PEOPLE MEANS KNOWING THEM AS INDIVIDUALS

Regardless of your job, you have an awful lot to learn about your people. Moreover, there are a lot of people to know. They include those who may report to you, those at your level and in other organizations who you work with (including in other companies), those higher up in the organization including your boss, and of course, your customers. Whew! That's quite a job. Furthermore, each is different and has a unique way of doing things. This fact constitutes one of the most fascinating, yet challenging aspects of knowing stuff about them.

Every single person thinks differently and may be motivated by different stimuli. Psychologist Carl Jung found that, faced with exactly the same situation, each of us have different preferred ways of acting, decision-making, or getting a job done.

Isabel Myers and her mother, Katherine C. Briggs, organized Jung's theoretical work about how different types of people like to work into a conceptual framework and a psychometric questionnaire called the Myers-Briggs Type Indicator. Based on a preference for alternatives in decision-making and the answers to a battery of questions, individuals are classified into one of 16 different personality types. Amazingly, these 16 personality types determine much about how each individual lives, loves, and prefers to work.

The Myers-Briggs Type Indicator or MBTI has become one of the world's most used research survey tools, everything from job preference to finding a mate. However, the MBTI is not a success indicator.

There are successful people in every single one of the 16 categories. The main lesson to be learned from MBTI is that we are all human beings.

We have had different experiences in life and have different beliefs and values. To influence, work with, lead, and do anything else with people you need to know and understand these differences.[6] Drucker maintained that one of the first things you have to learn about a new boss is whether he or she is a listener and prefers to hear things from you, or a reader and prefers to get information in a report. According to Drucker, get it wrong and you'll probably fail no matter what you know. If you are wondering how you find out, according to Drucker this is easy, you ask.

BECOMING AN EXPERT IS A LOT EASIER

It is generally thought that to become an expert in any field takes around five years. But, of course, this probably varies somewhat depending on the field, and how you define expert. Steven Spielberg took longer, although if you consider that his success came at an early age, it would appear that it took less time than it actually did for him to succeed.

Spielberg is arguably the most successful movie-maker of our time. Spielberg was only in his twenties when he directed the successful movie *Jaws*. he didn't stop with one big hit. This is the man who made *Close Encounters of the Third Kind*, *ET*, *Indiana Jones*, *The Color Purple*, *Schindler's List*, *Jurassic Park*, and the numerous others that followed.

How did Spielberg accomplish all this at such an early age? Wealthy parents with connections in the movie industry? Not quite. His father was an electrical and computer engineer and his mother a concert pianist at the time. They divorced when Steven was still in his teens, shortly after they moved to California.

Maybe Steven went to a great graduate film school like the University of Southern California (USC) in nearby Los Angeles? Then, he was hired right into a high-paying director's job. Right? Wrong! As a matter of fact, Spielberg applied to USC twice. And, he got turned down twice. USC probably regrets that decision dearly.

No, Spielberg's secret was that he took the time to become an expert at what he wanted to do. While only 12, he got his hands on an 8mm movie camera and began to turn out home movies starring relatives and friends. He decided right then on his life's goal: he wanted to make movies.

A year later, he won a prize for writing a fully scripted war movie. At the age of 16, he made a 2½ hour science fiction movie. It cost $500. He persuaded a local cinema to run it as a favour. It must not have been a great movie because they only ran it once. But that didn't bother Spielberg, because he was almost an expert.

While he was waiting to receive the second of two rejections from the USC film school, he was accepted at what was then Cal State College Long Beach and graduated in 1970 with a BA in English. While still a student, he was offered a small unpaid intern job at Universal Studios with the editing department. He was later given the opportunity to make a short 26-minute film for theatrical release. At age 22, he borrowed $15,000 from a friend and made a short film. It won a few awards and came to the attention of a vice president of Universal Studios who immediately recognized Spielberg's talent and expertise. He hired Spielberg as a director on a seven-year contract.[7] Spielberg had become an expert. He knew his stuff, and his many successes followed.

YOU MUST LEARN FROM EVERY EXPERIENCE, EVEN FAILURES

'Colonel' Harland Sanders got his first pension payment after retirement and decided it wasn't enough to live on. He then went on the road and spent two years trying to sell owners of fast food restaurants on the idea of using his recipe for Kentucky fried chicken. He didn't ask for any money up front, only that the owner try his recipe, and if successful, give him a few pennies from each sale. Every single owner he approached turned him down. He failed, probably hundreds of times. But Sanders learned from each rejection. He improved his presentation. He did more research. He learned to handle every possible objection. Finally, after two years, he got an acceptance. And then another, and another, and another after that.

No wonder when he was Governor of Kentucky, John Y. Brown, Jr, who was also former owner of Kentucky Fried Chicken, wrote about him: "Sanders took a bunch of people, most of whom had never been successful in their lives, and made them something of themselves. ...

In my lifetime, I have had the opportunity to meet and know nine US Presidents, most of the political and business leaders of our time, but the Colonel still stands as one of those great men you can count on one hand."[8]

Winston Churchill is one of my heroes. I know that he was one of Drucker's heroes too. He was a military hero when a young man. During World War I he was first Lord of the Admiralty and engineered the disastrous Gallipoli Campaign because he believed it would outflank the German forces and end the war sooner. It failed after a horrendous loss of life and Churchill resigned his safe civilian post, went into the English Army and immediately volunteered for front-line duty where the danger was the greatest. Everyone thought it would permanently end his political career. But as you know if you watched the movie *Darkest Hour*, he became prime minister and he not only led the United Kingdom when it stood alone against Hitler early in World War II, but he held things together until it all turned around, and today many credit him with having saved everything, even Western civilization. When you think that failure will end your project, it's good to remember his words: "Success is not final, failure is not fatal: it is the courage to continue that counts."

NEVER STOP LEARNING

If you think that you have learned all you'll ever need to know for your career you're making a big mistake, and I don't care at what point in your career you are, a new hire, or the president. There are always new ways of doing things. Technology changes. The business environment is constantly changing and is usually different as you become involved with new companies, industries, or geographical areas. I remember hearing one new college graduate proclaiming: "I'll never need to read another book again."

Drucker learned that a successful organization that continues to do what made it successful in the past will eventually fail. Why is this? Because of change. It makes what an organization knew or did to achieve success in the past irrelevant or even wrong. And this goes for everything. So, you must learn to keep up with change. You must constantly consider new approaches and new techniques with every task or project that you are assigned. It's all part of knowing your stuff. And it was the one big thing that Drucker learned which led to his professional success.

---

1. National Research Council with the collaboration of the Science Service, *Psychology for the Fighting Man*, 2nd ed. (New York: Penguin Books, 1944), 307.
2. Luth, Wolfgang. "Command of Men in a U-Boat". Speech given in 1943 at a German Naval Officers' Course reported in Harald Busch, *U-Boats at War*, trans. L.P.R. Wilson (New York: Ballantine Books, 1955), 162.
3. Montgomery, Bernard L., *The Memoirs of Field-Marshall Montgomery* (New York: World Publishing Co., 1958) p. 77.
4. Montgomery, Bernard L., *The Memoirs of Field-Marshall Montgomery* (New York: World Publishing Co., 1958), 77.
5. "Gordon Bethune". *Wikipedia*, https://bit.ly/2O5GcIQ, accessed 30 August 2017.
6. For those who want to know more about these Jungian concepts, the MBTI, and how it is used, I can recommend the following books: *Gifts Differing* by Isabel Briggs Myers with Peter B. Myers (Palo Alto, CA: Consulting Psychologists Press, 1980); *Please Understand Me*, 5th ed., by David Keirsey and Marilyn Bates (Del Mar, CA: Prometheus Nemesis Book Company, 1984); *Type Talk* by Otto Kroeger and Janet M. Thuesen (New York: Delacorte Press, 1988).
7. "Steven Spielberg Biography". *Encyclopedia of World Biography*, https://bit.ly/2I2Z3WF, accessed 30 August 2017; "Steven Spielberg". *Wikipedia*, https://bit.ly/2qAljJY, accessed 30 August 2017.
8. Pearce, John Ed. *The Colonel* (New York: Doubleday, 1982), dustcover, vi.

CHAPTER 7

EXPECTATIONS AND THEIR DECLARATION

Proper management requires balanced stress on objectives… It avoids the all-too-common business malpractice: management by crisis and drives.

– Peter F. Drucker

Sometimes it's more basic than you may think. It's difficult to reach any objective or goal if you don't have one or you don't have it clearly and precisely defined in your mind. If you don't have a clear objective or goal in mind, it's unlikely that anyone who works for you does either, and it's mostly unlikely that you will reach it. The chaos of management by crisis and drives is all too prevalent. Drucker knew that the way to the top for an individual or a corporation had to be spelled out exactly and it had to be declared to all, especially to one's self.

IF YOU ARE IN CHARGE, OTHERS EXPECT YOU TO SET THE STAGE

Drucker spent years working and consulting with Japanese companies. Commenting on 'Theory Z', the American version of Japanese management and the forerunner of TQM (total quality management) back when it was thought that this was always the best solution to managing American companies, Drucker maintained that it wasn't so much 'quality circles' or some other unique technique used in Japan that changed the quality of Japanese goods. Rather, Deming, Juran, and other quality leaders, simply made Japanese leaders aware of the problem. Once that happened, Japanese business leaders declared their own expectations regarding a focus on quality. This redirected the emphasis in their companies to a subject that had previously been ignored because it was thought unimportant. 'Quality circles' and other techniques that grew into TQM in the USA reinforced an effort that was begun with the understanding that this was something which needed to be done and was therefore emphasized.

Drucker realized that, "The foundation of effective leadership is thinking through the organization's mission, defining it and establishing it, clearly and visibly. The leader sets the goals, sets the priorities, and sets and maintains the standards ... What distinguishes the leader from the misleader are his goals. Whether the compromise he makes with the constraints of reality – which may involve political, economic, and financial or people issues – are compatible with his mission and goals or lead away from them determines whether he is an effective leader.

And whether he holds fast to a few basic standards (exemplifying them in his own conduct), or whether 'standards' for him are what he can get away with, determines whether the leader has followers or only hypocritical time-servers."[1] This applies to the individual as well. So, let's start with what your mission, objective, and goals are. What are your expectations? As you'll see, this applies to your leading an organization as well as to yourself. Let's look at the organization you may be leading first.

HOW DID FRED SMITH ESTABLISH A VERY SUCCESSFUL FEDERAL EXPRESS?

The almost mystical story of how Smith grew FedEx with a marketing plan that earned a 'C' grade from his professor in college has become a part of business folklore, but it is largely just that. Fred Smith actually credits the Marine Corps for teaching him good leadership. Smith's personal talent for leadership helped him to establish the world-famous company. It's not surprising. Smith declared his expectations to his employees very clearly. Declaring his expectations and communicating them helped Smith to found a new industry.

When employees meet his expectations, Smith follows through with a dramatic form of declaring his pleasure. New employees are taught that the highest compliment that can be given is "Bravo Zulu!" That's Marine Corps-ese for: 'Job well done, your performance rose above the call of duty.' Smith was a Marine and this fact had more influence than any 'C' grade earned on a marketing plan from a college classroom.

Once during a big UPS strike, FedEx was swamped with almost a million extra packages every day. Thousands of employees needed to work through midnight, weekends, and other inconvenient times after their regular hours. After the strike was over, Smith ordered bonuses and took out full-page newspaper ads congratulating his employees whose work had enabled FedEx to accept and fulfil this additional and unplanned work. All congratulations ended with the phrase "Bravo Zulu!" Some say it meant more than the extra money. Smith knew how to declare his expectations and reward his employees when these expectations were attained.

OK, that's for day to day operations. But at the top rung is the vision. And your vision is as important for setting personal goals for yourself and having expectations for an organization that you may lead.

VISIONS ARE AT THE TOP RUNG

A vision is an all-encompassing picture of the way you want an organization or yourself to look in the future. Without a vision, you and your organization will drift. Without a vision, you'll never get there and neither will your organization.

GREAT VISIONS ARE ALWAYS POWERFUL

The vision held by the one in charge is extremely powerful. This is true because it is always before him or her. Dr Norman Vincent Peale, who wrote the bestseller *The Power of Positive Thinking*, found that with great visions, "You have it, because it has you."[2] Such a vision is so strong that it can even appear in the subconscious to make things happen.

YOU CAN CHANGE EVERYTHING
WITH A COMPELLING VISION

In his most famous speech, Dr Martin Luther King told his listeners, "I have a dream." King went on to describe a very different kind of America than the one that existed at that time, one in which people weren't to be judged by the colour of their skin, but the content of their character. Dr King's vision galvanized the process that would help change America forever.

Sam Walton built a spectacular retail chain because he had a vision of providing quality goods to people at a competitive price, in geographical areas that major retailers were not serving. He felt so strongly about his vision, that he risked his personal future and wellbeing, and left a well-paid, executive position at J.C. Penny to implement it. Wal-Mart was the fruit of his powerful vision.

All successful organizations, whether small businesses, Fortune 500 companies, athletic teams, combat units, or even countries must be built on a clear and compelling vision. This vision provides direction for everyone in the organization. It guides all action and tells everyone exactly where the organization is going. Properly involved in this vision, members of the organization willingly work towards it. Almost miraculously, the organization usually attains the vision that the leader sees, sometimes in every single detail.

THE HEAD OF THE ORGANIZATION SEES THE VISION BEFORE IT EVEN EXISTS

When they opened EPCOT Center in Florida – a theme park at Walt Disney World Resort – a news reporter interviewed Roy Disney, Walt's brother. At one point in the interview, the reporter commented: "It's too bad Walt isn't here to see all this." He had died before EPCOT Center had opened. The reporter continued, "What would Walt have thought about EPCOT Center?"

Roy Disney didn't hesitate in replying: "Walt saw it years ago, before anybody else … that's why you and I are seeing it today."

The head of the organization always sees the finished product first, in his or her mind. Usually that proves to be a pretty accurate representation of the final product. Then, he or she declares these expectations to others (and to himself or herself), promotes them, and starts everyone making his vision a reality. Again, this happens long before the completed product appears.

In 1948, Disney took his daughters to an amusement park. He was distressed that the amusement park had frequently become run down, a place that parents no longer wanted to take their children. Walt Disney put out a memo for what he called the "Mickey Mouse Park" that very year. It read: "The Main Village, which includes the Railroad Station, is built around a village green or informal park. In the park will be benches, a bandstand, drinking fountain, trees, and shrubs. It will be a place for people to sit and rest; mothers and grandmothers can watch over small children at play. I want it to be very relaxing, cool and inviting."[3] And thus began Walt Disney's vision for "The Happiest Place on Earth".

SEEING YOUR OWN EXPECTATIONS AND DECLARATIONS

A vision must be so strong, that it outweighs the egos or negative thoughts that may block real attainable possibilities.[4] When he was a teenager, my oldest son, Barak, wanted to attend West Point for college. That's not an easy goal to achieve, I should know since I am a graduate myself. Barak studied hard and had a high grade-point average, but each congressman only gets one appointment for his district, and though Barak had a 3.8 grade-point average with honours, four others in our Congressional district had a 4.0 with honours. So Barak didn't attain his vision the first year he tried. But as famed motivational speaker, Tony Robbins says, "God's delays are not God's denials." Barak attended another college but kept his vision and asked for my advice. I advised him to make a business-card-sized note and to write on it: "I am attending West Point and will graduate in four years." He was to keep this card in his wallet, but to take it out and read it aloud at least three times a day and to visualize himself as a cadet and how it felt as he went through West Point after attaining the goal of being accepted, and to write down the benefits of being a West Point cadet. Barak followed my advice and did exactly as I had instructed. Several times a day he would take out the card from his wallet and read the positive instructions he had written for himself. The following year he applied for West Point again, was accepted, and on schedule four years later, he graduated.

THE BIBLE SAYS THAT WITHOUT VISION THE PEOPLE PERISH, BUT IS THAT TRUE FOR CATERPILLARS?

The Bible tells us "Where there is no vision, the people perish ..." (Proverbs 29: 18). Do you think that you can learn anything about vision from an insect? Well, I did. Jean-Henri Casimir Fabre was a French naturalist, an entomologist and author known for the lively style of his popular books on the lives of insects. Fabre became curious about a strange insect called a processionary caterpillar. What makes this species of caterpillar so unusual is the way it travels. A family of these caterpillars moves as a physically connected unit. They actually hook up, one behind the other and move in a long, undulating, connected line.

The one in front knows where they are going. The others simply hang on and have a rather spectacular view of the rear end of another family member as they hang on and keep moving forward together.

Fabre wondered what would happen if there were no vision of where they were going. So, he designed a little experiment. He took a family of these caterpillars that were already connected and hooked the leader up to the caterpillar who was last in line, so that there was no leader and therefore no vision.

Then he hooked up the circle of insects so that they were are travelling in the same direction. What he wanted to know was for how long would the caterpillars continue to travel around in a circle, going nowhere with no vision except the rear end of another caterpillar. How long would they continue with no vision of where they were going before they changed tactics, or at least stopped for a coffee break?

Fabre placed his circle of visionless processionary caterpillars on the rim of the flower pot whose circumference exactly matched the size of the circle of caterpillars. He placed water and mulberry leaves at the bottom of the flowerpot. Mulberry leaves are the processionary caterpillars' favourite food. As they began to travel in a circle, he looked at his watch and told his assistants to release the caterpillars and they watched and waited. He planned to calculate exactly how long the caterpillars would continue to go around the rim of the flower pot with no idea as to where they were going. In other words, with no vision.

Without a vision, the caterpillars never stopped to eat and drink. They kept going around and around until they fell unconscious for lack of sustenance. Yet, food and water were always only a few inches away. With no vision, the people perish, says the Bible. That appears to apply to caterpillars as well.

HOW TO DECLARE AND ACHIEVE
ALL YOUR EXPECTATIONS

It doesn't matter whether the expectation is a task, goal, objective, or vision for your organization or for yourself. The steps in declaring and achieving them are the same. They are:

- Get your expectations clear
- Make your expectations compelling
- Develop a plan
- Promote your expectations and implement your plan
- Listen to feedback (your own or others, if a group) and adjust your strategy.

GET YOUR EXPECTATIONS CLEAR

Now, I know this may sound oversimplified, but the truth is some individuals just don't know what they want for themselves and their organizations' futures. They may not know what they want period. They just want their organizations to be 'successful'. But until the one in charge defines exactly what success means to him or her and to the organization, there is no hope. Without clearly defined expectations an organization cannot accomplish tasks, reach its goals or objectives, and attain no object. It will simply perish like the caterpillars. Therefore, you must take the time to get your expectations very clear in your mind.

GET YOUR GOAL CLEAR, THEN YOU CAN FOCUS YOUR ENERGIES

The basis of all strategy or achievement is to concentrate superior resources at the decisive point. Since resources are always limited, where you concentrate them is of particular importance. Claude Hopkins founded and headed up one of the largest advertising agencies in the USA in the early 1900s. He wrote two bestselling books: *Scientific Advertising* and *My Life in Advertising*. One day a correspondent asked him to what he owed his success. "Simple," he answered. "I spend more time than any of my competitors on any given project." In other words, he focused his most limited resource where it counted, on his job, more than his competitors.

CHOOSE, DON'T JUGGLE

Many are proud of their ability to juggle many different objectives and goals. In some cases, these objectives may even be mutually exclusive if you look closely. For example, one company I know set certain short-term objectives in sales and profits. Yet, the way they set things up, to reach their sales goals they could not reach their profit goals, or vice versa. These corporate jugglers could not understand why they could not reach greater success in any of their expectations. Peak performance expert Dr Charles Garfield says, "Choose, don't juggle!" Choose each expectation very carefully and get it clear in your mind. Is it worth your and your organization's effort to attain it? If it is, then you can concentrate superior resources at the decisive points. Like Claude Hopkins, you will succeed by putting in more effort on any given project and focusing on worthwhile expectations while ignoring those that are less worthwhile. Once you achieve one major goal, then move on to another.

CLOROX'S CEO SHOWED HOW IT'S DONE

Clorox Chairman and CEO G. Craig Sullivan made clear some major expectations when he took over the company. With more than 25 years at Clorox after starting out in sales, he had time to think through his goals for Clorox with clarity. He knew exactly what he wanted to do, but it wasn't easy. Clorox stock fell 5% right after he was selected. Soon after taking over, he set up ambitious, but reachable, growth targets. Some senior managers balked at these expectations. Sullivan suggested that those who didn't want to participate had best move on and almost half of his old staff of senior executives did exactly that.

"I think I had the advantage of being 'an observer' in the Company for a long time so I had a pretty good idea of what needed to be done. Also, since I'm not smart enough to do complicated things, I tried to keep things simple and focused. That seems to have worked out pretty well."[5] Indeed it did. Earnings increased every year with Sullivan running things. Sales soon exceeded $2.5 billion, up 14% since he began.[6] Glenn R. Savage, Clorox's marketing director noted that, "There's power in giving people very clear objectives."[7]

Unlike others who are afraid to announce what they expect for fear they will not reach the goals stated, Sullivan declared his expectations to one and all. Here were some of Sullivan's goals for Clorox at that time:

- "To achieve sales of $3.5 billion by the Year 2000, requiring average annual growth of 12% over the following three years;
- "To grow the Clorox Value Measure (CVM) at a rate that exceeds 12% over time;

- "To generate total shareholder return over time that places us in the top third of the S&P 500 and the top third of our peer group;
- "To build an international business that by the Year 2000 is 20% of total company sales."[8]

Sullivan, was enormously successful as CEO at Clorox. He revitalized the company in the early 1990s by focusing its resources on a core set of closely related product lines and categories. Brands that didn't fit into the portfolio were sold to fund internal growth and the acquisition of brands that did. In 1999 Unilever announced that it would actually drop 1,200 of its 1,600 or so brands, putting most of its resources behind just 400 so-called power brands. This is a strategy that Drucker used too. It's based on a strategy concept which Drucker called 'Abandonment'. We'll see how Drucker implemented it in future chapters.

A 98-POUND WEAKLING MADE HIS EXPECTATIONS COMPELLING

Whenever I think of compelling expectations, I cannot help but think of Charles Atlas, of whom you may have heard, and Charles Roman, of whom you probably have not. Atlas was a poor Italian boy who immigrated to America around the turn of the 20th century. His real name was Angelo Siciliano. As a boy Angelo was painfully weak – a 98-pound weakling. After a painful beating by a bully, he cried himself to sleep, but swore an oath that no man on Earth would ever hurt him again.

He developed his own unique method of bodybuilding, which did not use weights. He had to, because he couldn't afford to buy weights or to join a gym. Health clubs didn't exist in those days, but it wouldn't have made any difference. He didn't have the money. However, in 12 months, he doubled his body weight using a method he originated which he called "dynamic tension". He entered bodybuilding contests and won. Then, he became a well-known artists' model. Among famous sculptures which used him as a model, are Alexander Hamilton in front of the US Treasury Building in Washington, DC, George Washington in New York's Washington Square, and the "Dawn of Glory" in Brooklyn's Prospect Park. Using the prize money from the contests and his modelling, Atlas developed a physical development correspondence course and began to sell it through the mail. However, he couldn't get enough customers with his advertisements, and he lost money more rapidly than he had put on weight. Married with two children, no income, and a floundering business, Atlas was in serious trouble. Enter Charles Roman.

Charles Roman was a new hire at the Benjamin Landsman Advertising Agency of New York. In desperation, Atlas asked the Landsman agency for help. Roman was a recent graduate of New York University. As the new employee, he was given the account with the worst potential. That was Atlas. Roman read over Atlas's course materials and realized that the ads simply didn't make Atlas's expectations for his prospects compelling. Roman came up with innovative ways of doing this. Four months after their meeting, Atlas and Roman became partners. "The Insult That Made a Man Out of Mac", one of Roman's headlines trumpeted. And Roman invited respondents to check the kind of body they wanted: Broader Chest and Shoulders, Iron-Hard Stomach Muscles, Tireless Legs, Slimmer Waist and Legs, More Energy and Stamina – the list went on and on. From a few hundred courses sold, the number climbed to 3,000 the first year they were in business together. Soon it reached 10,000. The year before Atlas died they sold over 23,000 courses world-wide.[9] The course is still selling today.

Now here's the point. Atlas declared his expectations for his potential customers, but until Roman came on the scene, he did not do so in a sufficiently compelling fashion. Once Roman made these expectations compelling, prospects were influenced to buy, and buy in a big way.

Drucker realized that those declaring their expectations to influence those who follow them are much like retailers attempting to influence prospects to buy. Those who reach the top do so by first making certain that their expectations are formulated in a compelling fashion.

IF YOU WANT EXPECTATIONS TO BE COMPELLING, ASK THE QUESTION 'WHY?'

To be compelling, expectations must offer strong benefits to the buyers once they are achieved. And you must do that for yourself as well. What benefits will result, once you have turned your expectations into reality?

If it's for an organization you head, will your customers be better off? How? Will the members of your organization be happier or achieve more in their careers? Will society benefit? Will your organization be acclaimed number one in its field? Think through and know the benefits of your expectations specifically and in detail.

WRITE DOWN YOUR EXPECTATIONS IN A NOTEBOOK

Once you have your expectations clear and know why you must attain them, write them down. Work on the wording so that it is clear, direct, and compelling. This is where you want your organization to go. This is what you want your organization to be. Keep working with them until they have the impact, clarity, and conciseness of the sound of a wet rag thrown against a wall. When you think you have written them down perfectly, let them sit for a couple of days and then go back and work on them some more. Once you have your expectations written down so that they are clear and compelling, you are ready to plan how to achieve these expectations.

Mark Victor Hansen, co-author with Jack Canfield of the "Chicken Soup" series of books, which have sold millions of copies says: "Write down 101 goals. Put them around your house and office so that you can see them. Then, as you achieve each, don't just remove it. Instead write, 'Victory!'<TNBS>"[10]

YOU MUST DEVELOP A PLAN

There is a very old saying that those who fail to plan, plan to fail. Yet when movie star Paul Newman was asked about future plans for his successful line of food products he answered, "If we ever have a plan, we're screwed."

While I suspect that Newman's answer was somewhat tongue-in-cheek, I have found that even though winners always have a plan to achieve their expectations, that plan is not always documented. However, each one can describe his or her plan without missing a beat or leaving out a detail, whether it is in writing or not. I think that Newman could have done this also. Drucker definitely did and taught his students its importance. Some people call this an elevator speech. They can describe their entire plan, without notes, to fellow travellers on a two-minute elevator trip.

Planning is a process of thinking it through. You have established precisely where you want to go and why you must get there. Now you must establish exactly how you are going to do this. Start by scanning your environment. Those who reach the top have been doing this for thousands of years. They look at alternative courses of action to reach their goals and objectives, and then decide on the best one. And that's what Drucker did. You must do the same.

Sometimes reaching your final objective requires breaking an objective or goal into smaller tasks. You can eat an elephant, but only if you eat it one bite at a time. So, you may need to break your larger goal down into smaller, doable bites.

Although you *can* do it in your head, many find it useful to write their plans down with firm dates for reaching each expectation. I know that I do. It's a way of even getting greater leverage on yourself and your organization to attain what you expect. And it's what you should do for your personal expectations as well.

PROMOTING YOUR EXPECTATIONS IS A BIG PART OF IMPLEMENTATION

Promoting your expectations means just that. It means promoting what you want your organization to do, what its values are, where you want your organization to go and what you want your organization to be. Think about it, use it as a basis of discussion – talk about it and write about it every chance you get. Tie it in with everything you do. Every time someone takes an action that moves you towards one or more of your expectations, let people know. Give them a pat on the back. As Mark Victor Hansen suggested, just don't just check them off your list, declare a victory. Again, do this in your personal life as well.

Successful individuals promote their expectations at every opportunity. To communicate his expectations to his salesmen, Elmer Wheeler, one of the most successful sales managers of all time, coined the phrase, "Don't sell the steak, sell the sizzle."[11] Approaching a century later, his words still live and are communicated to new salespeople in many organizations.

JUMP-START YOUR PROMOTION THROUGH DRAMATIZATION

Successful people following this universal law know that it is important to dramatize their expectations as they promote them. Many shorten their expectations into brief messages that have a dramatic impact and these are repeated again and again.

FINALLY, LISTEN TO FEEDBACK AND ADJUST YOUR STRATEGIES

Robert Townsend was president of Avis Rent-a-Car during its period of greatest growth. It was he who developed the "We Try Harder" theme which is still heard occasionally today. In the book, *Up the Organization,* in which he reported that one of his vice presidents who disagreed with a proposed action routinely sent him a note which was memorable. It read something like: "If you insist, it will be my duty to make it so. However, I must respectfully tell you that you are full of shit again."[12]

This got his attention and made him laugh without making him angry. He listened to the feedback and adjusted his intended action.

---

1. Drucker, Peter F. "Leadership: More Than Dash". *Drucker Management* (Spring 1994,), 3.
2. Peale, Norman Vincent. *The Power of Positive Thinking*, first Fireside ed. (New York: Simon & Schuster, 2003), 26.
3. Thomas, B. *Walt Disney: An American Original* (New York: Simon & Schuster, 1976). 218
4. Freiberg, Kevin and Jackie Freiberg. *Nuts! Southwest Airline's Crazy Recipe for Business and Personal Success* (Austin, TX: Bard Press, 1996), 49.
5. Sullivan, G. Craig, letter to the author, 22 October 1997.
6. *The Clorox Company 1997 Annual Report*, 1.
7. Hamilton, Joan O'C., "Brighter Days at Clorox". *Business Week* (16 June 1997), 62.
8. *The Clorox Company 1997 Annual Report*, 5.
9. Gaines, Charles. *Yours in Perfect Manhood, Charles Atlas* (New York: Simon & Schuster, 1982), 69.
10. Hansen, Mark Victor. Speech, Crystal Cathedral, Garden Grove, California, 10 November 1997.
11. Wheeler, Elmer. *Tested Sentences That Sell* (Englewood Cliffs, NJ: Prentice-Hall, 1937), Ch. 1.
12. Townsend, Robert C., *Up the Organization* (New York: Jossey-Bass, 2007) p. 55

CHAPTER 8

FORGING AHEAD WITH UNCOMMON COMMITMENT

*Unless commitment is made, there are only
promises and hopes… but no plans.
Unless there is personal commitment to the values
of an idea and faith in them, the necessary
efforts will therefore not be sustained.*

– Peter F. Drucker

D rucker knew that commitment was difficult to measure quantitatively, but it was of incalculable value for advancing in a career or leading an organization to move ahead. And he knew what it took to get what you want, and to have the level of commitment necessary to reach the top.

In his career, Drucker never doubted how he'd end up even though it was not always smooth sailing. Around the time that Hitler came to power, everything began to go wrong for him. He had an uncle at the University of Cologne, a prestigious, top-ranked university who had indicated he could help him gain a professorship there. Moreover, Drucker already had written books, in German. One was on the life of well-known conservative German philosopher Friedrich Julius Stahl, who was a converted Jew, and another entitled *The Jewish Question in Germany*. Unfortunately, they were both burned and banned by the Nazis.[1] In fact, Hitler, Nazism, and Drucker's Jewish blood ruined Drucker's plans at that time. Drucker was lucky and had the foresight to flee Germany for England while he could still leave relatively easily. People who are committed to a goal tend to be lucky in achieving their goals.

Drucker "looked through the window". This was his way of describing how he analysed issues and saw what events that had already occurred meant for the future. Consequently, he left Germany for England right away when Hitler came to power in 1933. However, Drucker's Austrian accent was heavy and his English speech was probably not perfect. He got nowhere close to a professorship in England. He was able to get work with an insurance company, and then a bank, the latter job attained through the good offices of a fellow ethnic Jewish Austrian. He didn't waste time and was soon hard at work at improving his English, and in the evenings he worked on his first book in the language that eventually made him and his ideas famous. He may have thought that it would help him attain his goal of a professorship at a major university in England. However, after struggling in England for four years, he decided that he would have a better opportunity for a professorship in America. The best he could manage at first was a part-time teaching position at Sarah Lawrence College, which in those days was intended to provide instruction in the arts and humanities for women.

It was located in Bronxville, New York. Then, in 1942, he finally attained the goal to which he had been committed since before he left Germany. He became a full-time professor at Bennington, a small college in Vermont for women. This was not the University of Cologne, but given his extraordinary situation as an expatriate Austrian, this opportunity was a progress towards his vision and goals.

Napoleon Bonaparte in his *Maxims* declared: "An extraordinary situation calls for extraordinary resolution … How many things have appeared impossible which, nevertheless, have been done by resolute men"[2] Drucker was indeed a resolute man.

Drucker continued with extraordinary commitment, and as we know eventually attained his goal after writing his book, *Concept of the Corporation*.[3] He became a management professor at New York University and later a world-famous professor at Claremont Graduate School in California, the school part of Claremont Graduate University is now named after him. To reach the top, immigrant or not, you have difficulties to overcome.

NICOLE DIONNE AND PRIMALSCREAM

Today, Nicole Dionne is famous in her field. She is CEO and Creative Director of one of the most renowned music production companies in the USA. She produces award-winning music for film, TV, advertising, branded content, movie trailers, all sorts of promos, and more. She has won Clios (the Oscar of the advertising industry) and many other top awards and developed multimillion dollar campaigns for some of the largest corporations in the US.[4]

I first met Dionne when I interviewed her more than 20 years ago. Dionne had only a few years' experience in the sound design industry then. She was in her mid-twenties and had recently been happily employed working for a local sound design company. What was to happen showed her uncommon commitment and tested her severely but, like Drucker's setbacks, eventually led to her success.

Sound design people are the folks that create sounds to fit the moods of commercial advertisements on TV and of movie trailers.

Dionne had some ideas for improving the business, and so she put together a 30-page marketing plan and gave it to her boss at the sound company she worked for then.

Some months later she was distressed to discover that her boss hadn't even looked at her ideas, much less approved or even considered them. Dionne talked to another employee, her sound designer, about the possibility of starting their own business to implement the plan. Apparently, they talked a little too loudly. They were still in the talking stage when her boss heard about it, and she and her would-be partner were both fired.

But taking advantage of being out of work, the two started their own sound design company. Or rather, they took the first step. They picked a name designed to attract attention: 'PrimalScream. Now all they needed was money. In an interview with the *Los Angeles Times* Dionne said, "I took the business plan that had started it all, but had been ignored, expanded it and started contacting investors based on the creative sound design talent of my partner, Reinhard Denke."[5]

Dionne met with dozens of venture capitalists. There was interest, but the investors wanted 60% of the profits and total control. That may have been normal in the industry, but as she saw it, it would be just as if she were back working for someone else. However, she didn't stop trying, even after numerous disappointments. She showed uncommon commitment.

Dionne next tried seeking a small business loan. She approached almost 60 banks all over the US with no success. Most told her that she had to have been in business for two years and have collateral. She and her partner cashed in their retirement plans, emptied their savings accounts, and came up with about $30,000. It wasn't enough. Some potential lenders told her she should first drop the name of the company. "PrimalScream is a terrible name," they said, "it violates all the rules." She ignored them and pressed on with her uncommon commitment.

One day, someone recommended a loan officer at a certain bank. She made a presentation stressing her business plan and her partner's creativity as an artist. She asked for $70,000. It was still a significant risk from the bank's perspective, but based on her uncommon commitment, the bank took it. Or, at least part of that risk. The bank loaned her $30,000. It was barely enough to get started, but it was enough.

Now, they had to find a location. After many false starts, the two found a house located in a commercial zone. The rent was barely within their budget. Then, they had to somehow get the expensive sound equipment they needed. It could have swallowed up their entire loan. Fortunately, the manufacturer was familiar with their work, and combined with Dionne's uncommon commitment, they were able to lease the equipment at an amount they could handle.

PrimalScream work was great and it was almost an immediate success. Within three months, they paid off the loan. Eight months later, they were able to expand their business into a full-blown music company with a 4,000-square foot studio in a suitable location. Then they won two Clio awards. Their annual sales when I spoke with Dionne at that time about 1997 exceeded $1 million, and after only two years, they were considered among the top firms in their field.

Dionne told me, "Whenever I start to worry, I press on harder. I always think of a herd of zebras being pursued by a predator. It's not the one that keeps focused and has extraordinary commitment that gets caught and eaten. It's the zebra that starts looking right and left to see whether other zebras are getting ahead, or worse, looking back to see how the lion is doing. The people I approached saw that. Whenever I heard 'no', I immediately started figuring how to turn it into a 'how'. Others take note of your commitment and behaviour accordingly. I have the same attitude in dealing with my people, and they know it. I am totally committed to whatever project we're working on. But I am not tied to a way of accomplishing the goal. In fact, I have what I call my 'no' rule. That is, if anyone disagrees, about an approach, we find another way. But we stay committed to the outcome. There is always an alternative when you are committed."[6] Drucker would have agreed: his attitude and Dionne's were similar.

WHAT WILL SHOWING UNCOMMON COMMITMENT DO?

What will demonstrating uncommon commitment, or extraordinary commitment, 'whatever it takes commitment' do for you? Why can just the fact of showing uncommon commitment affect your own performance and why are others readier to follow someone who demonstrates this quality? Psychologists who have studied commitment have identified two main reasons why showing uncommon commitment frequently yields dramatic results in getting not only others on board to help solve problems and attain goals, but also in getting yourself more likely to continue to achieve them:

- It proves to others and to yourself that the goal is worthwhile and important
- It proves to others and to yourself that you are in it for the long term and aren't going to quit.

FOUR WAYS OF DEMONSTRATING UNCOMMON COMMITMENT TO OTHERS

Anyone can show uncommon commitment to others and himself as well. Here are four ways you can do this – they aren't complicated, but they aren't necessarily easy either. Successful people like Dionne do all of them. They worked for Drucker and they can work for you too:

- Make a public commitment to your objectives and meet face-to-face if you can
- Keep going despite setbacks
- When the situation looks impossible, do it anyway
- Accept the risks, they are normal with any worthwhile goals.

MY FRIEND GEORGE PATTERSON GOT PEOPLE COMMITTED

As a young Air Force captain, George Patterson was one of my professors at West Point. Much later he became a general and years later he helped to publicize one of my books on leadership. He told me this story.

After he retired from the Air Force, he became president of Ohio Precision Castings in Ohio. The company contracted to supply a new type of fuel pump for the then ultra-advanced B-1 bomber. Several million dollars and many jobs were on the line.

As Patterson explained, "Moulding these new pumps was no easy task. It had never been done before. No matter how carefully the moulders worked, many of the pumps did not meet the specifications. There were so many rejects that we got behind schedule and were losing money. I was pretty worried."

Patterson could have renegotiated the contract. He could have asked for a delay. He could have scaled back the number of units he was required to supply. These alternatives were possible and would have been a viable solution. However, he felt it would have hurt the company's reputation and could have delayed production of the B-1. It would also have meant laying off some of his workers.

So, instead Patterson put everyone to work as they had never worked before. "I met repeatedly with the production crews and engineers. Everyone got into the spirit of solving the problem without asking for favours. I knew there had to be a solution and we tried all sorts of crazy things."

Patterson's employees saw his commitment. They saw he wasn't going to quit. So, they didn't quit either, they stuck with him. In general, when dealing with a single moulding material, normally the formula and moulding temperature for each part was the same for all. Only the shape of the part varied. But, Patterson's experts found something interesting: on this occasion this wasn't working. So what if they changed the formula and temperature to optimize it for each separate part?

Through experimentation, they found they could meet the specification by varying the temperature and formula for each individual part in this way. But there was still a problem. Since each part required a different temperature and a different formula, it was not clear that developing and using so many different casting formulas simultaneously was possible. It too had never been done before. Some of Patterson's people thought that this meant they could not succeed.

One said, "Well, boss, I guess this means we've got to renegotiate the contract?"

Patterson thought otherwise. Because of his uncommon commitment, they kept at it. Everyone was obsessed with finding a solution that would work. They not only worked overtime, they worked night and day. Eventually, they discovered the correct formula for each separate casting. "We posted it near the moulding production machine for each part," Patterson said. "We moulded each part differently." The number of rejects began to decline dramatically.

Unfortunately, they no sooner solved this than they ran into yet another problem. Patterson's engineers found that air contacting the exterior of the aluminium moulds caused the moulding temperature to vary. Varying temperature caused minor differences in the parts. Minor, but out of tolerance again. Consultants said that nothing could be done. They said that air always leaked around the exterior of the mould to some degree. "The specifications required," they maintained, "are just too tough."

But Patterson didn't give up. Because he wouldn't give up, his workers wouldn't give up. Because he was totally committed, so were his employees. "Finally, somebody came up with the idea of using ordinary plastic Saran wrap, to stop the air from escaping," Patterson says. "We tried it and believe it or not it worked."

Patterson's company got back on schedule and delivered the pumps on time. The company not only made a good profit and kept its reputation, but Pat's employees kept their jobs.[7]

OTHERS FOLLOW BECAUSE
THEY KNOW THE GOAL IS IMPORTANT

People don't exert themselves for little, unimportant goals. They work hard, take great risks, and let nothing stop them only for big, important goals. That's why those who try to play down the difficulty of a task make a big mistake. It is far better to tell people exactly what is expected of them, no matter how challenging the situation or how much effort would be required. Of course, you've got to hold everyone, including yourself, responsible for their own actions in their part of reaching the goal, and accept nothing less than their best effort. That's the essence of showing uncommon commitment.

I've said that Winston Churchill is one of my heroes. During the darkest days of World War II, when the United Kingdom stood alone against the power of Nazi Germany and its allies, Churchill wisely told his countrymen, "I have nothing to offer but blood, toil, tears and sweat."[8] Churchill was 100% committed, and the British people knew it.

Then, Prime Minister Churchill addressed the UK Parliament. Churchill said, "we shall not flag or fail. We shall go on to the end. We shall fight in France, we shall fight on the seas and oceans, we shall fight with growing confidence and growing strength in the air, we shall defend our island, whatever the cost may be. We shall fight on the beaches, we shall fight on the landing grounds, we shall fight in the fields and in the streets, we shall fight in the hills; we shall never surrender."[9]

Churchill's public declaration allowed no room for retreat or negotiation. It dramatized his intention to continue regardless of the outcome. Because of Churchill's uncommon commitment, the British came together and faced the future and their hardships with confidence. Hitler thought twice. His confidence was shaken, and he postponed the invasion of the United Kingdom when the Royal Air Force stood up to the Luftwaffe's air attacks and eventually he abandoned his plans to invade Britain altogether. Churchill's bulldog commitment of extreme trial and danger and his public announcement which demonstrated this uncommon commitment was one of the crucial junctures of the war. That was the central message of the movie *Darkest Hour*.

Making a public commitment from which there is no retreat, and which dramatizes your intention to continue regardless of the outcome works! It works for countries and it works for companies. In fact, it works for any organization and it works for yourself, too. Showing uncommon commitment is how one proves that the goal is important enough to sacrifice mightily to attain it.

OTHERS FOLLOW BECAUSE THEY KNOW YOU WON'T QUIT

People won't follow you if they think that your commitment is temporary, or that you may quit the goal short of attainment. Why should they? Why should they invest their time, money, lives, or fortune in something if the leader isn't going to lead them there anyway? Others will only follow when they are convinced that you won't quit no matter how difficult the task looks, and no matter what obstacles you encounter along the way.

There will always be obstacles. Someone said, "There are no dreams without dragons." When you show uncommon commitment, followers know that their investment of time and effort won't be wasted. They know that you won't walk away but that you will see the task through to the end. Yes, there may be dragons. But your uncommon commitment gives everyone confidence that with you, they can, and will, slay them.

If your followers are convinced that the goal is important and that you are not going to quit until you reach that goal, then watch out! There is nothing they won't do to show you that their commitment is equal to yours, and nothing will stop them until they reach that goal or accomplish that task with you.

NOT THE GRINCH, STILL, SHE GOT HER EMPLOYEES TO GIVE UP CHRISTMAS

Thirty years ago, the *New York Times* ran a story in which they reported that a woman by the name of Grace Pastiak got her organization to give up Christmas.[10]

As Director of Manufacturing, Grace Pastiak, worked for Tellabs in Lisle, Illinois. Tellabs designed, manufactured, and marketed expensive telecommunications products. Her department won a major contract. The only problem was that it was the Christmas season, and the job had to be completed by the end of the year. It looked impossible, but she decided to accept the contract anyway. It was probably one reason that Pastiak's organization was offered the contract.

Pastiak always took pride in her group's ability to take on any job and complete it successfully. As did her group. But now, she faced a particularly tough challenge. Accepting this job would mean time away from families during the holidays. Yet the contract was very important. She did not want to turn it down. Pastiak knew that she needed the full support of her employees. But how could she get it and get them to give up their Christmas holiday?

Pastiak did something she had never done before. She called her employees together and explained all the facts face-to-face. She told them that the job had to be completed by the end of the year. She told them that the job was so important that they were going to take the contract. To this, she was committed. However, she also told them that it would involve time away from home at Christmas and New Year. They would be able to attend religious services, but that was about it. She was willing and committed to the project. However, because of the extent of the sacrifice necessary, they would help make the decision. And there were alternatives. She offered several. They could contract to do only half of the order before the deadline. They could bring in part-time labour. Or they could subcontract some of the production to other companies. She told them again that she wanted to take the whole contract and accept the deadline as they had always done. But it was their choice.

One way or another, accepting the contract would require giving up their holiday. This showed uncommon commitment. Giving her workers a choice on how to do the job proved that this was not a regular job order and extremely important. Her workers voted to take the full contract and not to bring in part-time workers or to subcontract any of the work. The contract was completed during the holiday season without difficulty. Is it any wonder that subordinates and superiors alike call her 'Amazing Grace'.[11] Pastiak had taken a notable risk in what she had done. But Drucker had found that every business success required risk.

RISK TAKING IS NECESSARY FOR SUCCESS

Drucker found that every successful business situation required some kind of risk. If anything appears not to have any risk associated with it at all, something is probably wrong.

In 1939, a small businessman, W. Clement Stone of Chicago, assumed a significant risk. He had his own insurance agency and several insurance salesmen selling insurance for him throughout the US. He was making a good living, and his agency was growing every year. However, most of the policies his salesmen wrote were for a single company, Commercial Casualty Company of Newark, New Jersey, offering accident insurance.

Stone's operation was unique in that being a small business, he not only ran the company, he spent an extraordinary amount of time in selecting, training, and motivating his salesmen. So able were Stone's salespeople, that they sold far more insurance than did this major insurance company's salesmen.

One day while on holiday with his family in Miami Beach, Stone received a frantic call from his secretary. A salesman from the Commercial Casualty Company had complained about one of Stone's salesmen in Texas taking business away from him. His secretary explained that the CEO of Commercial Casualty Company had called and confirmed that from the beginning the following week, Stone's agency was forbidden to sell any insurance policies for this company.

You can imagine how quickly this message must have spread through the organization during the great depression. His salesmen probably didn't know what to do. With no product to sell, they could make no sales. A few probably wanted to quit right then and there, while others just wanted to know how Stone was going to phase out the business, and when they could start looking for a new job.

Stone immediately flew to the headquarters of the large insurance company and negotiated an extension of time that he could continue to sell Commercial Casualty's insurance. No doubt the CEO of this company was impressed with Stone's commitment to flying to New Jersey. Remember, this was back in 1939 when flying was more expensive and not the preferred method of travel for business travellers.

Stone returned to Chicago. The message he gave his salesmen showed them his uncommon commitment. The unthinkable thing he told them about and did saved his company.

Until this time, Stone's salesmen had only sold insurance for other companies who were the actual insurers. Stone thought that the business of selling insurance was complicated enough. The government laws and regulations having to do with actual insuring were complex. Stone had only a high school education. Becoming a real insurance company and the actual insurer rather than an insurance agency performing the sole task of selling insurance was unthinkable. He didn't even know where to start. It would be difficult, there would be so many problems to overcome. He couldn't even imagine them all. He would have to keep reserves of cash. How much, he didn't know. He would have to pay off the accounts when money was due. He would be subject to fraudulent claims which he would have to handle. He could get sued at times, it was part of the business! He would have to sue. But Stone decided to think outside the box and stayed committed.

"We won't be phasing anything out," he told his salesmen. "I'm starting my own insurance company, and each one of you has a place in it."

Stone founded his new company and called it Combined Insurance Company of America. Later he started the AON Corporation which included his insurance operation and other businesses. Annual sales eventually reached $6 billion and AON Corporation employed 27,000 people.[12]

Stone kept his company and his sales force by showing uncommon commitment and thinking outside the box when faced with an impossible situation. Since he could no longer sell someone else's insurance, he started his own insurance company, and sold his own.

COMMITMENT MEANS TAKING RISKS

Of course, commitment means taking risks. Some leaders are afraid to show uncommon commitment for this reason. Let's be frank. Some are afraid to show any commitment at all. Yet, risk is a part of life. Your willingness to accept this risk is part of your responsibilities as leader. Its acceptance is one clear way of showing uncommon commitment.

How did Drucker recommend dealing with necessary risks? He recommended analysing the situation and asking questions such as, what is the worst that can happen? When you know the worst that can happen, you can decide whether it is worth the risk. If it is, accept the risk and go ahead.

It is amazing that once you accept the worst that can happen, if your goal is worth the risk you will have much less difficulty accepting this risk. Then, you will have no difficulty making and showing an uncommon commitment.

You never know what you can do until you pull out all the stops and go all the way. So many people attaining success against all odds were able to do so because they showed uncommon commitment and attempted the impossible and they attained the extraordinary. Those whose examples I gave you did it. Drucker did it. You can too!

---

1. Byrne, John A. with Lindsey Gerdes. "The Man Who Invented Management," *Business Week* (28 November 2005). https://bloom.bg/2MoYFj6.
2. Bonaparte, Napoleon, "Maxims of Napoleon," LXVII, published originally in Paris in 1830 and translated into English shortly thereafter in *Jomini, Clausewitz, and Schlieffen* (West Point, NY: Department of Military Art and Engineering, United States Military Academy, 1954), 89.
3. Drucker, Peter F. *Concept of the Corporation* (New York: John Day, 1946).
4. *PrimalScream Music*. "Nicole Dionne: CEO/Creative Director", https://bit.ly/2KySSpO, accessed 20 July 2018.
5. Klein, Karen E. "Sound Approach". *Los Angeles Times*, 15 July 1997, D2, https://lat.ms/2vBEU0N.
6. Dionne, Nicole, interview with the author, 19 October 1997.
7. Patterson, George K. Telephone conversations with the author, 4 and 11 April 1996.
8. HM Government. *Hansard*, 13 May 1940, https://bit.ly/2M1isZa, col. 1502.
9. HM Government. *Hansard*, 4 June 1940, https://bit.ly/2MahJFh, col. 796.
10. Holusha, John. "Grace Pastiak's 'Web of Inclusion'<TNBS>". *New York Times*, 5 May 1991, https://nyti.ms/2M2cDLa.
11. Glaser, Connie and Barbara Steinberg Smalley. *Swim with the Dolphins: How Women Can Succeed in Corporate America on Their Own Terms* (New York: Warner Books, 1995), 12-17
12. Hill, Napoleon and W. Clement Stone. *Success Through a Positive Mental Attitude* (Chicago: Nightingales-Conant, 1988), Tape 3

CHAPTER 9

THE IMPORTANCE OF EXPECTING SUCCESS AND HOW TO DO IT

Only a tiny number of people can be outstanding successes, but a very large number are expected to be adequately successful.

– Peter F. Drucker

t is true that if you expect positive results, you may still not actually achieve them due to circumstances which may be beyond your control. But it is equally true that if you do not expect positive results you will probably not get them. So, while expecting positive results may not always lead to success, failing to expect positive results will more often lead to failure. You don't need to be outstandingly successful every time you attempt anything. You can still reach the top. But you do need to be adequately successful overall to progress to the top, and that is within all of our abilities.

WHAT A GREEK GENERAL SHOWED US ABOUT EXPECTING POSITIVE RESULTS 2,000 YEARS AGO

More than 60 years ago Drucker advised his readers to read "the first systematic book on leadership" in his own book, *The Practice of Management*.[1] These were part of the writings of Xenophon, a Greek general. The book Drucker referenced was *Kyropaidaia*. One source translates the title of this material as *The Education of Cyrus the Great*.[2] Xenophon was an Athenian general. From 401 BC to 400 BC B.C., he led 10,000 Greek soldiers in retreat from

Persia to the Greek Black Sea colony of Trapezus more than 1,000 miles away. They initially faced an enemy that was greatly superior in numbers, and they were continually opposed by unfriendly tribes through their escape trek, which took five months. Afterwards, Xenophon became known as a writer as well as a remarkable and successful general.

Here's what happened to Xenophon in his adventures which detailed how he had become a general and led those 10,000 Greek soldiers to safety. Cyrus the Younger, son of Cyrus the Great of Persia, had enlisted Greek troops as paid mercenaries to help him overthrow his brother, Artaxerxes, who was king of Persia. At the Battle of Cunaxa, they fought a Persian army many times their size and won. However, during the battle, Cyrus the Younger was killed. Even so, the Greek general Clearchus, who was second in command changed tactics, advanced against the right wing of the Persian army and, for all practical purposes, defeated Artaxerxes and won the battle despite the death of his commander,

Cyrus the Younger, who was challenging his brother for the kingship of Persia.

But since Cyrus, pretender to the Persian throne, was dead, there was little point to the victory of his troops. In fact, the Persians in Cyrus's former army deserted to Artaxerxes.

Artaxerxes told the Greeks that since Cyrus was dead, there was no reason for their continuing to fight. To use two cliques in one sentence, he was willing to 'forgive and forget' and to 'live and let live.' He offered a truce which was accepted by the Greek mercenaries. Artaxerxes told them that they could retreat and return to their own country unhindered. To celebrate their truce, he invited the Grecian generals to a great banquet. They were told to leave their weapons outside. Once Artaxerxes had them under his control without weapons, he surrounded and murdered them. And since Troy, and remembering the Wooden Horse, the warning is to beware of Greeks bearing gifts! Or in this case, Persians, but I guess in all cases we need to at least be cautious regardless of ethnicity.

In any case, Artaxerxes then offered a truce to the lower-ranking officers of the Greek army.

Xenophon was a young staff officer. But after the murder of the Greek generals, he wisely did not trust Artaxerxes. He gathered the surviving officers together and convinced them that if they accepted this truce, as did their generals, they would be probably killed too.

He persuaded them to elect new generals. Xenophon was one of those elected. Some Greek officers wanted to work out some sort deal with Artaxerxes. The other newly elected generals were uncertain as they saw no way of marching such a great distance through unfriendly country, not to mention the numerically superior and revenge-seeking Persian army that they had just defeated in battle.

Xenophon still had credibility as the one who had convinced them not to accept Artaxerxes word. He assembled all the officers and spoke to them. "All of our soldiers have their eyes on you, and if they see that you are downhearted they will become cowards, while if you yourselves are clearly prepared to meet the enemy and if you call on the rest to do their part, you can be sure that they will follow you and try to be like you."[3] You can see why Drucker liked Xenophon as a leader. Xenophon expected positive results. Through his positive expectancy, he convinced both officers and soldiers that they would return to their homes even though they had lost their most experienced and proven generals, were numerically inferior to their enemy, had hundreds of miles of unfriendly territory to traverse, and had no supplies of food and water. Because Xenophon expected positive results, his 10,000 followers expected positive results as well. They escaped from Artaxerxes and followed Xenophon on one of the most amazing long marches in history. They completed their journey successfully despite countless battles and hardships. No wonder Drucker called our attention to Xenophon's work as containing important lessons for leading in business. Never fear, you can learn to be a Xenophon, too.

YOU CAN LEARN TO EXPECT POSITIVE RESULTS

Bill Gates may be one of the wealthiest individuals in the world today. Gates started his first company, Traf-O-Data, with high hopes. Its purpose was to process and analyse the data from traffic tapes. Unfortunately for him, the process was flawed, and the company failed. But Gates didn't let this failure hold him back from starting famed Microsoft only a few years later. He expected success with Microsoft even though he had a major failure in the past, with Traf-O-Data, and with Microsoft, he got it.

HOW YOU CAN DEVELOP THE QUALITY OF EXPECTING POSITIVE RESULTS

Here are five ways you can develop the quality of expecting positive results:
- Develop your self-confidence
- Become a positive thinker
- Visualize the results you want to achieve
- Be who you are – don't pretend that you are someone else
- Maintain your enthusiasm.

DEVELOP YOUR SELF-CONFIDENCE

Few start out in life accomplishing what we think of as big goals. We all start as infants and accomplish trivial things like learning to walk and talk, and later to read, write, and reason. But are these really trivial things? Think back. At the time you first learned to do any of these things you probably didn't think it was so trivial. The truth is, even with these small things we started out by doing still smaller things first and slowly increasing the difficulty of the subtasks until we could accomplish the overall task – things like rolling over and sitting up, in preparation for the actual walking.

Today, you no longer doubt that when you stand, put forth one leg and then another, you are going to walk. As you read these sentences, unless you are just learning English, there is little doubt that you will understand what you have read. You automatically expect positive results.

With the more complex and challenging tasks and projects of adults, many fail to expect to succeed for only one of two reasons. Either they have been unsuccessful at similar tasks or projects in the past, or they have never tried to accomplish them in the first place. And by the way, those who have never tried usually haven't tried because they feel they would fail if they did. You'll learn more about developing your self-confidence in Chapter 13. Meanwhile, you can start right now by becoming a positive thinker,

BECOME A POSITIVE THINKER

You can think positively, or negatively. It's your choice. However, most negative leaders do not expect positive results. On the contrary, they frequently expect the worst to happen – and so it does. I don't know whether this is some kind of black magic or self-fulfilling nightmare, or what. It doesn't matter. It's a fact: what we think of we usually get, whether it's positive or negative. It's not that Drucker recommended that you become a wishful thinker or always think wonderful things no matter the situation. Not at all. You can be a steely-eyed realist. Still that shouldn't stop you from thinking positively. And that will help you to expect to be successful.

Positive thinkers keep their eye on the ball (what they want, their goals, tasks, etc.) and not what they don't want (what they want to avoid). To do this, they first ask themselves, "What is the worst that can happen?" Then they accept that as a result if all goes wrong. Next, they act and do what needs to be done.

Do you think that someone who has already considered the worst, accepted it, even planned ahead as to what action to take is less fearful and thinks more positively? You bet! No wonder such individuals expect to be successful.

GENERAL COLIN POWELL SUCCEEDED DESPITE THE ODDS

One of the most positive thinking men I have ever met is Colin Powell, former Chairman of the Joint Chiefs of Staff, the highest-ranking general in the US military.

I met General Powell when he addressed the *Los Angeles Times* Management Conference in March 1993, before he retired from his position as Chairman of the Joint Chiefs of Staff. I had been invited to do a piece on leadership for the *Los Angeles Times* internal newsletter for their managers. As it happened, Powell was slated to speak to their management conference shortly after my article was scheduled to appear. David Laventhol, then Publisher and CEO of the *Los Angeles Times* and Dickson Louie, a fellow graduate of the University of Chicago Business School who was conference president asked me if I would like to attend the conference and meet Powell. I was delighted and honoured to accept.

Powell was positive, upbeat and full of energy despite this being his third speech that day, and these were in three different cities located hundreds of miles apart around the US. The first was in Texas, and the second in San Francisco. Here it was, three o'clock in the afternoon in Los Angeles, his third speech in as many cities hundreds of miles apart, and Powell showed no sign of fatigue. He was still raring to go.

Everyone knew that Powell was in for some tough questioning. One of President Bill Clinton's promises prior to his election was over the issue of gays in the military. The rumour was that it was Powell who had convinced the President to adopt a compromise position.

This was before 9/11, but there were other issues. Why couldn't the military budget be cut further and faster? What was the future of the National Guard? Many were unhappy with the way they perceived that the Army's National Guard Roundout brigades had been treated during the Gulf War which had recently been concluded with Saddam Hussein's defeat. Powell was facing the media in the heart of the enemy camp. It was expected that he would be in for a rough time.

Well, it didn't happen like that. Powell was positive and in control right from the start. CEO Laventhol treated him to an elaborate introduction. During his accolades for Powell, Laventhol also revealed that before going into the newspaper business, he had once been a private in the US Army. Powell came to the podium and thanked Laventhol for his generous introduction. Then, with a twinkle in his eye, he added, "And, Private, that introduction was done very well."

Powell gave a five-star speech. His positive thinking won over every one of the 300 or so senior managers present even when he had tough questions to answer.

Powell was the highest-ranking officer in the US armed forces. Yet he came from the humble beginnings. He was raised in the South Bronx in New York. Both of his parents were working-class immigrants, only one of whom had graduated from high school. Despite competition and prejudice, Powell graduated from the City College of New York. There were no special admissions for minorities in those days and this was important as Powell is African-American. He competed for and got a regular commission in the Army through the Reserve Officers Training Corps (ROTC) at the City College of New York. He was not an affirmative-action success story as some have suggested. He was a Colin Powell success story, and as Drucker recommended, he expected to succeed.

There was real, live bigotry and prejudice as Powell rose through the ranks. There was no quota system to assist him. He completed not as a minority, but on his own ability. Powell made it to the very pinnacle of the US armed forces on sheer guts, an incredibly positive attitude, and his own merit and ability. Powell was a positive thinker and those who followed him became positive thinkers too.

His positive thinking culminated in leading our armed forces as Chairman of the Joint Chiefs of Staff during the most successful major military action since World War II: Operation Desert Storm.

While still Chairman of the Joint Chiefs of Staff, General Powell spoke to kids in the ghettos. And because he couldn't reach them all in person, he had 10,000 videotapes made which were sent to high schools across the USA.

Here's what General Powell told them. "There's nothing you can't accomplish if you're willing to put your mind to it, if you're willing to set aside the negative influences that are out there, if you believe in yourself, if you're committed to yourself, and if you believe in this country, and if you let nothing hold you back. Don't let the fact that you're Hispanic or black or any other attribute hold you back. Just go for it. I did it; you can do it. Don't look for a silver bullet. Don't look for 'a role model I'm going to follow'. Be your own role model. Believe in yourself."[4]

VISUALIZE THE RESULTS YOU WANT TO ACHIEVE

If you want to learn to expect positive results, you've got to see those results achieved in your own mind first. Psychologists call this mental rehearsal or visualization, and it is amazing what can be done with it. Mental visualization seems to work best in a very relaxed state, and I have witnessed, as well as been involved in, many experiments that illustrate just how powerful mental visualization is.

My wife is a clinical psychologist, and I studied psychology at the graduate level myself. Therefore, I attended a number of seminars on hypnosis, many with her. Under a hypnotic trance, a subject is extremely relaxed and open to suggestion. One sequence while so entranced is to have the subject imagine himself in a lemon grove, to pick a lemon, slice it in half, and squeeze a bit into his mouth and taste the lemon.

The amazing thing is that when you do this, your lips invariably pucker as you imagine the sweet-sour juice from the lemon in your mouth. One theory is that all hypnosis is really self-hypnosis, and anyway to enter yourself is quite easy. In fact, if you found yourself pucker your lips when you thought about the lemon juice now, you self-hypnotized yourself!

But there is more. When in a hypnotic trance, a subject, after some visualization techniques, can be told that a cube of ice applied to their bare skin is red hot. Believe it or not, it can raise a blister on the subject's skin!

However, one of the most amazing stories I ever heard about the power of mental visualization and self-hypnosis, especially regarding its use in expecting positive results comes from a psychologist by the name of Charles Garfield. I first heard about Garfield from an article in *The Wall Street Journal* in January 1982. The article said that through visualization techniques and visualizing a positive outcome, Garfield was able to significantly increase the speaking performance of top executives. Later, Garfield wrote a book, *Peak Performers*, in which he described the following incident.

In Milan, Italy, at a conference on peak performance, Garfield met some Russian scientists who began to discuss their current work. Learning that Garfield was an amateur weightlifter, they invited him to participate in an experiment. They learned that Garfield had been able to bench press 280 lb. They asked him what was the most he thought he could lift. Garfield told them 300 lb. After some encouragement from onlookers, and working up to it, he was good as his word and lifted 300 lb. However, Garfield said that the lift was made with great difficulty and required every ounce of his strength and concentration.

Next, the Russians put Garfield into a very relaxed, hypnotic state and took him through a series of visualization exercises that lasted about an hour. During these exercises, he visualized himself pressing not 300, but 365 lb in the bench press, which to Garfield seemed utterly impossible. However, after this preparation, when told to do so, not only was he able to accomplish the lift, but he felt that it was easier to lift 365 lb than when he had tried to lift 300 lb![5]

To use visualization to expect positive results is easy. Sit in your chair or some place that you can relax and simply visualize your goal in every detail. If your goal is to make a speech, then imagine yourself on the stage waiting to be introduced. Hear the introduction given for you.

Are there flowers on the dais? Smell their fragrance. Are some waiters still serving coffee? Listen to the sounds they make as they move about the room. Smell the aroma of the coffee. Sip some yourself and savour its taste in your mind. Use all five senses to make the scene as real in your mind as you possibly can.

If you are preparing yourself to give a speech, listen to the applause in your mind as you are called forward to begin your presentation. Imagine looking out into the audience and visualize the eager and expectant looks on the faces of those who are about to listen to you. Now, give your speech in your mind and note the audience's rapt attention. See yourself connecting with the audience, and see the audience responding to what you have to say and hanging onto every word. Now see yourself coming to a powerful conclusion, and see the audience leaping to their feet to give you a standing ovation in their enthusiasm.

After you have done this once, repeat the whole sequence again. If your project is several days ahead, I recommend repeating it several times a day. The night before your performance, you can repeat it a dozen times or more. You will be pleasantly surprised with the results that you achieve in your presentation by expecting success through mental visualization.

BE WHO YOU ARE
– DON'T PRETEND THAT YOU ARE SOMEONE ELSE

You can't be someone you are not. You're stuck! We all are. We're all different, but we all have the potential for being successful.

A.L. Williams, was an $18,000-a-year high school football coach in Georgia in 1977 when he founded a life insurance company based on a new concept. Most insurance companies make their largest sales through emphasizing ordinary life insurance. Williams pointed out that you can buy a lot more insurance for less money with term insurance and you can make even more by investing the difference. Obviously, his competitors were not thrilled.

Williams had no MBA and no corporate business experience. Still, his company became one of the largest of its kind in the world in less than ten years with over $81 billion in individual life insurance. Williams wrote a book on his experiences. Its title was *All You Can Do Is All You Can Do, but All You Can Do is Enough!*[6] What Williams is telling us with this title is that what we think our limitations are makes a slight difference. That it is still good enough to reach success and to become wealthy if that is what is desired.

Too many try to be what they are not. They may be kind and thoughtful, and yet are afraid to display these qualities. They may have read management books somewhere that promoted a tough management style. So, they want to be tough. Or maybe they heard that today's leader should have a participatory style. So, they strive for participation, even when it is inappropriate. Or maybe they try to be overfriendly, when by nature they are more reserved.

One senior vice president told me this story back when Total Quality (TQ) Management was all the rage as the latest management fad. "We hired a team to come in and teach us TQ. They got all the senior and middle managers together for four days. They told us we should all be more open and call each other by our first names. They made us wear big name tags that read 'Bob' and 'Bill' and 'Joe'. That's never been the style in our company, and it certainly wasn't the boss's style. Then we were supposed to spend three days coming up with a strategic plan. It was one of the worst experiences I ever had, and I suspect that the same was true for others, including our middle managers. We had to call the president 'Bob'. It was terrible. I never felt so much tension in relationships with senior leaders in the company. We came up with a plan, but we all knew it was awful. Fortunately, 'Bob' recognized it, too. We threw it out and redid the whole thing about four months later. This time, we got real and were ourselves. What a difference! And the conference was a lot more open and free of tension, too!"

It wasn't that calling senior managers by their first names was so bad. In many organizations that works just fine. Drucker used to tell his graduate students "call me Peter" and we did. It was doing what was not normal in this organization that was the problem.

I once taught the same graduate student at two different schools. One was Claremont Graduate School. There everyone was on a first name basis with professors. The other school was California State University Los Angeles. There professors were always addressed with his or her title as doctor or professor. "How should I address you?" my student asked. "Is it Dr Cohen or Bill?" "That's easy," I responded. "When you address me at California State University Los Angeles, you call me Dr Cohen. When you address me at Claremont you call me Bill." And that's what we did, and it worked just fine.

MAINTAIN YOUR ENTHUSIASM

Ralph Waldo Emerson once said, "Nothing great was ever achieved without enthusiasm."[7] Peter Drucker believed even more emotional investment was needed to reach the top. He thought that not only enthusiasm, but that *passion* was essential with each individual taking responsibility for his or her own results and continued learning.[8] Of course, you need to do this yourself as well.

One thing I can assure you is that if you aren't enthusiastic about something, no one else will be. That's a fact. You can't expect others to enthusiastically accept a challenge that you haven't enthusiastically accepted yourself.

1. Drucker, Peter F. *The Practice of Management* (New York: Harper & Row, 1955), 194.
2. Grant, Michael. *Readings in the Classical Historians* (New York: Charles Scribner's Sons, 1992), 101.
3. Xenophon. *The Persian Expedition*, translated by Rex Warner (Baltimore, MD: Penguin Books, 1949), 104.
4. Powell, Colin L. "Address to *Los Angeles Times* Management Conference", 19 March 1993.
5. Garfield, Charles. *Peak Performers* (New York: Avon, 1986), 71-75.
6. Williams, A.L. *All You Can Do Is All You Can Do, but All You Can Do Is Enough!* (Nashville, TN: Oliver-Nelson, 1988).
7. Emerson, Ralph Waldo. "Essay X: Circles". *Essays* [First Series] (Boston, MA: J. Monro and Co., 1841), https://bit.ly/2KumoNc.
8. "The Passion Puzzle". *Drucker Institute*, 27 September 2013, https://bit.ly/2KuCh6b.

CHAPTER 10

TAKING CARE OF YOUR PEOPLE

*So much of what we call management consists
in making it difficult for people to work.
Treat every worker as a volunteer because in today's
world of knowledge workers, that's what they are.*

– Peter F. Drucker

W hen I first wrote about the importance of taking care of your people as one of the eight universal laws of leadership, I thought only of employees or those being led. In fact, I quoted Xenophon, the author of the book Drucker frequently touted as "the first systematic book on leadership written two thousand years ago, and still the best".[1] Xenophon was first to document words to the effect that: "People are only too glad to obey the man who they believe takes wiser thoughts for their interests than they themselves do."

Later I expanded my thinking about "taking care of your people" to include not only subordinate employees, but customers too. And when I realized that taking care of your people was also a success principle, I expanded the definition to include all people that you meet professionally. Your success is always dependent on others, and if you truly want success, you need to take care of them as well.

HOW FAR SHOULD YOU GO IN TAKING CARE OF YOUR PEOPLE?

How far should you go in taking care of your people? Fortunately, most civilian careers do not normally require someone to lay down his or her life for people to take care of them. Some, such as police, firefighters, and others may do. But make no mistake. The more that you take care of the needs of others, the more they will help you on the way to the top. Of course, this does not mean helping others in unethical or illegal ways or that you should violate your own beliefs or standards in helping them. Years before President Trump, a friend of mine who was serving as a political appointee in Washington at the time explained to me why a senator had opposed and voted against and eventually stopped a nominee of his own political party from getting appointed as Secretary of Defence. My friend said that years before the nominee had publicly attacked the senator unnecessarily, for no reason other than personal disagreement. The nominee had done nothing particularly wrong, but as far as the senator was concerned, it was payback time. It would be nice if everyone would simply turn the other cheek, as Jesus advised, when disrespected or treated poorly. However, that's unlikely to happen. You may dislike someone, but you should still need to treat them fairly, honestly, and with respect.

DOES IT REALLY HAPPEN?

They say that Thomas Watson, who founded IBM and later instituted extensive programmes in education, healthcare, and recreation for IBM employees was continually visiting his factories and spent hours talking to his employees. On one occasion, he told an employee, "If you have any problem at all, let me know."

Later, the employee came to New York and asked to see Watson. On being ushered in to Watson's office, he told Watson that his younger brother had an incurable disease and he had been told he would not live long. Remembering Watson's promise, he asked whether anything could be done that was beyond the medical resources of his small community. Watson had the brother put in a top hospital under the care of a famous specialist.

At this point, the employee began to feel a little guilty that perhaps he had overstepped Watson's invitation and he began to apologize to Watson. But, Watson interrupted him. "When I said bring your problems to me, I meant exactly that."[2]

IF YOU WANT TO TAKE CARE OF YOUR PEOPLE, DO THESE THINGS

Normally, your duties will not require you to take care of your people to the extent that Watson did. However, the idea is on target. If you want to be someone that aims for the top like Drucker, here is my advice to you:

- Be the one others turn to when things go wrong
- Give others' needs priority over your own needs
- Really care
- Assume the responsibility
- Share the gain.

BE THE ONE OTHERS TURN TO WHEN THINGS GO WRONG

It doesn't make much difference whether it is your responsibility or not. Of course, if it is, it is more important. When the chips are down and times are difficult is when others really watch to see what you do. Do you really take care of your people, or is it all for show?

MR FEUERSTEIN HAD A ROUGH BIRTHDAY

Age or other factors have little to do with this concept. You either take care of your people, no matter how bad the situation, or you do not. A man from Lawrence, Massachusetts named Aaron Feuerstein did, and the situation was indeed bad. On the night of 11 December 1995, while Feuerstein was celebrating his 70th birthday, his factory, Malden Mills, suffered a major fire and destruction.

Malden Mills was a complex of nine buildings, and it employed 2,400 semi-skilled workers. Most of them were immigrants. The company, which manufactured upholstery and synthetic winter-wear fabrics, was one of the largest employers in the region. Feuerstein's grandfather, a Jewish immigrant from Eastern Europe, founded it in 1906. Feuerstein had earlier problems with Malden Mills. He had laboriously worked the company out of Chapter 11 reorganization and saved the company in the early 1980s. He had a reputation for taking care of his people and in paying what some termed the best wages in the textile industry. Productivity had practically tripled prior to the fire.

His losses in the fire were significant. One of three boilers exploded in a building where nylon velvet materials for chairs and other furnishings were made. Not only was this building destroyed, but three of his nine buildings were levelled. Thirty-three workers were injured, 13 of them severely. Almost half his work force had no work.

At a time when CEOs of bigger, wealthier, and financially stronger companies were firing employees simply to cut costs and improve their profit picture, Feuerstein pledged to continue paying wages and health benefits for as long as it took to rebuild even though many of his workers had no work to perform. This cost him $1.5 million a week just to meet his payroll. He even paid the previously announced holiday bonus of $275 to each employee. Rather than take the insurance money and run, he vowed to rebuild on the same spot.

Many bean-counting managers at larger companies said he should have pocketed the insurance money, and if he wasn't going to retire or take the money and run, have rebuilt down south where labour costs were lower. That would be a good business decision. I'm not so sure. I know it would have been a poor leadership decision. Feuerstein agrees. "Why would I go to Thailand to bring the cost lower when I might run the risk of losing the advantage I've got, which is superior quality?"

But Feuerstein was a businessman and nobody's patsy. Drawn into a discussion of Al Dunlap who about the same time fired a third of the work force at Scott Paper when it was in trouble, Feuerstein said, "If one-third of the people of that company were wastefully employed, then Dunlap did the right thing. Legitimate downsizing as the result of technological advances or as a result of good engineering? Absolutely. I'm in favour of it. And we do it here all day long ... We try to do it in such a way as to minimize human suffering, but the downsizing must be done." However, Feuerstein said that the trick is to do it "without crushing the spirit of the work force." He continued, that if all you are after is cutting costs, if you "just have a scheme to cut people – that sort of thing is resented by labour and never forgiven."[3]

Speaking at MIT, Feuerstein said, "Within four months, we had 85% of the people back. Were it not for the slow payments of the insurance company, we would have over 100% back today." At first, the company made an amazing recovery. As an example, Feuerstein said, "The fourth plant, which prior to the fire had never produced more than 130,000 yards a week, is producing more than 200,000 yards."[4] It would be nice if this kind of thing always had a happy ending. But that's not real life. Despite Malden Mills' recovery, it was only temporary. In 2001 Feuerstein had to declare bankruptcy and eventually sell the company. A new company, Polartec LCC was created which purchased its assets in 2007. The company was honoured by *Time Magazine* sometime later as the inventor of synthetic fleece.

Feuerstein's actions didn't cause the bankruptcy and we all face challenges of health and age which may have contributed to his latter business and personal decisions. However, when it counted, Feuerstein took care of his people when things went wrong, and he could do something about it. There is no doubt that both his example as well as synthetic fleece was part of his legacy. Drucker knew that our legacies are an important part of what we leave behind whether we are 100% successful or not.

WHAT IT MEANS TO GIVE OTHERS' NEEDS PRIORITY OVER YOUR OWN

Dave Whitmore was my classmate at West Point and my flying partner in flying school. After the Air Force, Whitmore joined IBM. Later he was promoted and became an IBM marketing manager for a new region in New York that serviced utilities and telephone companies. The two largest accounts in Whitmore's area were serviced by two of his most senior marketing team leaders. These accounts represented a considerable amount of money, and the pressure was incredible. If any of the computers went down, Whitmore could lose his job.

One day, Whitmore became aware of a fundamental problem concerning his two senior marketing team leaders. Neither one had ever held a staff job. So what, you may ask? Well, it could seriously affect the IBM careers of both. Whitmore was told that if they weren't assigned staff positions outside of his organization within the next few months, the chances were they would never get them. Many large organizations have personnel policies in place to encourage the best employees on their way to the top to seek assignments which will ensure they have the right experience for higher level positions. But sometimes these policies backfire and for one reason or another, employees don't get the required experience that the company has decided is needed to keep being promoted. Sometimes companies have emergencies and employees miss out on moving into the right jobs. Then for no reason of their own certain employees may miss out on promotion for top jobs, when they are compared to competitors who have the experience. That's what the danger was here. It was unlikely that either could ever get promoted to a more senior position without the experience in certain types of staff jobs. Yet, these were talented hard-working people who deserved the shot at higher positions, their timing was just bad.

First Whitmore talked to his two team leaders. He explained the situation to them. What did they want to do? Both expressed a willingness to stay if they had to, but both understood the necessity for obtaining the required staff experience. Both wanted a chance at future promotion if it were possible.

Whitmore was inexperienced in his work and had only recently assumed his own new job. He had no other experienced team leaders, and none would be available if Whitmore let these two go to staff positions elsewhere in the company. But it was Whitmore's decision, and it was his responsibility to take care of his people.

Whitmore's boss, a branch manager, counselled him. "Who cares whether they become managers or not? It's your fanny that's on the line. If you let them go, you're taking a chance on losing everything you've worked for. Screw up, and I can't guarantee whether you can ever become a branch manager. Your sending them to these staff positions may help them, but it may limit your own future chances at promotion in the company."

Whitmore knew what he had to do. He saw that both team leaders were offered staff positions in IBM immediately. They both accepted and left.

What happened to Whitmore? He made do without the two experienced team leaders. Later, due to his success at this job, he was offered what he called "my dream job": international account manager in Brussels. Before retirement from IBM, he was promoted to branch manager and served in that capacity in Saudi Arabia.[5]

AVOIDING LAY-OFFS: A SURE ACTION THAT SHOWS YOU CARE

Minnesota Mining and Manufacturing Company in St Paul, Minnesota, better known as 3M, was a $14 billion business when, back in the early 1980s, it had to address the possibility of lay-offs for the first time.

To avoid or at least minimize them, company leaders came up with a system called the unassigned list.

The unassigned list allowed employees whose jobs had been eliminated through no fault of their own six months to find another position within 3M. Meanwhile, workers continued to receive full salaries and benefits. Within the first four months, they had the option of taking an unassigned severance package. This included a week and a half's pay for every year of service, plus six months of paid benefits. Those who were over the age of 50 but hadn't yet reached retirement age could receive a pre-retirement leave package that continued until retirement. Those over age 55 received a special bridge to social security. For those who couldn't find a position within the company, 3M also offered extensive help in finding new employment.

The senior vice president of human resources said that this plan was all due to some thought that also benefited 3M, "We're a company of long service employees. That long service translates into less than a 3% turnover among the salaried staff. And pride."[6]

That plan for taking care of employees translated into real results. Revenue increased by 11.7% after the plan was implemented, and there were record sales and earnings in 3M's two business sectors in their US and international operations.[7]

Lands' End, Inc., the catalogue giant, was in trouble several years ago. Paper prices had doubled, and apparel demand collapsed at the same time as a significant postal hike. As a result, third quarter profits were down 60% and falling. Advisors told the then CEO, 34-year-old Michael J. Smith, that he should think about laying off employees to improve his bottom line. That should boost stock prices and please stockholders.

To Smith, that was an integrity issue. Laying off employees simply to make himself look good when business conditions were tougher was not doing the right thing.

Smith added benefits. What kind of benefits? He added an adoption assistance service and mental health referrals. And part-time employees received full health care benefits. He refused to lay anyone off. "If people feel squeezed, they won't treat the customer as well," explained Smith. Results? To everyone's surprise, the following year first quarter profits more than tripled to $4.4 million compared to the previous year. Sales rose 2.3%. Stock price of Lands' End shares increased 85%.[8]

Another company that avoided lay-offs by sharing the pain was Nucor. Ken Iverson was the CEO of the Nucor Corporation. Nucor consistently had high profits in what can only be termed a declining industry, steel manufacturing. Nucor's 7,000 employees were the best-paid workers in the steel business but had the industry's lowest labour costs per ton of steel produced. Nucor was a Fortune 500 company, but there were only 24 people assigned to corporate headquarters, and four layers of management from the CEO to the front-line worker. Nucor had no R&D department or corporate engineering group. Yet, the company was the first major operator of 'mini-mills' and the first to demonstrate that mini-mills could make flat-rolled steel, the first to apply thin-stab casing, which 'Big Steel' had determined couldn't be done, and the first to commercially produce iron carbide.

Iverson took over the company in the decline and built it into a highly successful giant. How did he do it? What happened during a period when times got worse might give us some insight.

Suddenly things got much worse and total number of steelworkers dropped like a stone from 400,000 to 200,000. At Nucor, they had to cut production in half. Iverson did not downsize anyone. How did he avoid doing what every other steel company did? Department heads took pay cuts of up to 40%. Iverson and other more senior company officers cut their salaries up to 60%.

It wasn't enough. So, Iverson cut back workweeks from five to four, and then, three days. This meant that on average his workers suffered a 25% cut in pay. "You know that had to hurt," said Iverson. "Still, as I walked through our mills and plants, I never heard one employee complain about it. Not one."[9] That's not surprising when those workers fully understood that their leaders were taking significant cuts also.

Iverson knew what he had to do to show his people that he really cared: "I took a 75% pay cut from $450,000 to $110,000," he said.

"It was the only right thing to do." But Iverson noted that nothing was written in stone. Of course, if lay-offs were necessary, he would do it, but not before he tried everything else first. Iverson called that "pain sharing". When times were good, they shared the benefits, and when times were bad, Iverson maintained that senior management, right up through to the president, had to share that as well. He believed in the success laws and that there is a duty that comes before personal interest, and certainly before any personal interest in times of crisis.[10] Not surprisingly, Iverson's legacy lived on, years after Iverson's retirement, and Nucor was ranked as the largest steel producer in the USA[11] and so it is as these words are written today (summer 2018) with revenues as high as $16 billion and more than 23,000 employees.[12]

IF YOU REALLY CARE, TREAT PEOPLE AS THEY SHOULD BE TREATED

Cutco Corporation manufacturers and markets some of the highest quality kitchen knives in the world. It was this company that first manufactured the KA-BAR knife, the official knife of the US Marine Corps during World War II. Its sales today are over $200 million worldwide.

But when Erick Laine took over as CEO in 1982, sales were only $5 million. That's a 2,000% increase in a field that older, established brands from Europe dominated. When Laine became CEO of Alcas (the old name of Cutco), his manufacturing arm was in disarray. In a nine-year period prior to his becoming boss, there wasn't a single contract that was settled without a strike! There were no less than 270 outstanding grievances on the books![13]

Laine was tough. He was born in Finland, and in addition to integrity, his parents taught him something that doesn't translate easily into English. The word in Finnish is *sisu*. *Sisu* means a sort of stubborn persistence wrapped up with sheer guts. He knew what he was doing, and he was no pushover. But he truly cared about his people and he insisted on treating them fairly.

From early on Laine met with his union in a spirit of openness and listened. And when the union was right, he acknowledged it.

And when he thought they were full of wrong, he was willing to tell them that, too. But then, a strange thing happened. This openness, honesty, and the willingness to treat people as they should be treated led to a spirit of camaraderie. They proceeded to work things through together. Over time they developed an unusual trust, and when they had a problem, they worked together to solve it.

Does your union present you with a yearly gift of cash collected from your workers? Every year at Christmas time during most of Laine's tenure, the union initiated an unusual act. It wasn't mandated, and neither Laine nor any of his managers recommended nor initiated it. No, this came from the workers and their union. What happened was this. The union leaders called Laine on the phone and requested a meeting. At the meeting, the union representatives presented a gift: money they collected from the workers on a volunteer basis. Ever heard of something like this anywhere else? The money was always used by management to purchase something that would benefit the workers – a TV for the cafeteria or a clock, that type of thing.[14] This practice lasted throughout Laine's tenure as president and CEO until his retirement.

Now why do you think the workers and their union did this? Obviously, they could just collect the money and go out and buy something themselves. Laine didn't tell me this, but I believe this informal ceremony during which Laine was presented with this money was a symbol of the trust between the union and its management, between the company leaders and their workers. It was rare and unprecedented. It happened only because Laine really cared.

TAKE PERSONAL RESPONSIBILITY

Whenever something went right, these leaders at IBM, 3M, Malden Mills, Cutco, and others gave credit to their people. But when something didn't go right, they took personal responsibility. Sometimes, taking personal responsibility must be expressed in the physical sense. At other times, in the moral sense. The leaders of these organizations did whatever was necessary in taking care of others. These were all organizations, but I'm certain that if we were to investigate we would see that these leaders treated friends or even someone they had never met in the same way. That's one reason that the customers of these organizations rarely complain and are usually the first to recommend their products and services to others. Former employees probably do the same. It's part of the reason that personal relationships are an important part of the way to the top.

YOU CAN BANK ON THIS BANKER

Marshall Carter was Chairman and CEO of The State Street Corporation. The State Street Corporation is a bank. Well, not exactly a bank: known as State Street, it is an American worldwide financial services company. State Street was founded in 1792 and is the second oldest financial institution in America. It is the largest processor of pension funds in the world. It has some $4 trillion under custodianship. Yes, that's trillion, with a T.[15]

When Carter took over State Street, there were severe challenges. There were talks of deep cost-cutting. There were talks of lay-offs. But Carter didn't see things that way. He expected positive results. And he declared his expectations, "We told people, We're going to change, but not by losing people. Who cares about losing people? I'm interested in hiring." He did everything necessary to make sure his ideas of expansion worked. And when they did, he gave the credit to his subordinates who worked to carry out his vision.

"I knew I was on the right track," he said. "If we were wrong, it would have been my fault, my responsibility. I didn't want to be wrong, but if I were, I would have taken responsibility. I would have done whatever was possible to take care of my people. A leader doesn't have that as a choice." In the years that he ran State Street, revenues tripled while the number of employees doubled.[16] No wonder Drucker considered taking care of people so important for success and that this was so high on his own list of must-do things on the way to the top.

THIS LEADER SHARES
THE GAIN THROUGH TRAINING

But sharing the gain doesn't need to be in ownership or bonuses. It's the concept of sharing the gain that I am talking about. Donald Weiss became CEO of White Storage and Retrieval Systems in Kenilworth, New Jersey. White Storage is a manufacturer of automated retrieval systems for the storage of small parts and documents. It is a small but profitable company. Through good leadership, the company grew.

Weiss decided to share some of the gains of raising the quality of life in his company by teaching his employees advanced management and professional subjects. At this point he discovered that most of his employees didn't have basic English skills. Weiss saw it would be rather difficult to teach them if they didn't understand English. So Weiss began by hiring teachers to come in and teach basic English. He started teaching after hours, but soon expanded to work hours as well. Before long, more than 100 employees were involved, and all sorts of topics, including mathematics, blueprint reading, manufacturing techniques, and team building were being taught. He started preparing employees for high school equivalency diplomas. Then he began inviting customers in to train his employees. IBM instructors came to White Storage and taught quality. At one point, they offered 7,000 hours in training.

This programme was initiated because Weiss wanted to raise the quality of life. But it had dramatic and unexpected results. Before Weiss retired as CEO he said, "Turnover used to be 25%; now it's below 10% … Workers' compensation claims filed have plummeted. We now pay one-tenth of what we paid four years ago … In one year alone, we saw the turn-around time on orders drop from seven days to one."[17] The company reported $50 million in annual revenues prior to Weiss's retirement.

That's certainly a win–win for everyone involved. Drucker used knowledge in pushing his career to the top. The head of any organization can use the same principle to boost the careers of others and boost their own organizations standing as well. Drucker wasn't a company president, but he took care of his students in the same manner, even years after they graduated. He knew this was important to get the right people to the top of their organizations, and the thing to do on his own way to the top of his profession.

1. Drucker, Peter F. *The Practice of Management* (New York: Harper & Row, 1955), 194.
2. Hay, Peter. *The Book of Business Anecdotes* (New York: Facts on File, 1988), 168.
3. Teal, Thomas. "Not a Fool, Not a Saint". *Fortune*, 11 November 1996. https://bit.ly/2AL63Eh.
4. Campbell, Kenneth D. "Malden Mills Owner Applies Religious Ethics to Business". *MIT News*, 16 April 1997, https://bit.ly/2AKmxwf.
5. Whitmore, David. Interview with the author, 8 November 1997.
6. Anfuso, Dawn. "3M's Staffing Strategy Promotes Productivity and Pride". *Personnel Journal* 74 no. 2 (February 1995): 28-34. https://bit.ly/2ncDIx8.
7. DeSimone, L.D. 3M *Annual Report*. 20 February 1997.
8. Chandler, Susan. "Lands' End Looks for Terra Firma". *BusinessWeek*, 8 July 1996, 128, 131.
9. Iverson, Ken, *Plain Talk: Lessons from a Business Maverick* (New York: John Wiley, 1998), 13.
10. Iverson, Ken. Telephone interview with the author, 30 October 1997.
11. "Nucor". *Wikipedia*, https://bit.ly/2swYyvv, accessed 20 July 2018
12. Ibid.
13. "Cutco". *Wikipedia*, https://bit.ly/2M50oNK, accessed 20 July 2018
14. Laine, Erick. Telephone interview with the author, 22 December 1997.
15. "State Street Corporation". *Wikipedia*, https://bit.ly/2ptQ1G5, accessed 20 July 2018
16. Carter, Marsh N.
17. Browkaw, Murphy & Seglin, "What It Takes."

CHAPTER 11

PUT DUTY BEFORE SELF

Above all, people demand that the manager take responsibility for his own work and performance.

– Peter F. Drucker

D uty is a synonym for responsibility, it is an obligation or task that you are required to perform. We may think of it most in the work environment. When you are hired for a position your duties may be written in a formal contract which you must sign to show that you understand and agree. In a smaller company, the position may only be explained verbally. That is a verbal contract, and one which may include a set of duties to which you agree to perform. There are also many duties from contracts in a non-work setting. When you are married you sign a contract and are given a marriage licence. In most marriage contracts, each side's duties are specifically noted. Also, some duties are implicit. For example, if you see someone in distress on the street, society expects you to stop and assist if you can.

DUTIES MAY BE IMPLICIT OR EXPLICIT

Many duties are legal and required even if you have not volunteered intentionally for them and not signed anything. For example, if you are in a car accident and someone is hurt or there is damage, you are required to stop and not leave the scene. Society also may assign you a social responsibility if you are a senior manager or a top executive and expect you to fulfil social responsibilities even if these are not noted in your hiring agreement. Sam Walton was lauded for social respon-sibility with his low prices and putting Wal-Mart stores in locations where larger stores wouldn't go. But he was attacked for lack of social responsibility as Wal-Mart grew in number and put many smaller local stores out of business. So, duty sometimes depends on perception and duties may be implicit or explicit. Either way, you are responsible and generally the more power you have in any situation or environment, the greater your responsibility.

A CEO has considerably more responsibility and power than a low-er-level executive and Drucker took notice of this fact and emphasized it. The importance of recognizing this fact and putting responsibility ahead of other personal needs at every level of management plays a key role in advancing or delaying your career or any endeavour to which we can attach the adjective, 'successful'.

PERSONAL RESPONSIBILITIES AND NEEDS

But wait, there are personal responsibilities as well as personal needs. What about your responsibilities to your family? Isaac Asimov was a famous writer. He had an extraordinarily successful career. He authored more than 200 books; many were bestsellers and not all were science fiction, in which he started his career and for which was best known.

In his family, Asimov especially adored his daughter. In one of two autobiographies that he wrote, Asimov related that when his daughter grew up he once asked her how she would best describe his time as her dad when she was younger. He expected her to say something like "You were a loving dad" or "You were an affectionate dad". Instead she surprised him completely by immediately responding, "You were a busy dad." Reflecting on this he wrote that she was, unfortunately, correct. Despite his efforts, he had frequently ignored his responsibilities as a father while furthering his career as a writer. This was not putting duties before needs, it was putting one type of duty before another.

Sadly, most of us, usually unknowingly, are guilty of this. The phenomenon even inspired the 1974 hit song "Cat's in the Cradle", by Harry Chapin and his wife, Sandra. The song related to how Chapin was always being too busy for his son: the voice of the story in the song had unwittingly trained his son to do the same. When the father grew old and suggested doing things with his son, the son answered the father in the same way the father had answered the son as he was growing up: too busy right now, but they would surely get together some day and have a good time when they did. The recording topped the *Billboard* Hot 100 in December 1974. It was Chapin's only No. 1 hit song and became the best known of his work and was inducted into the Grammy Hall of Fame in 2011.[1] About the song, Chapin said, "Frankly, this song scares me to death."[2] Once I wrote an article warning of the dangers in neglecting this duty and referring to the song. I received several strong responses which echoed the same sentiment from as far away as Australia.

What I am saying here is that while we think of success mainly in our careers, our families count heavily, and it is unfortunate that we may only realize this after we grow older and our children grow up.

Therefore, we need to remember Chapin's song as we proceed with Drucker's insights about our duties before our personal needs.

WHAT IS DUTY?

Not atypically, if you look up duty in the dictionary, you will find several definitions. Two definitions capture the sense of what is required as a part of this universal law of success: 1. The actions required by one's occupation or position and 2. A moral or legal obligation. We need both of these definitions, when we look at social responsibilities and duties to our families and legal duties as well as duties as managers and corporate executives.

THIS CEO PUT DUTY IN HIS WORK ABOVE PERSONAL DUTY TO SUCCEED

Herb Kelleher, was long the CEO of Southwest Airlines. Southwest Airlines had been the most profitable airline in the US, and the one picked as first in quality by customer surveys many times. Kelleher advised: "If there's going to be a downslide, you share it."

When Southwest Airlines ran into trouble at one point, Kelleher went to his board of directors and told them he wanted his salary cut. He cut his bonus by 20% and all corporate officers by 10%. These cuts were made before firing a single employee.[3] As we have seen, other successful CEOs have done the same. Here we will look only at his work life.

Managers who practise duty before themselves assist others in accomplishing difficult tasks when they face major obstacles. Yet, other managers with few work problems frequently fail to place their employees' issues first, even when they themselves face no major obstacles to their goals. Managers don't always need to attempt the impossible. They do need to put their duty first above personal needs while remembering that other duties, such as family duties, are also deserving of attention.

DUTY BEFORE SELF – DO MANAGERS DO IT ROUTINELY?

Is duty before self such as shown by Kelleher always practised in industry? Not always. In many companies, the automatic solution to any slip in profits or other business decisions are considered more important.

An article in *Newsweek* once stated: "After causing the problems through poor decisions, many CEOs offer up their employees as human sacrifices, hoping to get their stock prices up. If they do go up, they get a raise even while their employees suffer."[4]

Akio Morita, at the time chairman of the Sony Corporation, claimed, "American management treats workers as just a tool to make money. You know, when the economy is booming they hire more workers, and when the recession comes, they lay off the workers. But you know, recession is not caused by the workers."[5] Drucker spent a great deal of effort convincing others that people needed to be put on the asset side of an accounting ledger and not considered a liability.

Fortunately, all American managers do not treat workers "as a tool to make money". However, if you always put employees' or others' needs over mission, you are also likely to run into difficulties too. The same is true with family needs, as Isaac Asimov found out. There will always be times when you and your employees must work late and work over holidays or weekends to satisfy your customer. There are times when the personal wishes of individuals must be sacrificed for mission. But if you routinely do this you're asking for trouble. There are times when work must come first over people. But there are also times when needs of people – your employees, your family – must come first. Ignore them at your peril!

Concern for mission and people are closely intertwined, as without people, you cannot accomplish the mission. If you adopt the priorities of mission or people in the same fixed order every time, it will eventually be wrong for a particular situation which you will face.

GREAT CONCERN FOR BOTH MISSION AND PEOPLE IS NOT A NEW CONCEPT

The notion that you must have great concern for both mission and people may have originated elsewhere, but it has been well documented by researchers. Drs Robert Blake and Jane Mouton developed books in the early 1960s which investigated this issue. Their books, *The Managerial Grid* and *The New Managerial Grid*, described a system of measuring managerial effectiveness through a matrix showing concern for production on one axis and concern for people on the other. In a day when management books emphasizing people were only then gaining popularity, their original book sold almost 1,000,000 copies. Their conclusions are evident today, that a leader's great concern for both production and for people ("head and heart" they called it) led to many beneficial and synergistic consequences,[6] while a higher concern always for the same one in all situations was a mistake. In other words, both people and mission must be considered as very important, but not in a fixed and unchanging priority. There are times when the very top priority must be given to mission (work). At other times, your people must be given top priority (or a single individual) over mission. As someone who wants to use Drucker's methods to reach the top and be all you can be, you must ensure that both priorities are at the top of your list. You must judge which gets the primary call considering all factors in a specific situation.

REJOICE IN THE SUCCESS OF OTHERS

If you are an organizational head, you are responsible for everything your organization does or fails to do. Since your organization is made up of people, you are responsible for everything your people do or fail to do. If those for whom you are responsible are successful, you are successful. Conversely, if they fail, that makes you a failure.

Any leader who puts duty first rejoices in the successes of those responsible to him or her and does everything possible to help them to achieve success. Such leaders take full responsibility for failure but give as much credit as they can to their followers.

CONSIDER YOURSELF LAST

Sure, you've got to consider yourself. You owe something to yourself. As I've said, you have responsibilities to your family as well. If you never consider things like personal health, proper sleep, and spending time with your family, you are heading towards massive trouble which can negatively impact your entire life, not mention your ability to lead and certainly to reach the top.

The difficulty arises when those who are responsible almost always consider themselves first. If you are a leader, you've got additional responsibilities that you cannot avoid. You must take care of those who you expect to follow you. You've got to keep the wellbeing of those you lead in the forefront. You've got to consider the impact of any action you take or fail to take on the mission. And most frequently you've got to do this before you start taking care of your own wants and needs. Yes, as a leader you have certain privileges and power that others do not. But you also have much increased responsibilities as well.

As the one in charge, others will do as you do. If you always consider your own wellbeing first, before others, and before your mission, so will those you expect to follow you. In all likelihood, they won't willingly follow you at all. They will be too busy looking out for themselves, too!

SHARE THE PAIN

Sharing the pain means that when things go wrong, you are there to show your concern. However, showing concern isn't just a display. You must really share your subordinates' pain if you are putting duty before self. You must share their pain whether or not it is inconvenient, whether or not it is difficult, or whether or not it costs you time, money, or other resources.

THIS MAN IS FAMOUS FOR HIS COFFEE, BUT HE IS ALSO CONCERNED FOR HIS PEOPLE

If you want to embrace the concept of duty, you should note that actions speak louder than words. You don't need to run around saying what a wonderful people person you are. But you do need to show your concern by sharing the pain and hardship. That speaks louder than words.

Howard Schultz grew up in Brooklyn, New York and went to college on student loans and working as a salesman. In 1982, he joined Starbucks. Five years later he bought the company and became CEO. The Seattle company then had six outlets and fewer than 100 employees. Today Starbucks has more than almost 238,000 employees operating in 64 countries.[7] How did Schultz do it?

First, Schultz follows an earlier success principle which Drucker commented on. In his book *Pour Your Heart Into It*, Schultz wrote: "Our first priority was to take care of our people, because they were the ones responsible for communicating our passion to our customers."[8]

Years earlier, he had told a reporter, "Every dollar you invest in your employees shows up – and then some – on the bottom line."[9] And he backed that up with a generous and comprehensive employee-benefits package that included healthcare, stock options, training programmes, career counselling, and product discounts for all workers, both full- and part-time. "No one can afford not to provide these kinds of benefits," said Schultz.[10] So, Schultz shares the gain. But Schultz also shares the pain.

Yes, the universal success laws or principles we have been talking about overlap. So it's concern for people as a part of duty placed before self.

Once when Schultz was on a business trip to New York and asleep in his hotel room the telephone rang. Three Starbucks employees had been murdered in a Washington coffee shop. Schultz immediately dressed, left the hotel, and went to the airport. By the next morning he was on the spot comforting relatives and co-workers. In 1997, when Starbucks had over 200,000 employees, Schultz still knew in many ways that he was responsible for all of them. "It's very important for me – or any CEO – to be visible," he said at the time.[11] Sharing the pain, even if just to comfort those for whom you are responsible, is part of duty before self. In some situations, it can also be shown by simple things such as the size of your office or your lack of a private secretary.

BILLION DOLLARS IN SALES AND NO PRIVATE OFFICE

Michael Bloomberg is the founder, CEO, and owner of Bloomberg LP, a global financial service, mass media, and software company.[12] This is a billion-dollar company which, among other things, publishes financial news electronically through *Bloomberg News*. The subscribers are 100,000 financial professionals in more than 100 countries who pay a lot for the service and have helped create a personal fortune of over $53 billion for Michael Bloomberg. He left the job of CEO only to serve as three-time mayor of New York City and resumed his position as CEO in 2014.

Bloomberg News has 19,000 employees in 73 cities and 192 offices; it is a multibillion dollar conglomerate. Michael Bloomberg doesn't have the largest, nor the smallest office compared to any of his employees. That's because neither Bloomberg, nor any of his employees, had private offices nor do they have secretaries. "There are no private offices at Bloomberg," he insists. "My desk is exactly the same size as everyone else's."[13]

Moreover, Bloomberg believes and insists that as his employees are promoted, they shouldn't expect to work less and take more vacations. "You're more valuable, you get paid more, and your coworkers should get more out of you."[14]

The point isn't that Bloomberg executives don't have large offices, or other symbols of power. You can become successful at Bloomberg and this approach is exactly what Drucker recommended.

GREAT CONCERN FOR MISSION AND PEOPLE OVER SELF

Drucker was always proud when he saw businessmen who put duty before self. Homer Laughlin China Co. is a privately held company in Newell, West Virginia. Current estimates say this company has an annual revenue of $20 million to $50 million and employs a staff of approximately 1,000 to 4,999.[15] That's large for a company that manufactures china. In fact, it once claimed to be the largest china-manufacturing company in the world.

Yet Homer Laughlin China manufactures china in the USA, not overseas. The company managed to survive and even prosper during the Great Depression because cinemas were giving away dishes as door prizes to try and attract customers. However, in the late 1970s cheap imports almost did them in. By then, CEO Joseph Wells II and President Marcus Aaron headed the company. It was their grandfathers that bought the company from its founders in 1897.[16] It survived the latest recession, too. This is not so usual. Of the Fortune 500 companies listed by Forbes 60 years ago, only 71 have survived.

In fact, by the late 1970s, Homer Laughlin China was producing cheap dinnerware for the restaurant trade. Imports had wiped out their price advantage, and sales plunged. Neither owner needed the money. They were tempted to call it quits. However, both knew that liquidating the company would decimate the community. Said CEO Wells, "These plant employees are the fourth and fifth generation at Homer Laughlin. I went to school with some of them."[17]

So, the two owners decided to stick it out, not for their own good, but for the welfare of their employees, and maybe a little bit because of the traditions of their families' involvement with the firm. The decision to keep the company meant spending an additional half a million dollars on new equipment and reconfiguring their manufacturing process.

In this way, they eliminated dozens of steps, reduced costs by 15% and cut production time from one week to one day. This in turn enabled them to reduce inventories by 75% and they survived the challenge.

To do more than survive, they brought out old moulds from a once-fashionable design called Fiesta. Bloomingdale's launched the revived brand, and Homer Laughlin was back in business. Using cashflow from their Fiesta line, they moved into the custom china business with additional lines.[18] Naturally, Homer Laughlin workers responded to the high moral courage and duty before self displayed by their owners.

To summarize, what is illustrated by history is that putting duty before self means a focus on both mission and people and quite a bit of judging where your duty lies in different situations. It means always putting your own personal interests second to the mission and those who depend on you, including subordinates, customers, and family. That's quite a trick to pull off, because duties are frequently conflicting. You won't always be 100% successful, but it is worth the effort and Drucker's career proved that. Putting duty before self is difficult, but it can be done.

---

1. "Cat's in the Cradle". *Wikipedia*, https://bit.ly/2nj53xr, accessed 20 July 2018.
2. "Harry Chapin – 'Cats in the Cradle' Soundstage". *YouTube*, posted 21 January 2014. https://bit.ly/2OiGT1P, at 51s.
3. Waxler, Robert P. and Thomas J. Higginson. *Industrial Management* (July-August, 1990), 26.
4. Sloan, Allan. "The Hit Men". *Newsweek*, 26 February 1996, 44-48.
5. Waxler and Higginson, 24.
6. Blake, Robert R. and Jane S. Mouton. *The New Managerial Grid* (Houston, TX: Gulf Publishing Co., 1964, 1978), 95.
7. Statistic Brain Research Institute. "Starbucks Company Statistics". *StatisticBrain*, https://bit.ly/2vnfODz, accessed 20 July 2018.
8. Schultz, Howard and Dori Jones Yang. *Pour Your Heart into It: How Starbucks Built a Company One Cup at a Time* (New York: Hyperion, 1997), 182.
9. Rothman, Matt. "Into the Black". *Inc.Com*, January 1993. https://bit.ly/2OeAW5O.
10. Ibid.
11. Zachary, G. Pascal. "CEOs Are Stars Now, But Why? And Would Alfred Sloan Approve?" *The Wall Street Journal*, 3 September 1997, A-1, A-10.
12. "Michael Bloomberg". *Wikipedia*, https://bit.ly/25Ss7D2, accessed 20 July 2018.
13. Roshan, Maer. "Michael Bloomberg's Office Is … a Cubicle?!" *The Hollywood Reporter*, 9 April 2015. https://bit.ly/2OhfbCA.
14. Whitford, David, "Fire in His Belly, Ambition in His Eyes," *Fortune*, 12 May 1997. https://for.tn/2LUoeMR.
15. "Homer Laughlin China CO." *Manta*, https://bit.ly/2vK2jNo, accessed 20 July 2018.
16. "Homer Laughlin China Company". *Wikipedia*, https://bit.ly/2n5iLEe, accessed 20 July 2018.
17. Oliver, Suzanne, "Keep It Trendy". *Forbes*, 18 July 1994, 88.
18. Ibid., 89, 94.

CHAPTER 12

GET OUT
IN FRONT

During World War I the losses among higher ranking officers was rare compared with the losses they caused by their incompetence. Too few generals were killed.

– **Peter F. Drucker**

D rucker had read much on warfare and used military examples in class and in his writings. He knew that in battle, getting out in front of those you lead was important for success. He wrote the words that one reason for the failure of axis units during World War I was that "too few generals were killed". This was explained from one source as follows:

"When Peter Drucker was in high school in the mid-1920s, his history teacher assigned a number of books on World War I campaigns. When discussing the books, one student said, 'Every one of these books says that the Great War was a war of total military incompetence. *Why was it?* The teacher, who had been badly wounded in the war, shot back without hesitation: 'Because not enough generals were killed; they stayed way behind the lines and let others do the fighting and dying'."[1]

WHERE YOU NEED TO BE TO POSITION YOURSELF FOR SUCCESS

To be successful you must be at the front line in any job or human activity. Drucker knew that and followed the guidelines of being in front. In his youth he led fellow students in his conservative politics and as the Nazi party grew in strength, he publicly opposed the Nazis. His books in German supported, first, a Jewish convert to Christianity, and then addressed the entire question of being Jewish in Germany. Both books were banned by the Nazis. His first book in English, *The End of Economic Man* in 1939 continued this opposition. His book *Concept of the Corporation*[2] broke new ground in management. The 'Drucker Difference' was real even when Drucker was young. When necessary, he took an unpopular stance. When others cried for regulated 'business ethics' he maintained that there was no such thing, only ethics. When most academics said that all management should be participatory, he said no, it was situational. In some cases, a directive style was needed. He was a champion of decentralization when it was unpopular and was possibly the only management expert to point out that not only was selling not a subset of marketing, but that it could be adversarial to it. He was always out in front, and this contributed significantly to his success.

HOW TO GET OUT IN FRONT

If you want to be a success, obey this natural law and get out in front. Here's how to do it:

- Go where the action is and set the example
- Be willing to do anything you ask of those who follow
- Take charge
- Be an up-front leader.

CAESAR'S OUTSTANDING TRAIT: HE WAS ALWAYS WHERE THE ACTION WAS

Julius Caesar had one trait that set him apart from other successful Roman generals. It was not that he wasn't a deep thinker. He was. However, others like the 'philosopher emperor' Marcus Aurelius, were even deeper thinkers. It was not that he wasn't a good strategist or tactician, either. Again, he was, but there were other Roman generals who were at least as good.

No, what set Caesar apart, was the fact that he spent an inordinate amount of time up front in the company of his soldiers. It was said that he committed not only the names of his officers, but the names of thousands of his legionnaires to memory. He greeted all of them by name and he spent time with them out in front, in battle and, later, in the Roman senate. It not only made him popular, it brought him to the front rank of politics although he had little previous political experience.

Because of this, Caesar's troops knew they were not just numbers to him. They were important! Wherever the action was, and whatever happened, they knew he would be there with them.

In those days there was no way of leading from the rear during a war, and there is no way of leading from the rear in corporate life and other activities today. You must be out in front, where the action is. That way you can see what's going right and what's going wrong. You can make critical decisions fast, rather than those decisions working their way up and down the chain of command for approval. You can see your employees, and they can see you. There is no question in anyone's mind as to what you want done, and the fact that you are there on the spot lets others know just how committed you are to getting it done. It lets them know that you think what they are doing is important. It lets all who would follow you know that you are ready, willing, and able to share in their hardships, problems, successes, and failures in working towards every goal and completing every task. Moreover, going where the action is gives you an opportunity to set the example. Remember to get to the top you need to be a leader, and to be a leader, you must lead. To lead means that you need to get out in front. That's true for a professional like Drucker, too. Peter was known to all of us as Peter because he asked that we did not call him 'professor' or 'Dr Drucker'. He knew our names too, and after he met my wife once, he knew her name, also.

SUCCESS IN THE JUNGLES OF BRAZIL WITH THE HEADHUNTERS AND PIRANHAS

Dr Mark Chandler headed Inland Laboratories, a Texas company that sold toxins, viruses, and other biochemical products to medical researchers. At one time his company needed two rare plants to refine into a cancer medicine. Unfortunately, these plants grew only in the Brazilian rainforest hundreds of miles from civilization. Chandler couldn't buy the plants anywhere. Someone had to go into the jungle and harvest the plants, and he could have sent some of his employees to find this rare foliage. However, their job descriptions did not include facing piranhas, deadly snakes, and headhunters. This was a trip that no one wanted to make, let alone lead. So Chandler got out in front. He personally organized and led an eight-day expedition into the Amazon.

This wasn't easy. It was no adventure trip set up by a tour company. Several days into the journey, Chandler almost died. Burning up with fever and wracked by diarrhoea, he plunged into a nearby river to cool off, forgetting about piranhas and poisonous snakes. He was so sick, he just didn't care. Fortunately, he survived and two days later, the fever broke. Shortly after that, with the help of native guides, he got his plants. David Nance, president of Intron Therapeutics and a longtime customer for more than 10 years commented, "Mark is equally comfortable in a loincloth, a lab coat, or a three-piece suit."

Employees, customers, and suppliers all knew that Chandler could be counted on to be out in front where the action was. *Forbes* at the time gave Inland Laboratories a price/earnings multiple of 40.[3]

WHY YOU MUST GET OUT IN FRONT TO LEAD

There are leaders who feel they must maintain total detachment. They believe they must coolly and carefully analyse the facts and make decisions without being influenced by outside factors or complications. From their viewpoint, this must be done away from the action, where the noise, pressures of time, and other problems distract from their ability to think calmly and clearly. This is wrong. They forget that the action is where they must be to get current and accurate information and to make their decisions based primarily on what's going on where the action is.

There is a place for contemplative thinking and measured analysis in most situations in life. But many who would like to have success have their priorities about this all wrong. The priority when action is taking place is that you must go where the action is; where people are actually engaged and those that are doing the actual work are making things happen. You cannot lead such actions from behind a desk in an air-conditioned office and be the real leader.

WOMEN OUT IN FRONT

Only recently is this being recognized. The US armed forces recently opened equal career opportunities for women by allowing them to serve in battle. In the last few years women successfully completed such arduous programmes as Ranger training and the Amphibious Officer's course in the Marine Corps. Other women have fought in battle, undergoing the same dangers and hardships as men. And there are women who wear four stars, the highest general rank possible in peacetime in all US military services.

During the Hundred Years War, in the 15th century, a young French girl was despondent because of the English invasion of her country.

We know her as Joan of Arc. When she was 13, Joan began to hear voices which she identified as those of three saints. They gave her a mission: liberate France from English domination. For five years she was uncertain. She thought about it constantly but did nothing. Then she went to her monarch, Charles VII, and boldly asked for command of the French army. Can you imagine that? If you think that this would be difficult even in these days where men and women are at least moving towards equality in all fields, including the military, imagine how this would have been in Joan's time.

Charles VII and his advisors were so desperate that he actually gave her the command she desired. He had tried everything else with male commanders. The situation was so bad, that even the king's counsellors agreed that Joan might be their only chance.

Prior to Joan's appointment as French commander, the English siege of Orleans had lasted eight months despite the best efforts of the French army to relieve it. Joan lifted the siege in just eight days. Her orders to her soldiers before attacking were simple: "Go boldly in among the English." But she didn't just give the orders. She got out in front. "I go boldly in myself," she told the chroniclers of her age.

Joan personally hated fighting and killing. Though she commanded the French army, and gave the orders, she did not struggle in hand-to-hand combat. Mounted on a horse, she carried a huge banner. Everyone could easily identify her by this banner. Then she rode with these colours and her staff to the place on the battlefield where the situation was most critical. That's where most of the action was and where the danger was the greatest. The French soldiers saw that their commander was out in front; so that's where they went, too.

Being out in front is not just for show. In Joan's case, it eventually led to her capture while attempting to relieve Compiegne a year later. Her captors burned her as a witch. They thought for any commander to be so brave and so successful, much less a young girl with no military training, she had to have demonic power. She had extraordinary power all right. But it was the power of the universal laws with emphasis on the one that urges the leader to get out in front.

AN ACHIEVEMENT BY A WOMAN AIRMAN
NOT ATTAINED BY A MAN

In July 2018, a female general did something no man has yet accomplished. Lieutenant General Maryanne Miller had already become the first woman to become commander of the Air Force Reserves with 29,000 men and women and commanding a large percentage of the aircrew and combat aircraft engaged now in the Middle East. But yesterday, as I was writing this chapter, I received the announcement that General Miller had become the first reservist on active duty ever to be elevated to full general. That is, 4-star rank and to command Air Mobility Command a major active duty command not directly associated with the reserves.

Only one other reservist has ever worn four stars. Famed aviator Jimmy Doolittle, who led the Tokyo Raid, won the Congressional Medal of Honor, and commanded the 8th Air Force in Europe during the Second World War. Some years after his retirement and before he died, he was selected for a special honour (no additional pay) and elevated to four stars by Congress to recognize his distinguished past services. General Miller is a pilot with more than 4,800 hours flying a half of dozen different aircraft and she is still on active duty. She is in a different category.

There are modern Joans in the boardroom as well as the battlefield, who get out in front today. Beth Pritchard was the chief executive of the US leading bath-shop chain, Bath & Body Works. Pritchard got out in front and demonstrated a special power, too. In addition to her corporate duties and responsibilities, she spent two days a month working 'in the trenches', in a Bath & Body Works boutique. She didn't sit around observing or spend all her time handing out advice to employees. She saw and was seen; she taught, and she learned. She helped set up displays, stocked shelves, and arranged gift baskets. "Though," she claimed, "I'm not really good on the cash register."

Whether she was good on the cash register or not seems not to have mattered. The power of getting out in front paid off. Her cash registers were full. When she took over Bath & Body Works in 1991, it had 95 stores and sales of $20 million. Five years later, the number of stores had increased to a whopping 750, and sales hit $753 million. In July 2008, the company announced that it was opening six new locations in Canada.

Bath & Body Works currently operates more than 1,600 stores. In October 2010, it opened its first stores outside of North America in Kuwait. This demonstrated clearly the power of getting out in front, for male or female.

TIME MAGAZINE'S MAN OF THE YEAR WENT WHERE THE ACTION WAS

In 2017, Los Angeles was announced as the city of the Summer Olympic Games in 2028. Los Angeles last had the Summer Games in 1984. These Games were made famous among Olympic watchers in the US by Peter Ueberroth, who was still only in his forties. He became *Time Magazine*'s Man-of-the-Year for 1984[5] and the Games were a great victory for him personally as well as an unusual example of what can happen when a determined leader gets out in front. President Reagan invited him to the White House, and he was routinely introduced to audiences as "the man who brought honour to America". Yet before all this started, Ueberroth was practically unknown.

Ueberroth was a self-made businessman who made money and was successful in the travel business. He may not have been the first choice to run the Games. However, a headhunting firm suggested Ueberroth's name to a Los Angeles committee searching for someone to run the 1984 Olympic Games. No one thought it was a dream job and few predicted much success or glory for the person that got the job, so there wasn't a lot of competition and Ueberroth was offered the job, which he accepted, and he even took a 70% pay cut. Even the compensation wasn't that great. Later, he changed his status to volunteer worker. He refused to take any money at all for his work at the Olympics.

Some said Ueberroth declined to take a salary because there was no way the Games could turn a profit. Many experts said that it was unlikely that the Los Angeles Games could even break even. The media agreed. The Soviet Union and its satellites were likely to boycott the Games in retaliation for the Americans boycotting the previous Soviet Games in 1980. Other countries in the Soviet sphere of influence would probably follow. Other cities had had financial problems in hosting the Olympics even without the Soviet problem. How could Los Angles do any better? The conventional wisdom was that the US Olympic Games in Los Angeles were going to lose big.

His first week on the job, Ueberroth couldn't even get into his own assigned office. He and members of his staff could hear the phones ringing inside the office while they were locked outside. But, the landlord, like many others in Los Angeles, was so certain that the Olympics would lose money and not pay its bills, that he wanted his money first before handing Ueberroth the keys.

Harry Usher, who functioned as Ueberroth's Chief of Staff later said, "Leadership and inspiration are his managerial gifts."[6] Ueberroth plunged right in. He managed by getting out in front and going where the action was. Taking over an old helicopter hangar as his headquarters, he encouraged everyone to eat lunch in the hangar's cafeteria to save time. Ueberroth ate lunch there with everyone else.

Frequently, he would stroll through the hangar talking to his employees and asking questions. "Peter is demanding and self-demanding. That makes you try as hard as you can,"[7] noted Agnes Mura, one member of staff.

Ueberroth personally negotiated contracts totalling millions of dollars. As the cash flow slowly changed to going in the right direction, he went out of his way to cultivate the ministers of sport from each country. Once the Soviets announced they wouldn't be coming, Ueberroth spent even more time up front with his employees to make things happen. He kept the pressure on and did everything he could to stop other countries from joining the Soviet boycott. He flew to Cuba and met face to face with Fidel Castro to persuade Cuba to come. While Castro said he had to follow the Soviet lead, he did agree not to pressure other Latin American countries not to come.

Once the Soviets made their boycott official, the experts again announced that there was no way Los Angeles could do anything to avoid losing money. Big money. Ueberroth ignored the naysayers and stayed out in front. He claimed that even without the Soviets, they would make $15 million profit. The naysayers laughed. Make $15 million profit? Impossible!

As the Games opened, Ueberroth continued to go where the action was. According to *Time Magazine*, he was constantly on the move, racing to the scene of action and even riding a helicopter over Los Angeles freeways to check the traffic. Every day, he wore the uniform of a different Olympic worker as he made his rounds. One day it was a bus driver's uniform, the next an usher's, the day after, perhaps a cook's. And every time he spotted a security worker, he ran over to shake his or her hand. Ueberroth had been warned that Los Angeles was particularly vulnerable to terrorists, and Ueberroth was determined that they would not strike successfully at 'his' Olympics.

Both Ueberroth and the experts were proven wrong. The Los Angeles Olympics didn't make $15 million. Under Ueberroth, the Los Angeles Olympics made $215 million profit, $200 million more than Ueberroth himself had predicted.

And so, Ueberroth got to dine with President Reagan and his photograph graced the cover of *Time Magazine*. Many Americans thought he should run for president himself. But others said he was just very lucky. Ueberroth didn't say very much. He accepted an appointment as Baseball Commissioner. Ueberroth continued to be lucky and has been involved as a successful director or investor in many corporations, because he knows his real luck is that he always gets out in front.

HE GOT OUT IN FRONT AND WENT THROUGH GARBAGE

When Phillip Rooney was CEO of WMX Technologies, Inc. of Chicago, he found another way of setting the example. WMX Technologies manages waste, and every Founder's Day at the corporation, Rooney and other managers set the example by going through garbage. He and they took off their suits and ties and donned the appropriate clothing to sort through the garbage with everyone else. Rooney knew what he was doing. WMX founder, Dean Buntrock, hired him.

He was sent to Riyadh, Saudi Arabia to pull together a $250 million garbage-hauling contract. He set the example and got out in front then, too. To do this, he had to set up a functioning town for his workers.

He employed the town's entire population of 2,000 workers. Then he helped install the electricity and sewage systems himself. Not too many top executives do that.

Some years later, he was sent to Chicago to take over the main operation in the US. He was out in the field five days a week working with front-line managers and salespeople. He pushed sales managers to get out and talk to clients more. Or rather, he pulled rather than pushed, because he dropped in on customers himself as well.

Because Rooney set the example, others followed. WMX's head of sales and marketing said this about Rooney at the time: "He moves as easily among low-level [employees] as among CEOs."[8] And Rooney knew what he was doing. He acknowledged getting out in front as one of the keys to his success in both his professional career and other aspects of his life.

WHAT CAN AN ASTRONAUT DO AT A TROUBLED AIRLINE? GET OUT IN FRONT

On retiring from NASA and the Air Force, Eastern Air Lines recruited Astronaut Frank Borman as a vice president. Five years later Borman took the reins as president and CEO of a very troubled airline.

Eastern had once been one of the big four of US airlines. It was once headed by the 'Ace of Aces' from World War I, Eddie Rickenbacker. But now Eastern Airlines was in billions of dollars' worth of debt. Their planes were fuel inefficient, and mostly obsolete. Their best plane, the L-1011 was too big for most of their routes – and they had too many of them. Corporate headquarters were split between two separate locations: New York and Miami. This led to continual and unproductive in-fighting and friction between senior executives at the two locations.[9]

The company was top-heavy with useless managers. Management was so stratified that dozens of executives clogged the lines of communication between top executives and the people on the firing line. In one department, they had 60 people assigned to a job where a larger competitor had only 20.

A typical situation was when computer experts were hired to establish information control systems. However, after the systems were set up and running, the experts were never given any new work. They sat around doing virtually nothing. Bonuses were given to company officers based largely on subjective appraisals by fellow officers. Losing money, they furloughed or fired hundreds of employees. However, at the same time Eastern supported fancy cars and private jets for executives. Earlier, customer service had been so bad that a group of former customers had formed the WHEAL (We Hate Eastern Air Lines) Club. Things still hadn't quite turned around.[10]

When Borman became CEO, he got out in front and took charge. Here's what Borman did right away:

- He fired or forced into early retirement or demanded the resignation of 24 vice presidents.
- He sold the JetStar executive aircraft and informed executives that in the future they'd travel on regular Eastern Airline flights.
- He reduced the executive limousine fleet and its drivers to a single car and driver in each of three major cities.
- He cancelled the leased company cars for executives and eliminated the company's paying officers' membership dues in private clubs.
- He transferred all major executive functions to Miami, making this the single headquarters location.
- He sent a large number of people who had contact with the customer to a special school he set up based on the customer service training syllabus from a company that had a first-class reputation of dealing with customers: Disney World.
- He abolished the subjective executive bonus and established a new profit and deficit sharing plan that applied to everyone, rank and file as well as senior executives. It was tied in directly to how the company did and what the individual accomplished.
- He visited Eastern Air Line employees in almost every city in their system. In his own words, "I cajoled, pleaded, argued, and demanded. I courted not merely the rank and file but their union leaders on both the local and national levels."[11]

These measures proved effective. For the next four years, Eastern Air Lines had the most profitable period in its history. It made $45.2 million in the first year, $27.8 million the next, $67.2 million, in the third year, and $57.6 million in the fourth year.[12] Customer service went from dead last in the Civil Aeronautics Board's passenger complaint ratings to number two in the industry.[13] As Borman said, "You could actually see and even feel the new pride developing, growing, and taking hold in the way our people looked and worked."[14]

The need to get out in front is strongest when things go wrong, especially in an emergency. Borman showed immense strength in this respect when he was vice president of operations and Eastern Flight crashed into the Everglades at night. Borman heard the news and headed for the Systems Control Center. No one knew exactly where the plane had gone down and so Borman ordered the Systems Control director to charter a helicopter.

They located the crash site when they spotted a couple of Coast Guard helicopters in the area. Though it was pitch-black, they located a spot hard enough to land the helicopter in the swampy waters. It was 150 yards from the downed airplane. When Borman ran up, the scene was one of confusion and horror. Borman helped get the injured and the survivors into helicopters. "When I was satisfied that there were enough rescue personnel on the scene, I finally left on one of the last choppers," he said. With two of the surviving flight attendants, he flew straight to the hospital with a woman who had lost her baby.[15] It was no surprise that Borman obeyed the universal laws, taking charge and immediately getting out in front when he became president and CEO.

Later a new union president succeeded in destroying the incentive compensation system Borman set up. Then the company was sold. Borman was fired, and many of Borman's changes were dropped. Within months, Eastern Airlines ran out of money and was out of business.

What we're talking about here is not being a good guy and clapping people on the back. What we are talking about is being unafraid to be with your people, looking them in the eye, helping them when you can and listening to what they say. It is not important that they like you and think of you as a 'good guy'. It is important that they respect you and think of you as a human being willing to share their victories and defeats.

So, if you really want to reach the top like Drucker, get out in front and go where the action is whether you are a corporate leader or not.

My former boss and good friend General Ron Fogleman used to say that it's easy to be a leader, no matter your job or actual assignment. All you need to do is stick your arm up to volunteer and lead. "It's easy to tell the leader, he's the one that gets the job done," he told me.

---

1. "The Leader of the Future". *Executive Book Summaries* (Concordville, PA: Soundview Executive Book Summaries, n.d.) 2, original emphasis. https://bit.ly/2OLe2UJ.
2. Drucker, Peter F. *The End of Economic Man* (New York: John Day, 1939); Concept of the Corporation (New York: John Day, 1946).
3. Mack, Toni. "Indiana Jones, Meet Mark Chandler". *Forbes*, 23 May 1994, 100-104.
4. Bongiorno, Lor. "<TNBS>'The McDonald's of Toiletries'<TNBS>". *Business Week*, 4 August 1997, 79-80.
5. "Peter Ueberroth, Man of the Year". *Time Magazine*, 7 January 1985. https://ti.me/2vIecU5.
6. Ajemian, Robert. "Peter Ueberroth: Master of the Games". *Time Magazine*, 7 January 1985. In: *Time 1995 Almanac CR-ROM* (Cambridge: Compact Publishing Co., 1995).
7. Ibid.
8. Melcher, Richard A. "How Phillip Rooney Reached the Top of the Heap". *Business Week*, 17 June 1996, 80.
9. "Eastern Air Lines". *Wikipedia*, https://bit.ly/1INVp82, accessed 20 July 2018.
10. Borman, Frank with Robert J. Serling. *Countdown: An Autobiography* (New York: William Morrow, 1988), 329-330, 326.
11. Ibid., 323, 328, 335.
12. Ibid., 341.
13. Ibid., 334.
14. Ibid.
15. Ibid., 285-286.

CHAPTER 13

GAINING SELF-CONFIDENCE AND OVERCOMING FEAR

A person can perform only from strength.
One cannot build performance on weakness,
let alone on something one cannot do at all.

– Peter F. Drucker

I f you're going to make steady progress to the top, self-confidence and the ability to overcome fear is essential. Drucker recognized this and developed both of these traits. We can see this in his personal life and the decisions he made in his careers, as well as the decision to delay his longer-range goals in recognizing the realities of life in Germany and then changing course in England to find a new home five years later in US. The self-confidence and ability to face the fear of change and to overcome them to take up new challenging tasks of finding a home and a job does not come automatically. No one is born with it.

No one starts out in life accomplishing what we may think of as 'grandiose' things. You can see this by looking at toddlers. We start as an infant and accomplish what as adults we consider small potatoes, like learning to walk, talk, read, write, and eventually think and reason. But are these really minor accomplishments? Hardly. Think back. Today you might assume walking to be almost automatic and require little effort. At the time you first learned to walk or to do any of these things you probably didn't think it was so small. There are adults today who cannot read or write. They may be ashamed and keep their illiteracy a secret even from close friends and family. The truth is, even with these 'small' things we started out by doing still smaller things first, like rolling over, and slowly increasing the difficulty of the subtasks until we could accomplish the next step in our physical progress.

With the more complex and challenging tasks and projects of adults, we fail to expect to succeed for only one of two reasons. Either we have been unsuccessful at similar tasks or projects in the past, or we have never tried to accomplish them in the first place. And by the way, those who have never tried usually haven't because they think they will fail if they did. We may fail in our first attempts. Let me assure you that I have failed by falling many times, both as a toddler and as an adult, but I have developed the self-confidence to go on, and so can you.

A BABY MUST LEARN TO CRAWL BEFORE IT CAN WALK

The correct sequence is that the baby learns to turn over, begins to crawl, gains self-confidence and strength enough to stand up, gains a little more self-confidence and takes a step. Usually the first step ends in a minor disaster and the baby falls. But, the baby knows that at least it made a start, and so it eagerly tries again not long afterwards. Usually the parents are so elated about the attempt that they are full of praise and cheer the attempt. Talk to anyone who has had a stroke and they will tell you the same thing. It may be a little easier, because the stroke victim knows that he could do it once. He knows that it may be tough. He must build his strength and reconnect the neurons connecting brain and body. But he can do it. He has done it before. Trust me, I know. Having had a stroke, I had to do exactly that.

This points out an interesting fact about why people in general, and sometimes those you might never suspect to, lack self-confidence later in life. Babies usually have someone cheering them on. But even if they didn't, who's to say that that first step when they fell was a terrible attempt or a good one? But, as we get older, others may discourage us in learning physical things, many times even without malice. Some of these observers may be judgemental by nature and are almost certain to let us know when we do a poor job, perhaps only a little less so when we make an acceptable attempt, even if they generally support us.

Olympic decathlon champion Bruce Jenner said that as a child he was deathly afraid of being asked to read in class. His teachers criticized him, and the more he was criticized, the lower his self-confidence in reading became. And of course, the worse he did. He was attracted to sports because one day a teacher told him and others to run between two points in the school yard. He was the fastest. For the first time, others were complimenting him. "I didn't know you could run that fast." "Boy, are you good at running!" "I bet you could outrun anyone." Jenner's self-confidence soared, and as frequently happened, it spilled into other areas. In his opinion, this was his first step towards winning an Olympic gold medal in the 1976 Olympics.

When I was growing up my father was in the Air Force and we moved around a lot. Being from a military family I was from a different culture and sometimes the children at school made fun of me since none of them were from military families. Consequently, I lacked self-confidence and performed poorly. One day we had elections for student government. Almost as a joke one of my classmates nominated me as one of the five candidates for president. The class snickered. I tried to decline, but the teacher encouraged me, so I accepted the nomination. All candidates had to give an election speech. I discovered that this is why my classmates nominated me. They knew that I would do poorly and looked forward to embarrassing me. To get the parents involved, they were to act as campaign managers and assist in the writing of the speech. I came home that afternoon upset and depressed. However, my father was eager to become involved. He said that I should write the speech, and then he would go over it and add his suggestions and maybe use more appropriate words. My dad was not only in the Air Force, but after World War II he became an attorney in the Air Force. Attorneys sometimes love this kind of stuff.

I discovered that I was a fair speech writer on my own. But when my father got done with my speech, either Donald Trump or Hillary Clinton might have used it with positive effect. I practised the speech to a point where I could pronounce the more unfamiliar words he had added, many of the definitions of which I had only just learned. Came the big day of the election, I delivered the entire speech without missing a beat. The students, and even the teacher was speechless. There was no laughter. When the votes were counted, I had the second highest number, and was therefore elected to the vice president post. The attitude of other students towards me changed. Now when I entered a room, someone would shout, "Here comes, Cohen. Get your dictionary." But it was said in a friendly, respectful way. Their attitudes not only affected my ability to speak, but my general demeanor and self-confidence improved, and no doubt this assisted in my development and whatever success I attained later in life.

START WITH SMALL SUCCESSES
AND WORK UP

All anyone needs to do is select a relatively easy goal to accomplish and then go ahead and accomplish it. Every time you complete a task or goal successfully, celebrate and congratulate yourself. Then set a higher goal or a more challenging task. It's just like working out with weights or running. You build up the amount of weight slowly or run more swiftly as you develop your strength. Before long, you'll be doing things that you never thought you could. Motivational speaker Zig Ziglar once described how he lost weight by jogging. Every day he counted and increased the number of mailboxes he passed as he jogged by. Do this in your own life and you will acquire that self-confidence you need to expect positive results and reach the top in your profession.

YOU MUST DEVELOP YOUR OVERALL
SELF-CONFIDENCE FOR YOUR ORGANIZATION

As I mentioned in Chapter 1, Drucker wrote that your organization is not going to do better than you do yourself. Don't expect it to be any more self-confident than you are either.

Several years ago, I was surprised to read research that showed that most senior executives were more worried about speaking in public than they were of dying! Can you imagine that? Why was it true? What this means for many of us, even those having the ability to be extremely successful in some areas, is that we still lack overall self-confidence needed to reach the top. In many areas, we are afraid to expect positive results, because we have failed in these areas one or more times in the past. Now the question is, what can we do about this?

SELF-CONFIDENCE IN ONE AREA
CAN CARRY OVER INTO OTHERS

The military uses something called a confidence course to build self-confidence. It consists of man-made obstacles sometimes coupled with other mental challenges that each participant must overcome successfully before passing on to the next obstacle. All of them are designed to be from moderately to severely difficult and challenging, but doable if done right and provide the personnel with confidence to continue to the next challenge. One might require climbing down a 100-foot rope suspended from a cliff. Another might force the participant to jump out to catch a swinging rope suspended over a pool of water. Do it right, and you catch the rope and safely reach the other side by dropping off before the rope starts swinging back. Do it incorrectly and you end up in the water. Another is called a 'slide for life'. It consists of a rope drawn across a lake from a 90-foot tower on one side of the lake, to the bank of the lake on the other. The participant jumps off the tower holding on to a pulley attached to the rope. As he slides across the lake to the other side, he keeps his eyes on a visible individual signalling with a set of flags. On one signal, you raise your legs so that they are parallel with the water and you are in a sitting position. At the next signal, you let go of your perch and drop about 10 feet above the water. Like a stone, you go skipping across the lake to the bank of the opposite shore. If you don't let go and drop off the pulley, you impact the bank of the lake with some force, and you can get injured. Better to drop off as you were instructed.

While there is a real need for parachute training for some types of military duties, parachute training is frequently encouraged and given to almost anyone who applies for it for the same reason: confidence building, even if they are not assigned to paratroops. I knew a sales executive who got most of his sales force to do a parachute jump when sales were lagging for the same reason.

Motivational speaker Tony Robbins encourages fire walks using the same reasoning. Yes, this is no misprint, I mean walking on a bed of white-hot coals for 12 feet or longer. Robbins calls this seminar 'Fear into Power', and makes it quite clear that he isn't teaching party skills, but rather using the fire walk as a metaphor, "If you can do this which you think is impossible, what else can you do that you may also think is difficult or at least unpleasant."

What I am saying here is that there is a variety of confidence-building means available, some commercially, and they will work to raise your overall self-confidence.

PHYSICAL FITNESS AS
A CONFIDENCE BUILDER

George Patton once said, "Fear makes cowards of us all." He was right. When we are fatigued, our resistance is down. We make poorer decisions. We are more fearful. We cannot handle stress as well. We don't feel as well and are much less likely to expect positive results. Therefore, all the military services emphasize physical fitness for everyone, whether your job is that of an office clerk, a Navy Seal, or an Army Ranger. If you are sitting in a missile silo, responsible for the launch of a nuclear-tipped missile, your most physically demanding task may be pressing a button. Under these circumstances, the physical demands may not justify spending a great deal of time, energy, and resources on physical fitness. But those who serve in such a capacity know that there is far more to it than that and that physical fitness is crucial to the mental performance and handling the responsibility that goes along with 'just pressing a button'.

If you are physically fit, you look better, feel better, and have more self-confidence. Some years ago, I watched a TV show based on a fictional story of young men trying to get through Harvard law school. In one sequence, there was to be a debate between two teams of two students. One team consisted of the two top men in the law class. The other team was made up of a self-confident West Point-trained army officer and a smart, but fearful and slovenly introvert.

The West Pointer expected to win. He expected positive results. His partner, though a smart student, kept focusing on why they couldn't win. Finally, the West Pointer realized he had to build up his partner's self-confidence before he did anything else. So, he put his partner on a regime of physical fitness – push-ups, sit-ups, squat jump. His partner was subjected to a heavy dose. The brilliant introvert said, "We don't have time for this. We've got to prepare our arguments and legal briefs. What has this got to do with winning the debate?"

"Everything!" his ex-army partner told him. After several weeks, the introvert got fit, got self-confident, and together they won the debate. I don't know who wrote the play, but he was right on the money. So, if you want to develop your self-confidence, I recommend that you consider working out. I'm told that Peter Drucker did this until he was well into his nineties. I know that Doris Drucker, his wife was working out and playing tennis at the same time.

Start slowly at first. Jog from one mailbox to the next like Zig Ziglar. Then, every day add another mailbox. Or you can start working with weights. Do the same thing and work up slowly to heaver and heaver weights.

Drucker believed strongly in measuring everything. He recommended writing down your intended results and then looking at actual results some time later as you progressed to see what you achieved. This lets you see your strengths and weaknesses in bold print, too. But your progress is encouraging and builds your self-confidence.

TURN DISADVANTAGES INTO ADVANTAGES

If you really want to build your self-confidence, start turning disadvantages into advantages. When you know you can do that, you know that you can do anything. Back in the early part of this century, the richest man of his day, steel magnate Andrew Carnegie, commissioned a young reporter by the name of Napoleon Hill to research success. Carnegie offered to provide introductions to some of the richest and most famous men in America if Hill would investigate and analyse what had made them successful. It took Hill 20 years, but he accomplished his mission. One of his discoveries was that hidden within every problem, drawback, disadvantage, or obstacle, there was an equally powerful opportunity or advantage. Hill found that successful people looked for these opportunities hidden within the problems and used them. They always seemed to expect positive results. Later, Hill himself wrote the multimillion copy bestselling book, *Think and Grow Rich* which is still read by thousands every year.

Entrepreneur Joe Cossman bought 10,000 pieces of costume jewellery in a closing-down sale. Each piece consisted of a bracelet with seven imitation gemstones. Unfortunately, no one wanted to buy them. Always interested in innovative ideas, Cossman took a course in hypnosis from a stage hypnotist. He heard the instructor say,

"To induce a subject to enter a hypnotic trance, you need a point of fixation. This can be anything on which the subject can focus all of his attention."

"How about an imitation gemstone?" asked Cossman. "Sure," answered the instructor. "Suddenly," Cossman said, "I realized I had 10,000 points of fixation." Cossman made a deal with the hypnotist to record a hypnotic induction and other information on a record, together with some printed instructions and using a free 'hypnotic gem' as inducement to buy. Cossman sold tens of thousands of units and made more than a million dollars by turning a disadvantage into an advantage. As a young student in 1957, I was one of Joe's customers.

These were accidents, but they needn't be. Once you realize that no matter how difficult a problem, there are always solutions that can have a greater benefit to you hidden right within the problem. Moreover, the fact that you know that they are there (and they always are) will greatly increase your self-confidence in any situation.

ONCE YOU DEVELOP YOUR SELF-CONFIDENCE, YOU CAN SET BIG GOALS

People don't put everything on the line for unimportant, insignificant goals – at least, not if they can help it. People in organizations of all types are the same. They do not want to work hard and sacrifice for trivial things, only for big, important things. The sky is the limit on how big and how important. Successful leaders have powerful visions and goals because their visions are big, usually tough to reach, and always important. Then, there is little that their organizations cannot accomplish because you and they expect very positive results.

This concept can be used in sales too. Recently the Nightingale Corporation used this in promoting a product:

"Men Wanted for Hazardous Journey. Low Wages, Long Hours......"

This referred to another ad placed in the early 1900s by explorer Sir Ernest Henry Shackleton as he was looking for men to help him on a journey to find the South Pole. The ad drew more than five thousand candidates from which he selected the small crew he needed. On 15 December 1911 after much hardship (he spoke the truth in the ad) he accomplished this with the crew he had recruited.

The Royal Air Force has a motto that goes something like this: "What man can conceive, man can achieve." Note that this motto doesn't say "up to a certain amount" or "to a certain point". If you can conceive of it, you can achieve it. Period.

George Washington is known as 'the father of his country' because he had the self-confidence to go against the British, the superpower of the day. He conceived of an entirely new nation with freedom and liberty. He held this vision through the most trying times. Had he failed against the tremendous odds he faced, he would have been hanged. In fact, although the Continental Congress appointed him Commander-in-Chief in June of 1775, he was commander of only one soldier: himself. There was no Continental army. If Congress changed its mood and decided to accommodate George III, King of England, Washington would be left holding the bag as the most visible and conspicuous of traitors to the Crown. But it was Washington's self-confidence that enabled him to persevere through six years of war, and through incredible hardship, to ultimate victory. Washington's example continues to inspire not only Americans, but also others in the world, today.

If you want to become successful as a manager, or a professional like Drucker in any field, building your self-confidence is a good place to start. Remember, you cannot build on weakness, only strength – and strength of any kind starts with self-confidence.

CHAPTER 14

SETTING AND REACHING GOALS: PLANNING AND STRATEGY

*Management by objective works
− if you know the objectives.
Ninety percent of the time you don't.*

− Peter F. Drucker

Peter Drucker was very much into setting and achieving goals and objectives. It is little wonder that he originated the term "management by objectives" or MBO and first popularized it in his book *The Practice of Management* in 1954. Some say the basic idea goes back to Mary Parker Follett in her 1926 essay, "The Giving of Orders"[1] and others who had thoughts about similar systems, but it seems clear that it was Drucker that put it all together as a better system of managing and measuring an employee's performance by setting specific goals for the employee to attain. Drucker walked his talk in reaching and setting goals in his personal life.

THE RISE OF MBO

MBO (or goals) was adopted by many large corporations but was vigorously attacked by critics who pointed out that during the period of performance, many situations changed such that priorities were altered to the extent that any goals or objectives might have a much lower priority and might even make no sense at all. Drucker's defence was that MBO was not a "set and forget system", and that objectives had to be reviewed and adjusted continually, otherwise the correct objectives were unknown to the individual who was supposed to have the responsibility for attaining them and the supervisor who initially formulated them.

GOALS MUST BE UNDER CONTINUAL REVIEW

The first element we need to understand about goals is that they need to be reviewed periodically. Sometimes it is not the goal that needs to be changed, but the strategy we are using to attain that goal. In other situations, something has changed in our environment or in our lives such that the goal needs to be abandoned or seriously adjusted, and a new one substituted, just as Drucker abandoned his goal of a professorship at the University of Cologne due to the rise of Hitler. What this means is that before abandoning or otherwise changing a goal, you should first see if it is your strategy that should be adjusted and that your goal should remain essentially the same.

YOU CAN'T GET THERE UNTIL
YOU KNOW WHERE 'THERE' IS

Which brings us to the important point of fully defining each one of your goals because you certainly can't reach a goal if you don't know exactly what it is. So, it's important to fully define every goal. The definition should set out the goal with as many descriptors as needed and should include the times when each goal is to be attained. If you don't have a goal defined fully, this will certainly lead to less than optimal results with any progress towards goal achievement including MBO.

EXAMINING AVAILABLE RESOURCES

You also need to examine each goal and determine what resources are needed to attain it. It makes no difference if you don't have a resource so long as you can get it within a time that works for the time set for goal attainment. Drucker got a PhD in international law from the University of Frankfurt because he needed a PhD in any field, and the law degree was the easiest and quickest type of PhD to obtain for achievement of Drucker's overall goal. Your goal may be different and your immediate objective, if a PhD, might be one of the most difficult to get.

OBSTACLES MUST BE IDENTIFIED
BEFORE THEY ARE REACHED

When defining your goals, you must also consider obstacles to their achievement. The earlier in the process you can do this, the better. Drucker's original goal was a professorship at the University of Cologne. But with the rise of Hitler, Drucker's ethnic Jewish background would have stopped him. Drucker fully understood the risks this entailed in Nazi Germany. This was an obstacle he decided was best overcome by emigrating first to England and to get even further away, to the US, thus adjusting his goal at every step. In retrospect, this was clearly the correct decision although it delayed his attainment of his ultimate goal of a professorship at a major university. This also illustrates that we need to be wary of assumptions about obstacles and should analyse them completely and realistically at every step to avoid wishful thinking.

DEPENDENCE ON OTHERS

Along these lines, it is inevitable that we depend on others to help achieve certain parts of our goals much as we help others to achieve their goals. Here we need to incorporate a 'what if?' cautionary note. What if those we depend upon to act in some way or to do something for us do not do so? We need to think this through ahead of time. While defining goals and obstacles, all possibilities need to be identified along with potential alternative solutions. Of course, you don't achieve your goals automatically just because you have set them. That's where plans come in; you need to make plans to reach your goals and objectives. They are the road maps that take you from where you are now to where you want to go, the objective and goals you want to reach.

Planning: How You Reach Your Goals

Planning is challenging work and a good plan needs information gathered from many sources. It is used with the 'how' of strategy and tactics to accomplish specific objectives and goals. The process is not difficult, but it does require effort and organization.

There are many ways of organizing a plan. This applies to life planning as well as developing a project plan, a marketing plan, or any other type of plan. Some say you should just stumble on and figure out what to do as you encounter challenges, opportunities, and threats. You will need to do that eventually anyway. But it makes sense to struggle with each issue ahead of time to think things through before you encounter these as you execute your plan. You can avoid many obstacles and threats and exploit many opportunities if you can identify them before you begin. Even if you can't, better to have actions and alternatives ready before you start, than to try to deal with issues that might have been anticipated when you're under the pressures of time and execution during implementation.

I said there are many ways to organize a plan. Here is one I developed based on various concepts Drucker and other recommended.

INTRODUCTION

The introduction is the explanation of what the plan is about. Its purpose is to give the background of the project and to describe your situation so that you will understand exactly what it is you intend to do.

SITUATIONAL ANALYSIS

The situational analysis comes from taking a good hard look at your environment and the situation you face and contains a vast amount of information such as political situation, financial situation, economic situation, competitive advantages, trends, new technology, etc.

PROBLEMS AND OPPORTUNITIES

This is a summary that emphasizes the main points you have already covered in preceding sections. When you put your plan together and developed your situational analysis, you should have covered the problems and opportunities inherent in your situation. Group them first by opportunities, then by problems. Indicate why each is an opportunity or a problem. Also indicate how you intend to take advantage of each opportunity and what you intend to do about each problem.

GOALS AND OBJECTIVES

Goals and objectives are accomplishments you intend to achieve through your plan. In this section you must spell out in detail exactly what you intend to do.

What is the difference between a goal and an objective? An *objective* is an overall goal. It is more general and may not be quantified. *Goals* are usually quantified.

STRATEGY

Here you should describe what is to be done to reach your objectives and goals. You can also talk about obstacles to the strategies you discuss and how you will overcome these obstacles.

TACTICS

Just as strategy tells you what you must do to reach your objectives, tactics explain how you will carry out your strategy. List every action required to implement each of the strategies described in the preceding section and the timing of these actions.

IMPLEMENTATION AND CONTROL

In the implementation and control section you are going to forecast valuable information to help control the project once implementation has started. You will use this information to keep the project on track. Thus, if your budget is exceeded you will know where to cut back or to reallocate resources.

STRATEGY FOR IMPLEMENTING THESE PLANS

Drucker was opposed to any mathematical formulae for calculating strategy. He did not even discuss the once pervasive four-celled matrix of cash cows, stars, problem children, and dogs. He reasoned that following the advice of the four-celled matrix would invariably lead to acquisition as a main solution, and if the acquiring company had nothing to contribute but ownership it would have poor results.

Drucker maintained that in all cases you had to think your strategy through and concentrate your resources where they were decisive, abandoning those businesses or projects which had less potential.

Therefore, if you sat in a Drucker class you saw no matrices populated with cartoon images or curves or matrices that instructed a strategist to adopt one strategy or another. He maintained that a strategist needs to use his brain and think through actions and consequences.

The overall decision was made by executive's gut feeling. Quantitative analysis were inputs only to the evolving ultimate strategy which came from the gut.

ESSENTIAL PRINCIPLES OF STRATEGY

Strategy is important because by applying the right strategy and using the right tactics, you can dare the impossible and achieve the extraordinary in any human endeavour, not just business.

Many experts have maintained that there are certain principles of strategy. Unfortunately, while there is no collective agreement as to which all strategists agree, the following are ten principles from my book *The Art of the Strategist* to develop a strategy.[2] Some were advised and undoubtedly used by Drucker. A few came from others but I combined them with strategies that Drucker employed:

1. COMMIT FULLY TO A DEFINITE OBJECTIVE

Everywhere you look, you see people who logically should not even attempt what they attempt. But they are so committed to a definite objective that, more often than anyone can believe possible, their strategies are successful, and they are successful. Politics provides numerous examples. President Obama was told he couldn't win. And the election of President Trump is the most recent example. Did you know that Abraham Lincoln was not supposed to have any chance of becoming president? How do these things happen? We have discussed some of them previously. The basis is a fundamental principle of strategy: commitment to a definite objective.

2. SEIZE THE INITIATIVE AND KEEP IT

Nothing happens until you make it happen, until you take action. Putting things off until you can get around to it or until conditions are perfect almost always results in failure. W. Clement Stone, who rose from poverty to build an international insurance company worth hundreds of millions of dollars, asserted that to overcome procrastination, you need only say these three words to yourself, and then act on them: 'Do it now!'

Is it any wonder that the rewards in industry, in any organization, go to those who show initiative? Those who sit around waiting for something to happen or for someone else to tell them what to do are rarely successful. The same is true for the strategist who looks to the competition to dictate his own actions.

3. ECONOMIZE TO MASS YOUR RESOURCES

Good business strategists amass their resources where it counts. They know that they can't concentrate and be strong everywhere. Microsoft founder Bill Gates built the most successful technology company in the world virtually from scratch and along the way became the richest man in America. In an interview with *Fortune Magazine*, Gates said: "You know, the notion that a kid who thought software was cool can end up creating a company with all these smart people whose software gets out to hundreds of millions of people, well, that's an amazing thing. I've had one of the luckiest situations ever. But I've also learned that only through focus can you do world-class things, no matter how capable you are."[3]

If our resources are greater than those of our competitors we have an automatic advantage from the start. We bring these resources – money, people, time, skill, know-how, influence, or whatever – together, by massing them, concentrating them, or focusing them at the right place and at the right time.

4. USE STRATEGIC POSITIONING

The strategic position is the decisive point that will make the difference in attaining your well-defined objective. Some strategic positions should be obvious but are still ignored in the heat of business and competition. For example, at the height of the e-commerce frenzy, dot-com companies advertised all over the web. Yet. Although other factors impacted on the decision of where to advertise, these firms generally should have economized elsewhere to concentrate on these sites. This should be basic stuff. Yet, supposedly sophisticated strategists continue to violate this lesson repeatedly, with predictably poor results.

5. DO THE UNEXPECTED

It doesn't make any difference whether you are a large organization or a tiny one, or even an individual. You can use boldness and creativity to create surprise and win.

In the preliminaries to the California recall election in the fall of 2003, it was obvious that Arnold Schwarzenegger would be a major candidate if he decided to run. Still, the word went out that Arnold's wife, Maria Shriver, didn't want the actor to be a candidate. For several weeks, the media published stories that Schwarzenegger would announce his decision not to run on an upcoming NBC's *The Tonight Show* appearance.

On the night of Schwarzenegger's appearance, the host Jay Leno made the introductions and the expected jokes. Then all grew quiet as the cameras focused on Arnold. He began explaining that it had been a difficult decision. As he started to state what this decision actually was, the screen went blank, and one of the old black and white NBC logos from the 1950s appeared with the caption: "We are experiencing technical difficulties, please stand by." When Arnold appeared again, he was concluding, "and that is why I made the decision that I made."

Of course, the whole thing was a joke. Schwarzenegger made other jokes before making the surprise announcement that he was a candidate after all. According to the *Los Angeles Times*: "His announcement landed with the force of an explosion from a Schwarzenegger movie."[4] The resulting excitement brought the new candidate tremendous media attention much to the consternation of his rival candidates and the sitting governor, Gray Davis, who was trying to avoid a recall election. Schwarzenegger rode this wave of excitement all the way to the statehouse.

6. KEEP THINGS SIMPLE

An analysis conducted by the Booz Allen Hamilton consulting firm showed that in one industry after another large, traditional companies made an identical mistake in their strategy: overcomplicating their business. The strategies they developed to run their businesses had become so complex that profit margins had almost disappeared.

Naturally this left them vulnerable. As these market leaders struggled under the burdens of the complicated business models they themselves had devised, smaller, nimbler competitors with less complex strategies swallowed up market share by meeting customer needs at a lower cost.

According to the Booz Allen Hamilton analysis the large US airlines industry is a good example because of their complex strategies. It costs these carriers twice as much per seat mile as low-cost carriers to complete a 500-mile flight. This is because their solution to take anyone, anywhere led them to massive physical infrastructures, fleets of dissimilar models of aircraft, expensive information systems, and large pools of labour.[5] Keep your strategy simple!

7. PUT ADVERSARIES ON THE HORNS OF A DILEMMA

There is an example in game theory known as the Prisoner's Dilemma. It goes something like this. Two men are caught after committing a robbery. The District Attorney (DA) knows that these two are guilty. They were arrested with the victim's wallet. They fit the description of the robbers. They both have done time in jail for similar crimes using the same MO. Unfortunately, it was dark and the robbery victim fails to correctly identify either in a police line-up.

The two prisoners are kept separate and can't communicate. The DA goes to one prisoner and offers him a deal. If he will identify the other prisoner as one of the two robbers, he will be released since neither prisoner has been positively identified. His partner, of course, will go to jail.

The prisoner is left alone to consider the offer. If he does nothing, both he and his partner stand a chance of being convicted and going to jail because of other factors than positive identification. If he identifies his partner as a robber, at least he will go free, even though his partner will go to jail. He is about to accept this alternative, when he realizes that the DA has used a strategy of putting him on the horns of a dilemma. It is likely that the DA has made the same offer to his partner! If both identify each other as involved in the robbery, they will both go to jail. If he does not identify his partner as a robber and his partner identifies him, he will go to jail and his partner will go free. The DA, a clever strategist, has arranged things so that he wins no matter what the robbers decide to do. He has used the principle of putting them on the horns of a dilemma. The worst case scenario from the DA's perspective is that both refuse to betray the other. But the DA is in that situation anyhow. See if you can put your competitors on the horns of a dilemma.

8. TAKE THE INDIRECT ROUTE TO YOUR OBJECTIVE

It was English strategist Liddell Hart who came up with the indirect approach. He said that it was far better to approach a competitor indirectly than to meet him head-on. If you have ever watched a magician's performance, you may have wondered at his ability to perform impossible feats. In fact, doing magic is based on an application of the indirect approach. While you are being misdirected by him to focus on something unimportant, he accomplishes something that you may well have noticed if you had not been distracted.

9. TIMING AND SEQUENCING

Timing is critical in so many fields – sports, politics, and military strategy all come to mind immediately – but it is especially important in business. Doing the right thing at the wrong time can result in a great waste of money, time, and effort, with no results to show for it. To some, this may seem like a no-brainer. Yet many otherwise savvy businesspeople are convinced that it is the amount spent that is more important. Even if they recognize that timing is more important in some areas, like seasonal advertising, it is not generally true overall, they maintain. They couldn't be more wrong.

Let's look at something entirely different like a simple strategy for motivating employees: reward them with money. Which is more important in this situation, how much you give them or when you do it? William T. Quinn Jr, owner of a publishing company in Somerset, New Jersey, wanted to motivate his employees in this manner. He discovered that when handing out bonuses for extra or exemplary effort, it was timing, not the amount of the bonus, that mattered most. The key was to dispense his motivational dollars when his employees were most stressed, and to do so on the spot, not to wait for some collective time to reward everyone together in the future.[6]

This finding is psychologically sound. If you want to motivate someone, the desired action and the motivator should be as close together as possible. It should be no surprise that timing is far more important than the amount of money intended as a motivator in business. Doing the right thing at the wrong time can be a disaster. You must consider timing a primary principle of strategy.

10. EXPLOIT YOUR SUCCESS

The success process always involves two phases. First, a critical mass either exists or is created. This critical mass is the environment in which we are trying to achieve the success. Building this mass into the critical phase may take years, a few months, a few days, or perhaps just a few hours.

As we continue to pursue success, at first nothing or very little is likely to occur. Suddenly, the second phase comes, and everything seems to happen at once. Like a nuclear chain reaction, the environmental mass becomes supercritical. And just as the chain reaction results in a nuclear detonation, if we manage things correctly at this point, a complete triumph results.

Because events happen so rapidly in this second phase, the perception may be that the success was instantaneous. However, a closer examination of any achievement will show that only just before the triumph occurred did the pace speed up to near light-speed velocity. Whether the earlier phase lasted years or days, the pace of the first phase would have appeared to be slow.

Unfortunately, because of this variance in time between the phases, there are two traps that we can fall into which can block the very triumph we seek. First, because the first phase may be glacially slow, we may not realize that the mass is becoming supercritical. In this case, we may abandon the process before the chain reaction can occur, so we never reach the success we seek. But another error can also occur. We may fail to exploit our success for maximum gain. Both are important principles of strategy and failing to take note of them can impede our success.

Let's look at another historical example, but for an organization. Lever Brothers was a subsidiary of Unilever of London, a giant worldwide corporation as we first examine its situation. Having been successful with many products in the US, during the late 1920s, it now sought another new product to launch in America. A vegetable-shortening product seemed a good potential candidate. Lever's competitor Procter & Gamble (P&G) had already proven there was a market through its introduction of a product called Crisco. Although Crisco was well established, its dominance also meant that there were no other major competitors or competitive products to contend with. In the States, both business and economic conditions looked pretty good.

In initiating a deeper analysis in the situation, Lever Brothers also discovered that Crisco had weaknesses. Although women generally liked Crisco, there were some things that they definitely didn't like. If refrigerated, Crisco became hard and difficult to use. The alternative was to leave it unrefrigerated. Unfortunately for P&G and housewives, it then turned rancid rapidly. The color was not consistent, and while housewives were OK with a pure white coloration, Crisco was more a shade of dirty white. This was unappetizing for a food product. Moreover, the packaging was not uniform in the cans in which it was sold. That wasn't popular with housewives either.

ARRIVING AT A STRATEGY WHEN AN OPPORTUNITY WAS SPOTTED

Looking at principles of strategy, we can see how some were integrated with the situational variables noted to this point. Lever Brothers seized the initiative and committed to a definite objective. It planned to concentrate resources at the strategic position of vegetable shortening. P&G thought its product, Crisco, was pretty much invulnerable. This thinking is always dangerous when you are employing a strategy that involves competitors or potential competitors. It seemed apparent that P&G had paid little attention to these issues and did no further research with the consumer after the product had been introduced. If that were not enough, P&G had also allowed quality control in manufacture and packaging to get out of hand. P&G thought that competitors, even a major one like Lever Brothers, would not even attempt to introduce a product to compete with Crisco. To P&G it was unthinkable that Crisco was vulnerable in any way. Lever Brothers capitalized on this mistaken notion and introduced its own product, Spry, which took advantage of Crisco's deficiencies. The introduction of Spry was a complete surprise.[7]

LEVER BROTHERS HAD THE RESOURCES AVAILABLE AND USED THEM

Lever Brothers decided which of the situational variables could be taken advantage of and did. Unilever had made major technological advances in Europe in the manufacture of soap, and the technology was directly transferable to the production of vegetable shortening. The problems with Crisco noted by consumers were easy for Lever Brothers to overcome. Some simply had to do with a stricter quality control. Financial resources and know-how were on Lever Brothers' side, but it even had one additional major advantage.

LEVER BROTHERS EVEN HAD A SECRET WEAPON IN ITS LEADER

Francis Conway had become president of Lever Brothers in 1913 when sales were but $1 million. By the late 1920s, sales were over $40 million largely due to his personal leadership. Conway was a competent leader and had met every challenge thrown at him. Moreover, he had the confidence of the parent company leadership back in the United Kingdom. Unilever invested the money to build the manufacturing plants to make the product. By the early 1930s, Lever Brothers was geared up and ready to proceed.

ENTER THE UNEXPECTED

The Depression began in October of 1929 and pre-empted Lever Brothers' product launch. By mid-1930 it was clear this was not an economic condition that would change anytime soon. Lever Brothers had planned on introducing the product by then. There was tremendous pressure from within the company and the parent corporation to do so. The company had sunk a lot of money in Spry up to this point. They wanted to get on with it. However, Conway knew his strategy and the importance of timing. He made the decision to wait. Meanwhile he noted that the sales of Crisco did not slow as the Depression deepened, so vegetable shortening was still a winner as demand remained constant. While Spry was shelved, fine-tuning went on and research into the best promotional approach was initiated.

THE PRODUCT LAUNCH

In late 1935, lard and butter prices rose. This created a situation whereby the higher-priced shortening would be more price-competitive. Lever Brothers did not intend to compete with P&G on price, which would be a direct approach. Instead, although it was competing with essentially an identical product, the approach was indirect in the sense that problems with Crisco, recognized by consumers but not by the manufacturer, were all corrected in the new product, Spry. The day it first appeared on the market, therefore, Spry was already free of the problems that Crisco still presented to the consumer.

Conway economized elsewhere to concentrate and initiate a massive promotional campaign. Until this time, conventional wisdom was to introduce advertising for a new product and let it be assimilated gradually by the consumer. Conway avoided this approach and gave it everything he had from day one. This included door-to-door salesmen distributing sample cans and free Spry cookbooks. Discount coupons and advertising were even put in small-town newspapers. Conway also launched a mobile cooking school that went around the country doing two-hour demonstrations. P&G was stunned, and though it improved its product and manufacturing, it never recaptured the market share it had lost. Conway and Lever Brothers integrated the relevant variables with the principles, and using the resources available, developed and initiated a plan which made Spry a success despite the seemingly overwhelming advantages enjoyed by P&G.

As Drucker maintained, planning is never easy; however, even seemingly impossible goals that have been well planned can be achieved with the right strategy. Drucker thought through the direction of his own career to use planning and the right strategy to reach the top. No formulae, he simply thought it through.

---

1. Follett, Mary Parker. "The Giving of Orders". *Scientific Foundations of Business Administration* (1926): 29-37.
2. Cohen, William A. *The Art of the Strategist: 10 Essential Principles for Leading Your Company to Victory* (New York: AMACOM, 2004).
3. Schlender, Brent. "All You Need Is Love, $50 Billion, and Killer Software Code-Named Longhorn: An Up-Close Look at Why Bill Gates Still Holds the Key to Microsoft's Future". *Fortune*, 8 July 2002, https://for.tn/2vt2KfM.
4. Mathews, Joe and Doug Smith. "Role Reversal: 'Predator's' Prey Stalks Statehouse". *Los Angeles Times*, 7 August 2003, A24, https://lat.ms/2vqutOl.
5. Hansson, Tom, Jürgen Ringbeck, and Markus Franke. "Flight for Survival: A New Operating Model for Airlines". *Strategy+Business*, 6 December 2002, https://bit.ly/2M3GwuD.
6. Inc. Staff. "Instant Gratification: Timing Is the Key when Handing out Motivational Dollars for Morale and Motivation". *Inc. Magazine*, January 1989, https://bit.ly/2AQUCLe.
7. Robert F. Harley, Marketing Successes, 2nd ed. (New York: John Wiley & Sons, Inc., 1990) pp.68-78.

CHAPTER 15

BECOME A CHANGE LEADER AND INNOVATE

Innovation means to create change.

– Peter F. Drucker

Drucker wrote that there were only two elements driving any business: innovation and marketing. These two essential ingredients are also essential in self-development and personal success. You will need to do both to reach the top. We look at innovation in this chapter, and personal marketing in the next. Both will help boost you to the top in any environment.

Drucker maintained that any organization that continued to do what made it successful in the past would eventually fail. The solution for survival and success is to become a change leader and to innovate. He demonstrated that this must be done by individuals as well as organizations. A perusal of Drucker's many career changes, his drastic shifts in emphasis of his research and conclusions in his analysis demonstrates this. He looked at leadership in the 1950s and concluded that leadership could not be learned or taught. He changed this strong statement drastically to reflect a new belief 40 years later to write the opposite that leadership not only could be learned but must be taught.

One could also see in his career brief flirtations with small business and entrepreneurship to a major shift from management of large corporations to a brand-new stress on the management of non-profits which lasted to the end of his long career.

WHAT HAPPENS WHEN ORGANIZATIONS FAIL TO PRODUCE CHANGE LEADERS?

It is easy to find examples of organizations whose heads failed to become change leaders and the resulting disasters that followed. The parade of once highly successful organizations that have disappeared is almost endless. Railway companies, once the king of people transportation in the USA, failed, and were largely replaced by the airlines. Their presidents saw their businesses as companies totally synonymous with the instrument they used and not companies producing a need output, transportation. In even more recent memory, companies like Blockbuster Video, Borders Books, Circuit City, Pan American Airways, and Toys "R" Us have all disappeared by failing to adapt and change through innovation.

In the US, there was failure by a government agency that at one time held all financial resources and was the largest and possibly the most important government agency and the Federal Reserve Board of its day. It was even more powerful in some ways. This was the United States National Bank. The bank was chartered by Congress for 20 years and was needed because of growing inflation due to a major war debt from the War of 1812 and the increasing bank notes issued by state banks. It was a very efficient agency and not only of vast importance when the country was growing but was well managed and popular. In a survey prior to the bank's demise 20 years later, 126,000 people signed papers supporting the bank's rechartering versus only 17,000 opposing it. Its existence was most popular among the wealthiest segments of the country.

The problem was in its organizational structure. When the bank was first chartered, like any ordinary bank its management was answerable to a board, not the President of the USA or Congress. Congress itself favoured rechartering the bank in 1832 and the US electorate generally supported it. However, President Andrew Jackson vetoed the rechartering bill from Congress and withdrew all US funds, which he had the authority to do although theoretically it was the Board which controlled the bank. Almost immediately the once powerful, successful, and well-run National Bank of the United States failed and disappeared from the American scene forever.

PERSONAL INNOVATION IS EQUALLY IMPORTANT

Personal innovation is at least as important, as Drucker demonstrated by his own activities. This is not only true for organizations, but as we will see, on much closer related, personal levels, as well.

THE BRIGHT IDEA

There is a great danger that we as individuals will be stopped in our advancement without innovation, and if we head an organization, it will not succeed if we don't innovate, even if we have done well in the past, by any measure are efficient, good managers, and are even liked by our customers, associates, and supervisors. What can we do? Can we call everyone together and have one of those brainstorming sessions that psychologists and others sometimes recommend? Or maybe you, or someone else in the organization, has a sudden bright-sounding idea that can be adopted and that almost everyone in the organization will support without the time wasted on meetings or a more thorough analysis?

WHY BRIGHT IDEAS FREQUENTLY FAIL

Drucker thought that the idea of analysing the issue together with others was a possible tactic. However, he cautioned us that there would always be more clever ideas than time, money, and employees available to develop them. At the same time, I learned about his belief that there was always a built-in danger of what he called 'the bright idea'. The bright idea was his term for an innovation that was not thoroughly evaluated and frequently consisted of 'blue-sky' statements that were accepted for development without much real thought or analysis. He did not disagree that one could hit a home run with a single bright idea and he was happy to give us examples of bright ideas that had gone on to make millions of dollars for their originators. But he said that these were exceptions and should be ignored.

"The problem is," Drucker said, "that bright ideas are the riskiest and least successful source of innovative opportunities." He estimated that probably only one in 500 made any money above their investment costs and suggested that relying on the bright idea for innovation was akin to gambling at Las Vegas and was almost certain to lead to comparable results. The correct solution, he maintained, was systematic analysis using seven precise sources of innovative ideas. This, he declared, was purposeful innovation, the kind that all of us must pursue regardless of our speciality, discipline, or functional area. He recommended that we avoid the bright idea.[1] And he did so himself. What did he recommend? He championed these seven sources.

THE FIRST SOURCE:
THE UNEXPECTED

Drucker said that the unexpected was the richest source of opportunity for successful innovation, though this was not only neglected, but frequently actively avoided and rejected, by individuals and managers of all disciplines in many organizations. Unexpected innovation can be adopted to great benefit. During World War II, rubber was in high demand. The enemy controlled the primary sources of rubber and the US was desperate. Synthetic rubber existed but was expensive. In 1943, a GE engineer combined boric acid and silicone oil. The raw goo that resulted couldn't be hardened and thus it failed as a synthetic rubber substitute. However, the material had strange and unexpected properties. It would bounce when dropped, it could stretch to a rather amazing size without tearing and when pressed against printed images on a newspaper, it would transfer that image. The engineer showed his manager. He wasn't impressed and told him to discard the material.

The war ended, and over several years, word of mouth carried the unexpected invention along as a party toy. Then one day an advertising man by the name of Peter Hodgson who was seeking an innovative toy for a client found the product. He invested $147 and packaged the 'liquid solid' into one-ounce balls. He gave the product a new name. 'Silly Putty' went on to become one of the most successful toys in history and achieved worldwide fame. It made millions and millions of dollars for Hodgson and his backers. Even with toys, innovation is the key to success.

Or consider Eastman Kodak Company's engineer, Harry Coover, Jr. He asked a lab associate to try a cyanoacrylate as a heat-resistant polymer for jet plane canopies. The associate accidently destroyed an expensive instrument when he brought two prisms in contact while taking a reading. He thought he would be fired, but instead Coover tried sticking everything together using the polymer. Not only did it work, but the bond was amazingly strong. He realized that through these unexpected results they had stumbled on an extraordinarily strong adhesive. In 1958, Eastman Kodak began marketing the powerful bonding agent now known worldwide as Super Glue.[2]

THE SECOND SOURCE: THE INCONGRUITIES

Incongruities may be unexpected too, but in a different and unique way. You expect a certain result, but instead the opposite occurs. The opposite is the key word. It needn't be a product; frequently, it has to do with economic results. In the 1950s someone found that companies that dominated markets were more profitable. This led to portfolio management and the well-known Boston Consulting Group's matrix (the BCG matrix) in which relative high market share was considered desirable and became either a 'cash cow' or a 'shooting star'. So, if you could acquire a large share of the market, success and high profits were yours. The only problem was that the matrix wasn't working. A small firm with 96 employees called ICS, Inc. looked at this incongruity and uncovered the problem. It depended on how you defined the market and focused on the customer. If a larger company selected too broad a definition, a smaller company could beat a larger one in the market place. So, at a time when mighty IBM dominated large computers, ICS, Inc. concentrated on smaller computers for the educational market and dominated this niche from which IBM then withdrew. That too was a innovation: niche marketing.

In more recent times, famous coffeemaker Starbucks fell into the trap by concentrating on expansion instead of its customer. Afterwards, CEO Howard Schultz said in an interview with news interviewer Katie Couric, "We made expansion a strategy instead of an outcome of service."[3] The expansion led to great losses until Schultz spotted the problem and turned things around.

When my West Point classmate Fred Malek was an administrator in the Nixon Administration, he co-conspired with then army major Colin Powell to use the desire for expansion among his fellow politicians that held positions in the Administration to his advantage. Fred had a problem. Appointed to the prominent position of Deputy Director of the Office of Manpower and Budget (OMB), Malek was frustrated. Malek couldn't get things done quickly because of layers of career bureaucrats who occupied key positions. Early on he spotted then White House Fellow and army major Colin Powell. Malek made Powell his Executive Assistant.[4]

I'll let General Powell pick up the story. "Fred went about gaining control of the government in a way that opened the eyes of this fledgling student of power. ... Fred started planting his own people in the key 'assistant secretary for administration' slots in major federal agencies. Let the cabinet officials make the speeches, cut the ribbons, and appear on *Meet the Press*. Anonymous assistant secretaries, loyal to Malek, would run operations day to day, and to the Nixon administration's liking. ... I learned much in Professor Malek's graduate seminar."[5]

However, bureaucrats already occupied many positions in OMB, and the budget couldn't be increased for more positions for the young Harvard, Stanford, and Wharton graduates Malek wanted to bring in. So, he thought out of the box again.

"Thereafter, I started phoning agency officials, explaining that I was calling on behalf of Mr. Malek with good news. Their power was about to be broadened. A function currently being handled by OMB was going to be transferred to their agency ... music to any bureaucrat's ear."[6]

Then, Powell explained that the agency would get the function and the bodies, but not the positions and funding.

"<TNBS>'We don't have jobs for them. We haven't budgeted funds for them.' 'Mr. Assistant Secretary,' I would say, 'Fred Malek has every confidence that between attrition and some imagination on your part, you will work something out.' Soon the unwanted OMB bureaucrats were gone, their offices and titles freed up, and Malek's youngbloods moved in. Out of that experience emerged one of my rules: you don't know what you can get away with until you try."[7]

Drucker found that consultants were supposed to know more than clients. The old saying was that a consultant is someone that borrows your watch to tell you what time it is. But Drucker found that the client usually had greater knowledge and the experience regarding the issue, the industry, and the corporation. From this fact, Drucker decided that what he brought to the consulting engagement was not so much his knowledge or experience having to do with any company, industry, product, or service, but his ignorance and lack of experience. Based on this incongruity, Drucker began a unique consulting practice in which he asked his clients five basic generic business questions such as, "What business you are you in?" followed by more questions of the experts (his clients) which led to the clients solving the problem while Drucker facilitated the process.

THE THIRD SOURCE: PROCESS NEED

This has to do with the old proverb that necessity is the mother of invention. So, this source is straightforward. You need something done and you simply work on this something until you figure out how to do it. The Wright brothers, Orville and Wilbur, struggled to invent a workable flying machine. They calculated that they would need an engine weighing less than 200 pounds which would generate eight horsepower. They searched and discovered that no such engine existed. All existing engines were either too heavy or too weak to meet these specifications. They decided that they needed to develop such an engine themselves. They estimated that they would need one made of four cylinders with four-inch bore and four-inch stroke, weighing not over two hundred pounds, including all accessories. This they did. However, by itself, an engine was useless if it could not generate the artificial wind thrust over the wings to create lift. Where to find a propeller to generate the wind for thrust? No data on air propellers existed, so the Wright brothers found themselves working in a theoretical vacuum. They concluded that a propeller was simply like a glider travelling in a spiral course.

As they could calculate the effect of a glider travelling in a straight course, they realized that theoretically there was no reason why they could not calculate the effect of one travelling in a spiral course. But what in theory does not appear difficult, may be misleading. It was hard to find even a point from which to make a start; for nothing about a propeller, or the medium in which it acts, remains stationery. Eventually they solved that problem which led to yet another problem which they eventually solved too: their invention of three-axis control allowed the pilot to control his machine. Step by step they innovated as they solved problem after problem. Finally, everything came together on 17 December 1903 with man's first powered flight.[8] Where there is a need, there is always a way.

John Dewey, economic philosopher, Charles Kettering, who headed research for GM, and Peter Drucker concluded that defining the problem was of primary importance and that in effect a problem well stated was half solved. So stating the problem well is not to be ignored. Think about the importance of a medical doctor diagnosing the right disease before deciding on a treatment.

THE FOURTH SOURCE:
INDUSTRY AND MARKET STRUCTURES

People tend to keep doing things the same way forever, and this carries through to industries and markets. I heard a story once about a husband who asked his wife why she cut the ends off her roast before cooking. Her answer: "That's the way it's done." The husband noticed that his wife's mother made her roast in the same way. Her response was the same: "That's the way you cook a roast." One day, he and his wife visited her grandmother. She prepared a roast, too. But she didn't cut the ends off. So, the young husband asked her why she didn't. "Well," she said, "for many years I did. But finally, about the time our daughter left home and got married we bought a pan large enough to hold the roast without my having to cut off the ends." Amazingly that way of roasting passed through two generations as 'that's the way it's done'. How many 'roasting processes' do you have in your organization done that way because 'that's the way it's done?'

All organizations make these assumptions. What was magic about Henry Ford and his Ford Motor Company? Contrary to widespread belief, Ford did not invent the assembly line. Moreover, the assembly line wasn't even needed for enormous success and high profits. Rolls-Royce proved that. They never had one. What Ford did was to observe that the market structure had changed such that the 'horseless carriage' was no longer just a rich man's toy. Ford designed a car that could be mass-produced at a relatively low cost and driven and maintained by the owner himself. The assembly line was only part of this innovation. In developing his cars, using the assembly line and cutting costs to the point that a customer could have any colour car he wanted so long as it was black, Ford changed both the way the industry and the market worked. He changed an important part of market and industry structure.

As Drucker pointed out, innovation could work equally well going another way, but still using existing industry and market structure in the same business as a source. About the same time as Ford was innovating, Rolls-Royce introduced its own innovations. But it was the exact opposite of what Ford introduced. It more than quadrupled its already high price, abandoned the assembly line and returned to manufacturing methods and materials that had been used since the Middle Ages. Unlike the Ford Motor Company, Rolls-Royce guaranteed its product would last forever. It made a vehicle that was not designed for the owner to drive or maintain. Rather than envision everyone as its future customer, it sought to restrict sales to royalty, or those that had the financial resources equated with royalty. Rolls-Royce, too, achieved great success and high profits.

THE FIFTH SOURCE: DEMOGRAPHICS

Demographics have to do with the characteristics of a human population. These may be characteristics of education, culture, income, and more. These characteristics are not static. They change over time. For example, people live longer and tend to be in better health at older ages than in generations past. They say that today's age demographic of the eighties were previously that of the sixties. Can you see sources for innovation in this? These changes have caused an explosion in the interest in and maintenance of health among seniors, which has led to health maintenance organizations, health newsletters, vitamins, spas for seniors, and more.

Approximately 20 years ago Drucker predicted that the future of executive education was online. His prediction was based partially on technology and convenience, but also on the fact that computer literacy and computer ownership was growing even faster than the demand for executive education. Many traditional educators disparaged the idea of so-called distance learning. They said it had to be done in the classroom face to face by lecture as it had been done in antiquity. They said that discussions had to take place and questions be asked and answered in this environment or it wasn't effective. Students might be exposed to information and ideas online, but they just wouldn't and couldn't learn this way. It had to be in the way done over the millennia in the classroom. Well, Drucker was right again. Research found that learning online was even faster and more effective than classroom learning in many instances. This is probably because students tend to focus on the material to be learned more efficiently. Today leading universities, Harvard, Stanford, and the like, all have online programmes. Others such as Boston University even offer doctorate degrees entirely online.

THE SIXTH SOURCE: CHANGES TO PERCEPTION

How we look at things is critical. There is a very old example from psychology that demonstrates this well. When I first encountered it, I was amazed. It was an ambiguous picture either of a young, attractive woman, or an older, ugly one. It all depended on how you looked at the picture. You could see either depending on your perception at the time. Later, I discovered that you could influence which picture viewers would see by simply having them first view a picture of an image in which a few lines were redrawn, in doing so viewers would only see the young woman, or the old one, but could not see both in the same drawing as in the full drawing.

Here's the way I used this in the classroom. I would put the doctored picture in which viewers could only see the young, attractive woman in one set of envelopes and the doctored picture in which viewers could only see the older, ugly woman in another set. I would distribute envelopes with the young woman to students in the left side of the room, and the envelopes with the old woman to students in the right side of the room. I would than instruct everyone to open their envelope and look at the picture for 10 seconds and then return the picture to the envelope. Next, I would project the ambiguous picture on a screen by a projector.

I would then ask innocently: "How many see a picture of a young, attractive woman?" The hands on the left side of the room would go up. Those on the right side of the room would look puzzled, and I would appear puzzled, too. "How many see an old woman?" I would ask. The arms on the right side of the room would be raised, and now those seated on the left side of the room would look puzzled.

Drucker employed a much easier example which required no props, that was by asking, "Is the glass of water half full, or half empty?" It all depends on how you look at things. Moreover, your mood, values, beliefs, or what you see or know previously can all affect that perception. How can we take advantage of perception as a source of innovation? At one time a rip in clothing would have caused quality inspectors to reject the product and it would have been destroyed or if the tear was minor, it might be sold at a significant discount. However, the 1960s began the onset of the hippie generation, with young people wearing clothing which was frequently intentionally ripped. Almost overnight stressed, faded, frayed, and yes, even ripped, jeans became status symbols and desirable. In response to this new perception of what was considered desirable, jeans manufacturers began to manufacture clothing that was intentionally produced to resemble clothing that would once have been considered damaged and thrown away or donated to worthy organizations that could recycle it.

THE SEVENTH SOURCE: NEW KNOWLEDGE

You might assume that new knowledge would immediately become the source of innovations and competitive advantages which would encourage companies to advance positions in their industries at the same satisfying needs and wants, some of which were not even recognized until the innovations were introduced. Sad to say, this simply is not true. It frequently takes years, sometimes decades or longer, before new knowledge is applied to result in innovations.

Consider the 'wonder drug' penicillin. Alexander Fleming is generally credited with the discovery of penicillin in 1928. But the first documented cure didn't occur until 1942. That would be 14 years. However, the first published paper on the use of these fungi as a cure goes back to the 1870s, which would place the time between knowledge and innovation as considerably longer. However, hold on. The blue mould of this antibiotic on bread was observed to help speed the cure of wounds of battle in the Middle Ages. So, between knowledge and innovation could more accurately be described as about a thousand years.

The knowledge needed to develop the internet became available in the early 1960s. The knowledge for the internet's close relation, the personal computer, has been around since 1962. Even ideas not requiring high technology may take a surprising amount of time. Consider the marketing plan. Search in vain for examples prior to World War II. Postwar articles in the *Journal of Marketing* began to tout the idea of a marketing plan like plans of strategy that became more familiar during the War. But it took more than another 20 years before most organizations began to innovate and adopt the process and produce the marketing plans resulting from it.

What this says is that 'there is gold in them thar hills'. That is, there is knowledge that has been uncovered and is available today which is the potential source of innovations but is yet unseen and unexploited until some innovator comes along to utilize this knowledge.

Drucker was a change leader and as innovation demands change, he was an expert in change and innovation leadership and practised what he preached. However, he didn't stop at proving that we must innovate or suffer the consequences of failing to become change leaders ourselves. He showed us exactly what to do and what we should avoid in using innovation to build and maintain the success of our organizations and ourselves with the best sources of innovative ideas.

He strongly recommended becoming change leaders to ensure the survival and success of futures and our organizations.

1. Drucker, Peter F. *Innovation and Entrepreneurship* (New York: Harper & Row, 1985), 130-132.
2. McLellan, Dennis. "Harry Wesley Coover Jr. Dies at 94; Inventor of Powerful Adhesive Super Glue". *Los Angeles Times*, 31 March 2011, AA4, https://lat.ms/2nh7aCa.
3. Schultz, Howard, with Katie Couric on TV CBS *Sunday Morning*, 27 March 2011.
4. Malek, Frederic V. Telephone interview with the author 21 January 1998 and fax 22 January 1998.
5. Powell, Colin L. with Joseph E. Persico, *My American Journey* (New York: Random House, 1995), 167.
6. Ibid.
7. Ibid.
8. For a complete and detailed discussion of the Wrights' innovative processes in inventing the aeroplane, see Wright, Orville. *How We Invented the Airplane* (Mineola, NY: Dover Publications, 1988).

CHAPTER 16

MARKETING AND SELLING YOURSELF

The aim of marketing is to know and understand the customer so well the product or service fits him and sells itself.

– Peter F. Drucker

t may seem strange to consider marketing and selling yourself as one of Drucker's recommended ways to the top. Drucker never seemed to do this. But as we'll soon see, these are necessary actions that Drucker not only recommended, but followed in his own career, and which led to his success. It is one thing to invent or to do something for the good of humankind that has the potential for the betterment of all, but the challenging work that goes into such an accomplishment is utterly worthless if no one takes advantage and uses it. Drucker would have said that it is a societal obligation to do the marketing and selling required to let the maximum number of others know about and take advantage of your contribution to society. Drucker learned from his work with General Motors that he could contribute to organizations from his knowledge and methods of analysis. Yet he did not market and sell what he had to offer organizations or even to his associates in academia in the usual fashion, and his success with organizations as a consultant and as an academic was not achieved by marketing and selling himself in the ordinary way. Yet the ideas and a methodology he used were effective in enabling him to reach the pinnacle of his several professions.

THE METHODOLOGY DRUCKER USED TO MARKET AND SELL HIMSELF

The usual steps recommended for academic success and an eventual 'Father of Modern Management' title would probably be, first, completion of a terminal degree in management (a doctorate), then acquisition of a tenure-track position at a top research university. Harvard would do nicely. Drucker did neither of these and that's just for starters. And remember Drucker began his academic career by obtaining a PhD in law, not management.

In academia in the US, a tenure-track position is usually one that leads to tenure at a university and is not a temporary or short contract teaching position. A tenured position is a contract of lifetime employment with the university from which the professor can only be terminated for a serious offence. Attaining the position is just the beginning.

Acquisition of tenure is the next step. The common model for the period of probation is six years until a 'new' professor is recommended for and reviewed for tenure. Of course, tenure may be, in infrequent instances, granted early. More and just as often, it may be deferred indefinitely or deferred for an additional fixed period of trial before it is given. That's a lot more common than getting early tenure and sometimes even attaining it on the first attempt when a professor is eligible is uncommon. The non-tenured professor may be given three chances at achieving tenure through an annual tenure and promotion board's review. Frequently there are three levels of boards of review, any one of which can veto the recommendation of a lower board. So, one starts with approval at the department level and proceeds to the school level (the school of business, for example). And then, if one has been successful so far, it goes to the university level. A board may not be able to overturn the rejection of a lower board. Finally, it goes to the president of the university, who makes the final decision, thumbs up or thumbs down.

The primary determinant for tenure at most universities is important research published in peer-reviewed research journals that have an established reputation as being of high quality. In Drucker's discipline of management, highly quantified articles of research are usually considered better than so-called think or theoretical pieces. Books, by the way, are usually not considered as important a vehicle for disseminating research or theories for tenure as articles published in academic journals. Neither is teaching considered an overly important aspect for gaining tenure.

Drucker did not follow this usual, well-travelled path. He did complete a terminal degree at the University of Frankfurt in international law, but that was about it. He used his PhD and initial books such as *The End of Economic Man* to obtain a tenured position in politics and philosophy at Bennington, then a small school for young women, lacking the typical multiple schools or colleges, each headed by a dean. According to Drucker's widow, Doris, Bennington had no dean at the time. "It was too small," she told me. He did however occasionally do work for the president normally done by a dean.

Thanks to the numerous books he had written, Drucker became well-known as a business thinker and consultant. He was able to negotiate a tenure-track professorship of management at New York University, a highly respected university, not as prestigious as Harvard perhaps, but certainly enough to satisfy his ambitions at the time well enough. Tenure track, is not itself tenure. But it means that a professor can get tenure if he or she accomplishes the right research and publication described in the coming years. This was pretty good for a professor coming from a small school and a different discipline, and few previous research articles in academic journals. He remained at New York University for 22 years, building a worldwide reputation and authoring a further 10 books that focused on management and business. Although he was one of the first business authors to recognize the difference between marketing and sales *he wrote no quantitative, research-based articles that I am aware of*. However, he became one of the most prolific authors for the *Harvard Business Review* (HBR), which is not an academic research journal, but a vehicle read mainly by business practitioners. He wrote article after article such that today *HBR* has published many of his articles in book form by collating them by topic on some of the hottest issues of the day. In those days, some in the academic world did not appreciate *HBR* as a valid vehicle for disseminating academic research; but it was considered easier to attain publication while reaching a ready market for the type of articles Drucker wrote, as did the *Wall Street Journal*, for which he wrote a weekly column for 20 years. These two publications were read less by academics and sometimes were not given the credit they deserved, though they were extensively read by practitioners, even then. And that was a crucial factor in Drucker's rise. It was good marketing.

Jagdish Sheth, who made a well-deserved name for himself as an academic researcher in consumer behaviour, once explained it to several hundred amazed professors in a keynote speech at an academic conference some years ago, he said: "Over the last 25 years I've written extensively for the best academic journals," he continued, "over all that time and dozens of articles on my research and theories, I received exactly two letters, they were both from professors. From my single

Wall Street Journal article last month, I received over a hundred queries from business executives."

Now well-known, Drucker left New York University for California. I've already described how Drucker applied to two universities and how one of his criteria was that he be given an appointment which would allow him to teach Japanese art. But he had another item on his wish list. Claremont's dean, Paul Albrecht, saw that there was a growing demand by executives for advanced degrees. This included both the MBA and PhD in management. This was exactly the market that Drucker was interested in reaching and was a major area to which he had decided to contribute. It was a perfect match. Drucker had what Albrecht wanted, and several years later they founded what may have been the first PhD in executive management, where I was honoured to be the first graduate. Their theory was that management was so complex that you really needed a PhD to master it. An examination of Drucker's career yields his rules for achieving success.

DRUCKER'S RULES FOR
THE WAY TO THE TOP

Drucker followed several rules which included ideas from strategy, sales, and marketing.

1. HIT 'EM WHERE THEY AIN'T

Drucker later called one of his entrepreneurial strategies, "Hit 'em Where They Ain't". Two substrategies were "Creative Imitation" and "Entrepreneurial Judo", described in detail in Chapter 2. However, Peter erred by ascribing "Hit 'em Where They Ain't" to a Civil War general in his book, *Innovation and Entrepreneurship*.[1] These words did not originate from a general in the Civil War or any other war. Instead they came from Baseball Hall of Famer Wee Willie Keeler. At 5' 4" Keeler was one of the shortest players ever to play for a major league team. Despite his short stature, his .385 career batting average after the 1898 (yes, that's 1898, not 1998) season is the highest average in baseball's history at season's end for a player with more than 1,000 hits.[2]

His strategy was simple: hit the ball to parts of the field not well protected by opposing players either because the player was less skilful or had a habit of not fully covering a particular part of his assigned area on the baseball field. Every batter tried for success by hitting the ball as hard as he could and trying for a home run. That was one way to the top. Wee Willie instead strived to hit the ball to areas of the outfield that were ill-protected. He "Hit 'em Where They Ain't". This is similar to the popular Blue Ocean Strategy of today. This is a marketing theory explained in a book of the same title by W. Chan Kim and Renée Mauborgne.[3] It is based on their analysis of 150 strategic business situations over 100 years in 30 different industries. In a nutshell, the authors maintain that companies can succeed by creating areas of uncontested market space which they call blue oceans. This is opposed to red oceans where there are numerous competitors, which like sharks attacking prey, fight viciously against competitors and turn the area red with blood.

2. APPLY THE LESSONS FROM ONE FIELD TO ANOTHER

Drucker maintained that the major advances in any field or industry usually came from someone bringing it from another field or industry and he applied this principle. For example, in his book *Management Challenges for the 21st Century* he wrote "the management of people is a marketing job".[4] He did not mean only to incorporate the persuasion of a salesperson, he meant the whole of marketing, including considerations of all marketing aspects that must be included in the management situation such as marketing strategy and planning.

3. BE YOUR OWN CEO

In other words, Drucker maintained that you needed to be the one in charge on your way to the top. This required that you look at the facts and do the analysis and you take responsibility for the decisions you make. If you think that you need additional training or education, you don't sit around waiting for someone else in your organization to make the decision to send you somewhere to get it. Take whatever actions to get what you think necessary yourself.

4. FOLLOW THE WAY OF INNOVATION

Make plans to be a change leader and innovate as you proceed on your journey. You must innovate. It is essential for your progress and, like an organization that does not innovate, no matter how successful that you are currently, you will ultimately fail if you do not innovate.

5. APPLY THE CONCEPTS OF MARKETING AND SALES TO YOUR CAREER

Drucker meant these should be applied as if coming from another industry. He devoted an entire course once to a subject that he entitled "Marketing Yourself to Your Boss". He was serious about this. I still recall him saying that you first had to agree with your boss on what your job was and if possible to get it in writing, and then you were to discover how your boss preferred to communicate. Drucker said that all of us prefer to communicate in one of two ways: either in writing or verbally. He went on to say it was critically important to communicate with the boss in the way in which he or she preferred. To apply these concepts, you need first to understand that these had to be accomplished by the new employee.

THE WAY TO THE TOP REQUIRES THE TECHNIQUES OF MARKETING AND SALES

You first need to understand marketing and sales before you can follow these concepts. There are many definitions of marketing. Drucker's definition mainly delineated the differences between marketing and selling. Professor Philip Kotler is closely associated with Drucker in thinking and has been acknowledged by many with a title very much like Drucker's as the 'Father of Modern Marketing'. Kotler, S.C. Johnson Distinguished Professor at Northwestern University in Chicago, defines it this way: "Marketing is the social process by which individuals and groups obtain what they need and want through creating and exchanging products and value with others."[5]

Note that marketing according to Kotler is an exchange. It is not deceiving someone or cheating them in some fashion. It reminds me that you can only become successful by helping others to become successful.

Or said another way, you can only reach your goals by helping others to reach their goals. Drucker was not recommending that you engage in office politics. Working once with another professor, the other professor was the object of much jealousy due to his work with Drucker and was sometimes verbally harassed by his colleagues. "Ignore them completely," Drucker told him, "and stick to your work."

To put marketing into operation as an aid to reaching the top may require using the internet, advertising, sales promotions, face-to-face selling, publicity, and different distribution channels considering your goals and the target market selected. This is what Drucker did, he used what was available to him. It also requires that you treat others as you would like to be treated. Better yet, if possible treat others as they prefer to be treated, which is a step further.

You receive intelligence from both the target market and the distribution channels in your situation as you proceed. Done correctly, both receive something, tangible or intangible, in exchange for what they provide, as in the definition of marketing.

CAN MARKETING ELIMINATE SELLING? THE MARKETING CONCEPT

Earlier we noted that selling and marketing are not the same. Marketing professor Theodore Levitt, then teaching at Harvard once described the difference pretty much as Drucker: "Selling focuses on the need of the seller; marketing on the needs of the buyer. Selling is preoccupied with the seller's need to convert his product into cash; marketing with the idea of satisfying the needs of the customer by means of the product and the whole cluster of things associated with creating, delivering and finally consuming it."[6]

But Drucker went even further to explain: "Selling and marketing are antithetical rather than synonymous or even complementary. There will always, one can assume, be a need for some selling, but the aim of marketing is to make selling superfluous. The aim of marketing is to know and understand the customer so well the product or service fits him and sells itself."[7]

The difference between marketing and selling brings us once more to noting marketing's close involvement with strategy, and with tactics. If it is strategy that we use to attain objectives, it is tactics that must be employed to implement our strategy. Then marketing is your strategy and selling is but one of many tactics to implement whatever marketing strategy is pursued. Were our strategy perfect we would still need some selling (tactics) to implement it. But even more important to understand is that, no matter how good our selling may be, if our strategy is bad, wrong, or inappropriate selling cannot make up for deficiencies in that strategy. In fact, a tactical success in selling may even be wrong. And you must be careful of your tactics becoming the enemy of your strategy.

Consider American car companies in the early 1970s. Their positioning strategy was dependent on products emphasizing comfort and power as opposed to fuel economy and, later, quality. When the oil crisis struck, some tried to make up for an inappropriate strategy by selling. It didn't work. But what if it had? Good selling might have helped to buy time for devising and implementing a new and more effective strategy. But it could not overcome the basic problem of the wrong strategy. Furthermore, conceivably, remarkable success in selling might have masked the very real need to adjust strategy until the company, though initially benefiting from tactical success, was in even more difficulties because of delaying changing its strategy. During the oil crisis Chevrolet rushed a small car into production called the Chevette. Introduced in September 1975, the Chevette sold 2.8 million units over 12 years. The Chevette was the best-selling small car in the US for the years 1979 and 1980. The selling and advertising campaign was first rate from the start. However, after about a year of use the first-year model owners found that their cars would not start again soon after having been driven and had to cool down first. Rather than a recall, dealers were on their own as there was no fix. This problem had to do with the vehicle frame being worn down and resulting in an electrical disconnect after about a year of use. This resulted in bad feeling among customers who had bought the car and were stuck with it before the problem was corrected in design and production. I know. I was one of the unfortunate owners.

The same is true in self-management. Just after getting her bachelor's degree a woman I know got interested in law. She had little knowledge of the profession or what it was all about, and the recruiters (salesmen for the school) did an excellent job selling but misrepresented what she could expect as a law student and what the work entailed. She became a law student and hated every minute, though she made passing grades and passed what is called the Baby Bar exam, which was necessary to continue her studies after the first year. However, she wisely decided that after one year she'd had enough and entered the study of psychology. Today she is a highly successful clinical psychologist. Message: good selling, but poor analysis prior to spending time as a law student combined with an excellent job of selling by recruiters, but bad marketing by the law school resulted in a lose–lose for both the individual and the law school.

This brings us back to Peter Drucker's position, which says essentially that if we get our marketing (strategy) right, we can reach our objectives with a lot less work in selling (tactics) and more efficiently and effectively in performance.

YOUR ORIENTATION TOWARDS YOUR SELF-MANAGEMENT

Business historians have found an interesting phenomenon in the development of the basic orientation of businesses since the concept of the business was born and began moving towards a marketing orientation eventually integrating both marketing and society. All organizations that ignore marketing, or give it a low priority, suffer. This is true in moving ahead in a career and profession as well and anyone seeking to use marketing in their careers or professions like Drucker must pay close attention to how his or her self-management is oriented.

PRODUCTION ORIENTATION

Gutenberg's development of the printing press by inventing movable typefaces made books much cheaper and more available than before, and book ownership became more widespread. In fact, the demand for books still far exceeded the supply, even after Gutenberg's invention. As a result, organizations manufacturing books did not need to give marketing much emphasis. They could sell all the books they could produce. Production orientations persist today. A company with this orientation believes that customers will buy its products if the products are priced cheaply enough. Some individuals make the same mistake. They underprice themselves significantly, thinking that this will help them get a job or, if in business for themselves, they focus on low price because they think that this will bring in business. This may work for a while, but pricing also has an image value. Most shoppers will tell you that if you don't know anything about the product and want quality, you should be willing to pay a higher price. In other words, most believe that high price always equals high equality. If you price yourself too low, this has a self-limiting effect. Drucker didn't do this. As he progressed in his career he raised what he charged as a consultant and what he demanded as a professor. It wasn't a case of seeking wealth. He might require a corporate client to pay $10,000 for a few hours of consulting, but the money didn't go to him; it went to his foundation.

PRODUCT ORIENTATION

Other companies still maintain a product orientation. The Wright brothers built their first working aeroplane in 1903. Yet it was four long years before the US government made its initial purchase from them. Think of this for a moment. Here was an invention that enabled us to realize humankind's dream of flying. It had the potential for revolutionizing virtually every aspect of civilization, not only warfare, and eventually it did. Yet it took the US government four years before contracting with the Wright brothers to obtain even a single unit to test. This is not necessarily an indictment of government; rather it is a partial description of a marketing characteristic. The Wright brothers were bicycle repairmen and inventors. They knew little about marketing and how to effectively market their extraordinary breakthrough. You have a great product, but you need to market that product to reach the top.

SALES ORIENTATION

A company with a sales orientation takes a product as a given and the market as a given and tries to sell the product to the consumer or the industrial buyer. It is the opposite of the marketing orientation because it focuses on the product and convincing someone to buy it rather than the customer and having what the customer wants. Such a company has a philosophy that a good salesperson can sell anything to anyone. It is true that there are those who are superior salespeople and they can maximize the chances of selling once a product has been produced. However, from a marketing perspective, this is the more difficult way to create a sale because this task is far easier if a market already exists for the product that you have developed. In Drucker's words, "the product or service fits him and sells itself".

MARKETING ORIENTATION

The previous business orientations stretch back over the centuries, but the marketing orientation has become popular only since the mid-20th century. An organization having a marketing business orientation focuses on the customer. Its philosophy is: "It is not what you want to sell but what your customer wants to buy." Accordingly, an individual who seeks to reach the top wisely has at least a marketing orientation and seeks to find a need and to fill it.

Drucker was a genius who became known as the father of modern management. But was Drucker always interested in management or social ecology? Early in his career Drucker wanted to be a professor. But he studied for a PhD in law because, according to him, in Germany it was the easiest to get at the time. If his real interest in management was always so great, why were his early books and teaching in other disciplines?

Drucker acquired his intense interest in management only after some success and his work with General Motors. Opportunity knocked, demonstrated its wants and needs and Drucker recognized this demand. Further, he was ready: he had the tools, interest, and wisdom to answer. According to Drucker, that is about the best we can do, since we usually do not know our real interest at an early age, sometimes not until much older. Moreover, interests change. About the best that we can do is to have the necessary tools and wisdom ready when a new interest arises. So, Drucker, while still a young man in his thirties, could hit the ground running and take advantage of a brand-new career in management which would eventually morph into a career as a social ecologist.

SOCIAL RESPONSIBILITIES

In recognition of social responsibilities, many companies have modified their approach to include a social emphasis. For example, R. Gordon McGovern, at the time president of Campbell Soup Company, stated that the goal for Campbell was, "To be positioned with consumers as somebody who is looking after their well-being."[8]

The clear implication here is that firms with a social emphasis do not seek profit as their only purpose. Instead, profits are viewed as a business requirement in order as Drucker determined, to create a customer.

Of course, without profit, business stops. Drucker discovered that the purpose of a business was to create a customer, for without a customer there can be no business. To succeed, a business must produce goods and services that a sufficient number of customers will want to buy at adequate prices. Since production wears out the machinery that produces the product and is necessary to financially support the employees who run and manage the machines, to keep the business going there's got to be enough left over to replace what's being worn out. That 'enough' is profit, no matter what the accountants, the tax authorities, or anyone calls it. That is why profit is a requisite, not a purpose, of business.

If we translate this into a person striving to reach the top in any profession we run into the same issue. There are necessities like food and shelter for ourselves and our families that we need to keep going. But the purpose of our success must be to 'create a customer' that is, to contribute to society by producing value. Call it a positive unit of something.

If this be social ethics, Drucker simplified it for those striving to reach the top. He suggested a straightforward method that he called the mirror test. When you look in the mirror every morning, who do you want to see looking back at you? He told us once that procuring prostitutes for visiting executives didn't make you unethical. It merely made you a pimp. Is a pimp what you want to see in the mirror?

Drucker figured this out early along the path and lived his life not to acquire, but to contribute and to maintain a value system that he could support at the same time.

---

1. Drucker, Peter F. *Innovation and Entrepreneurship* (New York: Harper & Row, 1985), 220.
2. "Baseball Reference: Progressive Leaders & Records for Batting Average". *Sports-Reference.co*m, https://bit.ly/2vMxR5r, accessed 21 July 2018.
3. Kim, W. Chan and Renée Mauborgne. *Blue Ocean Strategy: How to Create Uncontested Market Space and Make the Competition Irrelevant* (Cambridge, MA: Harvard Business School, 2005).
4. Drucker, Peter F. *Management Challenges for the 21st Century* (New York: Harper Business, 1999), 2
5. Kotler, Philip, quoted in in Mike Thimmesch. "What Is Marketing? How 10 Experts Define It". *Skyline® Tradeshow Tips*, August 8, 2010, https://bit.ly/2vNbAEI.
6. Levitt, Theodore. "Marketing Myopia". Harvard Business Review (July-August 1960), 45-56. https://bit.ly/1xtBSn8.
7. Drucker, Peter F. *Management: Tasks, Responsibilities, Practices* (New York: Harper & Row, 1974), 64.
8. "Marketing: The New Priority". *Business Week*, 21 November 1983, 96-106, 103.

CHAPTER 17

HOW DRUCKER INFLUENCED OTHERS

*To be effective you have to know the strengths,
the performance modes, and the values
of your co-workers.*

– Peter F. Drucker

T o be successful you must lead and practise the eight universal laws of success as described in Chapters 4 to 12. Knowing and practising these laws are especially needed. In most cases people, no matter how capable or talented, don't achieve success alone. Others help. In addition, you must know how to lead others for positive results whether you are their supervisor or not. Leading and influencing for positive results means learning how others prefer to be treated and as much as possible treating them as they prefer even in moving towards your own goals and objectives. To do this you must influence others on an individual basis and if you work with groups you must consider how to influence the group for positive results. This chapter discusses eight strategies of influencing others depending on the situation, relative power you hold or do not hold in the situation, and what you are trying to accomplish. As we will see, that's what Drucker did throughout his career.

DRUCKER, A MAN OF APPLICATION, NOT THEORY

Drucker was a man of application and not just a theorist. He knew that to accomplish anything you had to work with others and that the others were human beings who are always different in their likes and dislikes as well as their preferences. What this means is that to influence them positively, you need to know how each wants to be treated. You may think that there is only one correct way of doing anything, and that is wrong. There are many. As Drucker noted, others have the perversity to behave as human beings.[1] There are frequently many 'best' ways depending on the situation and the individual or individuals you are dealing with. Each of us prefers a different way and feels that our own is best. Motivational speaker Tony Robbins had one explanation for this which Drucker would probably have agreed with. We were each raised differently and given different rules within our family, which we are taught is the way that things must be done.

One person is taught that he must never participate in adult conversations, 'a child should be seen, but not heard'. In another family, a child is encouraged to speak out whenever adults converse. As the child grows up these differing rules may result in differing approaches in dealing with others. Growing up with rules like these carry over into other relationships we have later in both our personal and professional lives.

THE TALE OF THE TWO COMPETING VICE PRESIDENTS

The story of the two competing vice presidents was a management problem based on an actual occurrence that Drucker asked his students to solve. The situation was that as the president of a company grew older he made the decision to retire in five years' time. The president had two outstanding vice presidents who had about equal experience and were both equally competent in their performance although each had his own way of getting things done. The president called each into his office and explained that each was a candidate to replace him when he retired, and that the decision would be based on their performance over this five-year time frame.

Over the next five years both worked diligently, and both did outstanding work in performance of their duties. However, the way in which each performed was quite different. One vice president felt that he should not bother the president. He worked every challenge given to him in on his own and he performed brilliantly. He went to query the president only when he had a particular challenging problem which he was having difficulty in solving. After he completed the project, he gave the president a briefing on why he had made the decisions that he had made.

The other vice president performed brilliantly also but operated quite differently. He discussed all issues with the president before he made a decision. He briefed the president weekly on these problems and on their status.

Drucker asked us which vice president became the new president after five years. Most of us thought that it was the vice president that showed he could work on his own, independently, while keeping the president informed as to how things had gone. Much to our surprise

Drucker told us that it was the other vice president, the one who discussed every issue with the retiring president. The answer surprised most of us but Drucker explained that it was the one that kept the president *involved*. This president desired this.

Drucker's reasoning on this outcome was that this particular president wanted to be involved and to understand everything that was happening within his company. Drucker's point was that either answer could have been correct, but that with this particular president since he preferred, above all else, to be kept informed during any work that was done it was important for the subordinates to understand and do this. This is why the outgoing president made certain that the board would appoint a replacement much like himself. People are different in this way.

THE STORY OF THE THREE GERMAN COLONELS

During World War I, a captain in the German Army described a classical example of the use of different influence tactics by a brigade commander and how he influenced his three colonels before an important operation.

The first regimental colonel wanted to do everything himself, and always did well. His second colonel executed every order, and performed well, but usually demonstrated little initiative on his own. He had to be told the smallest detail of what was expected. Finally, there was the colonel commanding the third regiment. He opposed almost everything he was told and was outspoken about wanting to do the contrary.

In battle, the brigade came up against a heavily defended allied position that had to be captured. The brigade commander issued different orders to influence each regimental commander for the same operation.

To his first colonel he said: "My dear Colonel 'A'. We will attack. Your regiment will have to carry the burden of the attack. I have, however, selected you for this very reason. The second regiment will be your boundary on the left. The third regiment will be your boundary on the right. Attack at 1200 hours. I don't need to tell you anything more as I have full confidence that you will use your own initiative in carrying out my orders to capture this position. Do you have any questions?" On answering the few points that his first colonel asked, he left and went to his third colonel, C, who generally opposed everything.

To him the brigade commander spoke quite differently. "We have met a very strong enemy position which we have been told to capture. I am afraid however that we will not be able to attack successfully with the forces at our disposal."

As he thought, his third colonel didn't agree.

"Oh, General, certainly we will attack and capture it. Just give my regiment the time of attack and you will see that we will be successful."

"Oh, very well. Go, then, we will try it," said the brigade commander and he gave his third colonel the formal order for the attack that he had prepared previously and again as with his first colonel, he answered any questions and then departed.

As for the colonel commanding his second regiment, he simply sent the attack order with many more details than he had given his other commanders.

All three regiments attacked successfully.[2]

In this chapter, you will learn the primary influence tactics and when and how to use them in practice over a wide variety of situations. Drucker applied these to influence his superiors, his associates, his clients, and his students. Your proper use of these tactics will equip you with the arsenal to make you a powerful influencer recognizing, as Drucker maintained, that these are human beings and must be treated differently.

HOW OTHERS PREFER TO COMMUNICATE

But before we start, you should first recognize, as Drucker did, that different people prefer to receive knowledge and communicate in two ways: verbally or in writing. To be effective in dealing with others, you need to know which method they prefer. In a lesson Drucker taught on influencing your boss, he stated that it was extremely important to find out which method of communication that your boss prefers. Later he wrote:

"Typical are people who, in their first assignment, work for a man who is a reader. They therefore were trained in writing reports. Their next boss is a listener. But these people keep on writing reports to the new boss – the way President Johnson's assistants kept on writing reports to him because Jack Kennedy, who had hired them, had been a reader. Invariably, these people have no results. Invariably, their new boss thinks they are stupid, incompetent, lazy. They become failures. All that would have been needed to avoid this would have been *one* look at the boss and ask a question: 'How does he or she perform?'<TNBS>"[3]

In fact, all people prefer to receive knowledge and communicate in these two ways. It is important to know which. You can find out which by asking or by observation. But how you influence them, and others means that you depend on other things including the situation and the power you have in the situation.

1. THE INFLUENCE STRATEGY OF DIRECTION

There are three situations where simply giving orders with no discussion is your best choice. But first, to employ the direction strategy, you must have more power in the situation than those you intend to influence. If you try to influence your boss this way, not only will you probably fail, but you may damage the relationship permanently.

The first situation where you may want to use direction is where there is little time. What you need done needs to be done now, with no time for discussion. For example, there is no time for dilly-dallying when stakes are high or when a slight delay can result in a significant negative impact.

The second situation when you should use direction is when the action you want done may be good for the organization but is less desirable for the individual. You need a report written by tomorrow morning, but the person who must do this has their own plans that conflict with getting the report finished on time. While you can try to use the other influence strategies first, eventually it may come down to using direction.

Unfortunately, the direction strategy is much overused. One reason is that when you have power it's so easy to use it and have things done your way. All you do is tell someone what to do and they do it. And that's the danger of overuse. As President Eisenhower commented about overuse of direct orders: "You do not lead by hitting people over the head – that's assault, not leadership."[4] It's a holding a gun to the head style of influence. It works. At times it is necessary, but overused, it is counterproductive.

When is direction right? Drucker said that a certain decision should be taken even when there are many reasons why it should not be done, but one right reason why it should. And that leads to the third situation, something is right, or at least you believe it is, but you are the only one that can correct it, and others may fear the consequences if you make this decision and force others to accept your position.

Late in 2017, President Trump announced the decision to move the American embassy to Jerusalem as the capital of Israel. Most of his senior advisors in government recommended against it. So did the Pope and many other foreign leaders. Some Arab and Palestinian groups threatened terror and "days of rage".[5] Trump pointed out that every country in the world had the right to declare its own capital, and despite this, for 70 years Israel's capital as Jerusalem had not been recognized by the US or other countries. They said that the decision was controversial because it needed to be negotiated. "This," he said, "is wrong."

Already, in 1995 a US law had been passed recognizing Jerusalem as Israel's capital, but the law was ignored and each US president, both Democrat and Republican, gave himself a waiver.

Trump's decision recalls President Truman's recognition of Israel's very existence as a country in 1948. President Truman's own Secretary of State then, General George C. Marshall threatened to resign if President Truman recognized Israel as an independent country. Arab countries threatened to invade the territory that was to become Israel and destroy it if Truman gave Israel this recognition. Truman ignored both threats. He recognized Israel anyway.

Secretary of State Marshall reconsidered and did not resign. However, seven Arab countries did invade the new State of Israel but were unsuccessful in destroying it, which may be just as well for them and for the rest of us, too. From voicemail technology, to the mobile (cell) phone, and the first fully computerized, no-radiation, diagnostic instrumentation for breast cancer, and other scientific breakthroughs and more, all were developed in Israel.[6]

Regarding his announcement, Trump clearly recognized the credible threats made, but felt that the correctness of the decision outweighed the consequences. Rather than any other influence strategy, which he correctly said hadn't worked in bringing peace between the Arabs and Israelis over the preceding 70 years, Trump chose direction.

The point is not whether you favour Israel or its adversaries or if Israel should have been recognized, or the American embassy moved, but rather if you believe something to be right that overrides possible negative consequences, and you have the responsibility for making the decision, then it is wiser to make the decision you believe correct even if others disagree.

2. THE INFLUENCE STRATEGY OF INDIRECTION

Before he became president, Donald Trump became well known for the television show *The Apprentice*. After a session in the boardroom he would lean forward, gesture dramatically, and tell one of the contestants, "you're fired". That's direction with a capital D.

Yet Trump was a strong believer in using indirect influence strategy. In his book, *The Art of the Deal*, Trump tells the story of how the manager of the Grand Hyatt was successful in influencing him through indirect strategy after a predecessor had failed and was discharged when he bluntly tried to influence Trump by direction.

Trump built the Grand Hyatt and still owned a 50% interest. The former manager objected strongly to the interference of Trump and his wife. Though lacking the power, he tried direction by complaining to the head of the Hyatt Hotels. This got the manager himself fired. His replacement was much more skilled at using the influence strategies. According to Trump, "The new manager did something brilliant. He began to bombard us with trivia. He'd call up several times a week, and he'd say, 'Donald, we want your approval to change the wallpaper on the fourteenth floor' or 'We want to introduce a new menu in one of the restaurants' or 'We are thinking of switching to a new laundry service.' They'd also invite us to all their management meetings. The guy went so far out of his way to solicit our opinions and involve us in the hotel that finally I said, "Leave me alone, do whatever you want, just don't bother me.' What he did was the perfect ploy, because he got what he wanted not by fighting head on against my interference, but by being positive and friendly and solicitous."[7] Some would say, why doesn't Trump use the indirect strategy more often as president? That, you'll have to ask President Trump himself. I know that there were occasions when I would have used the indirect approach myself. But then, I wasn't elected president, and I don't have all the facts, and most importantly I don't have the power or the responsibility.

The writer James Clavell gave us another good example. He unintentionally gave us an example of the use of indirection in his book, *Tai-Pan*.[8] *Tai-Pan* was about the founder and head of a great British Trading Company in 19th-century China. The head of the company was known as the "Tai-Pan". At the end of the book, the Tai-Pan is killed in a typhoon. His 18-year-old son, with little experience or training, is suddenly thrust into major responsibilities as the president's successor and the company's head. At first, he is frozen into silence. He doesn't know what to say or do. His subordinates are standing around waiting for him to take charge and give his first orders as the new Tai-Pan. There is a pause when none of the new Tai-Pan's senior managers say a word. Suddenly, the former Tai-Pan's right-hand man, who is Chinese, turns to the new head of the firm and in a pleading voice asks: "Tai-Pan, Tai-Pan, what should we do?" This man had years of experience and could have instantly given the orders that needed to be given and usurped the leadership from the teenage Tai-Pan. However, his deferring to the 18-year-old shocked the young man into the realization that he was now in charge and responsible whether he was ready or not. He had to take over the organization and assert his authority, or he would never be able to do so. And he did. This was a perfect example of influencing a superior and doing so using the indirection influence strategy.

3. THE INFLUENCE STRATEGY OF REDIRECTION

I once heard a story about a woman who was poised a hundred feet above the water outside the safety bar of a bridge, threatening to commit suicide. A policeman a few feet away on the bridge talked to the woman and tried to persuade her to climb back to safety from her perch. He first tried to convince her that regardless of her problems, life was always worth living. That didn't work. He tried to order her down: the direction strategy. That didn't work either. He tried negotiation and all the techniques taught by law enforcement and psychologists in suicide situations of this type. Nothing worked. The woman remained in place, getting ready to jump to her death. Finally, in desperation, the police officer shouted: "Lady, you can jump if you want, but I sure wouldn't want to jump into that dirty water. It's full of sewage and garbage and smells awful." She hesitated, and after a few minutes consideration returned to relative safety where the police officer was able to pull her to safety. That police officer had used the redirection strategy in his successful rescue. He had redirected her thoughts from suicide to the filthy water she would be jumping into which was more important to her than her life at that time.

4. THE INFLUENCE STRATEGY OF REPUDIATION

In using the repudiation strategy, you persuade someone to do something by disclaiming your own ability or power to do it. For example, an analyst goes to his supervisor and asks for help in doing some problems. "Gee, I'd like to help," his supervisor says, "but I haven't worked on this kind of analysis in quite a long time. How would you approach it? Why don't you begin. Maybe I'll remember a little." So, the analyst begins the work. Whenever he gets stuck, his leader gets him going again. The supervisor uses the influence tool of repudiation to get the analyst to learn to do the job and to do the job at the same time.

The repudiation strategy can also be used by subordinates to influence their bosses, or by managers to influence other managers. "Boss, I have a problem and I wonder how you would handle it?" The boss is flattered to be asked. Many bosses are more than willing to help. However, you must be careful to understand your boss when using this strategy.

As Drucker demonstrated in the problem of the two vice presidents, some bosses prefer that you work things out on your own and you certainly don't want to overuse this strategy.

5. THE INFLUENCE STRATEGY OF ENLISTMENT

All you need to do is to ask for help. That's the basis and beauty of the enlistment influence strategy. This strategy is especially effective in situations where you don't have the power, or may have the power, but may not want to use it. Surprisingly, just asking works very well in more situations than you might think. Psychologist Dr Robert Cialdini looked at the use of motivation in influencing. In studying the literature on persuasion, he found that frequently the request need not even be phrased logically. It may depend primarily on how the request is made, and the words used rather than the logic of the request itself. In one study that Cialdini looked at, Harvard social psychologist Ellen Langer discovered that the number of people who would allow someone to get ahead of them in a line to use the office copier depended primarily on a single word even if the reason given for the request made no sense at all. If the requestor said: "Excuse me, I have five pages. May I use the Xerox machine because I am in a rush?" the positive response was 94%. That's pretty good. However, if the request was: "Excuse me, I have five pages. May I use the Xerox machine?" with no reason given, the positive response rate dropped to 60%. That's a significant drop, and before we go any further, it's pretty good evidence that we should always give a reason why we want something done, time and circumstances permitting.

Now I know what I am going to tell you next will sound crazy, but if the requestor phrased the request as, "Excuse me, I have five pages. May I use the Xerox machine because I have to make some copies?" you might think that the acceptance of the request would remain pretty low, if the recipient didn't burst out laughing. After all, why else would someone ask to use the Xerox machine if not to make copies? That's just plain ridiculous. Yet, the positive response was 93% – almost identical as if a reasonable reason were given![9] One interpretation of these results is that this was due to use of the single word 'because'.

But it may also be since the word 'because' alerted the recipient that an explanation was forthcoming, even if the explanation itself was nonsense. The point is that your asking may be more powerful than you think, if you give a reason for what you want done. However, allowing someone to get ahead in line is not asking for much of a sacrifice. I'm sure that you can think of a better reason for your request. What about challenging work?

CAN YOU MAKE CHALLENGING WORK FUN?

People accept difficult and challenging work voluntarily, no matter how difficult or dangerous, all the time. Why? Because they have decided that what they are doing is not work, but fun. Why else do people choose to jump off bridges attached to a bungee line? Or parachute out of a plane, or play a sport in which injuries are frequent, or climb mountains? Playing high school or college football is difficult and challenging. Yes, a few go on to play professionally, but that's a tiny percentage. And of those who do participate, players are injured all the time. Some 3,800,000 concussions were reported in 2012 in the USA alone, with 47% occurring in high school football.[10] Yet there are many more that volunteer to do this than the players needed to play.

Are people crazy or what? Not at all. Even the most challenging, difficult, and dirty work will not only be gladly accepted, but sought after, if that work is considered fun or desirable.

You may not even need to emphasize the critical need. What you need to do is convince others that it would be fun or will gain respect from their peers. This can be an essential element in using the enlistment strategy.

6. THE INFLUENCE STRATEGY OF PERSUASION

Persuasion differs from enlistment in one important way. With enlistment, all you need do is to ask. Of course, asking in a dramatic or creative way with the word 'because' helps. However, with persuasion, the emphasis isn't on just asking. You must go one step further and convince someone to do something, and that requires reasons to be explained with a stronger convincing rationale as to why they should do it. Everyone wants to know why you want him or her to take a certain action. This is true whether you have authority over them or not. My personal feeling is that this is something that you owe to those you might want to do what you say. And giving reasons has an important fringe benefit. When the situation changes, and you aren't available to give new instructions, this person knows *why* you are doing what you are trying to do. He or she can alter their actions based on that information. You will find that you will be much more successful at influencing someone to complete the act you want than would otherwise be the case.

7. THE INFLUENCE STRATEGY OF NEGOTIATION

Another important influence strategy is negotiation. Negotiation means that you influence by conferring with others to arrive at a settlement which you (and those you want to influence) find acceptable. It may involve compromise and usually involves exchanging something that the other person wants or wants done for what you want done. Negotiation may be required under certain circumstances. Does the task offer little or no perceived benefit to the person or persons that you want to influence? Do you and those you want to do something have about equal power? Can both sides help or hurt each other almost equally? If any of these conditions exist, you may find the negotiation influence strategy extremely useful.

Let's look at an example of a university, where the addition of new courses must be voted upon by all departments. New courses may be perceived as attracting students from one department to another. Thus, there may be no reason for one department to vote for another department's proposal if they are going to lose students. If you want to get the university to offer a new course, part of your work may involve using a negotiation strategy. How can you do this? You could offer to support another department's proposal for a new course. Or you could offer something else that the other department wants in exchange for its support for your proposal while showing (if true) that you won't be taking their students.

George Washington gave us a successful demonstration of the negotiation strategy that was important in winning American independence.

By the summer of 1781, during the American War of Independence, the British strength was divided into two strongholds: New York and Chesapeake Bay. The French allies had a contingent of the French Army with General Washington under General Jean Rochambeau. However, British forces were stronger than the combined American–French force. But together, the combined allied force was stronger than either British force if faced separately. If the two British forces could be cut off from each other they could be defeated individually.

The French had a strong fleet under the command of Admiral François de Grasse. However, the hurricane season started in late summer and grew progressively worse in the autumn. De Grasse did not want to get involved in a campaign in the north for fear of having his fleet destroyed at sea by these storms.

Washington's original plan called for defeating the British in the Chesapeake Bay area, and then moving south for an attack on Charleston or the British base at Wilmington. He got De Grasse to support him by the negotiating strategy. Washington let Admiral De Grasse know that: "If you sail north and keep command of the sea during my operations against the Chesapeake Bay force, you can return to the West Indies immediately thereafter." In other words, Washington let De Grasse off the hook for supporting other allied operations earlier that year in return for his immediate services against the British Chesapeake Bay forces. De Grasse answered that he would make his fleet available until mid-October.

On 30 August, De Grasse's fleet arrived off Yorktown, Virginia. He also brought reinforcements and shipborne artillery support. More importantly, he isolated the British land forces under Lord Cornwallis from the one in the New York area. Six weeks later Cornwallis surrendered. The Battle of Yorktown is known as the decisive battle of the War of Independence. Based on the battle's results, the British opened peace negotiations the following spring.[11]

8. THE INFLUENCE STRATEGY OF INVOLVEMENT

If you can get others involved in what you want done, they are more likely to adopt your goals as theirs and become committed to their attainment. Because of this, involvement is a very powerful influence strategy, and usually can be combined easily with one or more of the other strategies we've discussed. Drucker discovered that this is one of the secret major elements in how the Japanese manage. The Japanese call this technique *ringi*. What Japanese leaders do is to take extraordinary pains to ensure that leaders and workers at all levels contribute to a proposed action. No action is taken until everyone has had the opportunity to study and comment on the proposal. Decisions which take days in the US may take months in Japan and so executives from other countries who do business with the Japanese sometimes get extremely frustrated with *ringi*. However, once the decision is made, the entire Japanese organization is involved and committed to a successful outcome. The Japanese then implement their decision amazingly quickly and effectively. In comparison, decisions made in US organizations are sometimes taken quickly, but are sometimes time-consuming to implement. The reason is that many members in the US organization are not involved and may not be fully committed to the action or goal.

THE IMPORTANCE OF OWNERSHIP OF IDEAS, STRATEGIES, AND GOALS

Why is involvement so important? One important dimension is ownership. We work much harder for things that are our own. That's human nature. As a consequence of this, ideas from someone else do not become our own instantaneously. Dr Chester Karrass has devoted much of his life to the science of negotiation and has written several important books on this subject.

In his seminars, Karrass cautions us to allow enough time when introducing our latest ideas. "Introducing ideas," he says, "is like introducing new friends. It takes time to know and understand people before someone else's friends become our friends as well. Therefore, when you introduce new ideas to someone else, you must give them sufficient time to get to know them before you can expect agreement." So, involving people succeeds as an influence strategy because it gives those you need ownership. But we must allow sufficient time for this ownership to take place.

Someone said that there are a lot of ways to skin a cat. I believe they were speaking rhetorically. In any case there are a lot of strategies and combinations thereof to influence others on your way to the top. Your job is to pick the right one according to the situation and the people involved including your own relative power with others and other variables which will define what you can and cannot do. That's what Drucker did in his career.

<hr />

1. Drucker, Peter F. "Managing Oneself". *On Managing Yourself* (Boston, MA: Harvard Business Review Press, 2010), 26.
2. Von Schell, Adolf. *Battlefield Leadership* (Quantico, VA: The Marine Corps Association, 1982), 15, my retelling.
3. Drucker, Peter F. *Management Challenges for the 21st Century* (New York: Harper Business, 1999), 184.
4. Attributed. Included in "Quotes on Leadership". *LeadershipNow.com*, https://bit.ly/2vqpE7O, accessed 8 August 2018.
5. "Palestinians Call 'Days of Rage' over US Jerusalem Move". *Al Jazeera News*, 6 December 2017. https://bit.ly/2OVD5or.
6. "Amazing Israeli Contributions to the World". *United with Israel*, 12 May 2009, https://bit.ly/2MbLp4N, accessed 27 July 2018.
7. Trump, Donald and Tony Schwartz. *Trump: The Art of the Deal* (New York: Warner Books, 1987), 140.
8. Clavell, James. *Tai-Pan: A Novel of Hong Kong* (New York: Atheneum, 1966).
9. Cialdini, Robert B. *The Psychology of Influence*, rev. ed. (New York: William Morrow, 1993), 4.
10. "Sports Concussion Statistics". *Head Case*, https://bit.ly/1uaKnFY, accessed 26 July 2018.
11. Selig, Robert A. "Francois Joseph Paul Compte de Grasse, the Battle of the Virginia Capes, and the American Victory at Yorktown". AmericanRevolution.org, https://bit.ly/2OU6oaM, accessed 28 July 2018.

CHAPTER 18

HOW TO DEAL
WITH RISK

People who don't take risks generally make about two big mistakes a year. People who do take risks generally make about two big mistakes a year.

– Peter F. Drucker

Y ou cannot eliminate risk if you want to reach the top. Drucker realized early in life that to eliminate risk is futile. He took a risk by not immediately going to college after graduating from Döbling Gymnasium, what we in the US would call high school. Even his parents probably wanted him to enter college immediately afterwards. Instead, he took an apprenticeship with a cotton import–export firm in Hamburg, Germany. But this wasn't his last risk. He took a risk when he left the apprenticeship after a year and entered study for a doctorate in international law, a far cry from the cotton business. He took a risk when he left Germany for England in 1933. He took another risk when he left England for the United States in 1937. He took a risk when he accepted an academic appointment at Bennington College to teach not law, the subject of his PhD, but political science and philosophy. Of course, there was another risk when he committed himself to take the time to accomplish what apparently was a full-time social scientific analysis with General Motors for two years. And then he took a risk when he left Bennington to relocate to New York City to become a professor of management at New York University, yet another new discipline but at least this was somewhat aligned with his consulting work at General Electric though he had never taught management previously. He then took a risk again on leaving New York University and a full tenured professorship 20 years later to relocate 2,800 miles across the country to become a management professor at a small, little-known university, in California. He didn't have a job when he left New York. He was 62, which many consider retirement age today and many more did then, when he began work in California.[1]

THE GENERAL AND THE GENIUS

Drucker, like General James Doolittle, was a master of the calculated risk. Doolittle was a famous flyer who left the Army to join Shell Oil in their public relations department. But he then resigned and returned to the Air Corps when war threatened. Only four months after Pearl Harbor was bombed, he led the desperate raid on Japan as the head of 16 B-25 medium bombers taking off from the aircraft carrier *Hornet*, something that had never been accomplished by a heavy bomber-type aircraft even then having only enough fuel for a one-way trip to bomb Tokyo and other Japanese cities successfully before running out of fuel. He was a master of the calculated risk. So was Drucker. Drucker even defined progress in economics as the ability to take greater risks.[2] However, Drucker went one step further than General Doolittle. While Doolittle analysed the risks he took, Drucker studied risk as a concept and analysed it thoroughly.

DRUCKER'S FOUR CATEGORIES OF RISK

Drucker categorized risks into four types.[3] First, there is the risk you must accept because its built into the business or profession that you are engaged in. If you are a professional boxer or professional football player you risk bodily injury and those risks are considered routine. You must accept these associated risks because it's part of the activity.

The second and third categories consist of risks that you can afford to take and those you cannot afford to take. To lose money and effort in pursuit of an opportunity must always be a risk that you can afford to take. Of course, if you don't have the money and must borrow it and the amount is excessive, compared to your means, it may not be a risk that you can afford to take regardless of the attraction of the opportunity. In other words, it is a risk that you cannot afford to take. That's Drucker's third category.

Drucker's fourth category are risks that you cannot afford *not* to take. To lose money, time, and effort in pursuing an opportunity is a risk that you should always be willing to take. Of course, if the money or resources are more than you can lose and still survive, you cannot afford the opportunity. To put this in other terms, if General Doolittle (he was a lieutenant colonel at the time) could not have afforded to lose the 16 bombers for his one-way mission, the risk should not have been taken. In fact, 13 of the 16 aircraft were lost because they ran out of fuel, but this possibility was considered at the time the aircraft were launched and it was calculated that the impact of the successful completion of the mission on the war was worth this loss.

The one risk you cannot afford to take is the risk of being unable to exploit success. The initial investment needed is frequently misleading. A new business requires certain resources to reach initial success. Unfortunately, Drucker found that the initial success in acquisition of capital for a new venture is sufficient only if it fails completely. If it succeeds at all it will always require more money to take advantage of the opportunity of continuing its growth. To be unable to obtain this money when it is needed is a risk that you cannot afford to take.[4]

You can also find yourself in trouble by seeking an attractive opportunity, but outside your business. I remember a friend who owned a successful management recruitment firm. During a slow period his business saw a decline and he decided to shift resources into a multilevel marketing opportunity until things improved. He had been a successful headhunter for more than 20 years and he and his firm had built a strong reputation and image. It was true that his business had slowed down during this period. It was also true that he had the necessary qualifications to do well in the multilevel marketing opportunity. However, this other opportunity was well outside his normal business operations and he failed, fortunately without too much harm to his established business. This probably was another reason why a leading method of business portfolio analysis was eventually abandoned when it suggested that a firm's routine acquisition of other businesses was the way to success since it automatically enabled an increase in sales. It is probable that although the acquiring company had certain qualifications including financial resources that could be of assistance to the company acquired, it was an entirely different business and this caused problems later down the line and was one reason mere acquisition of other businesses frequently led to failure rather than success.

Unfortunately, it is not only resources that will eventually fall short after obtaining a certain initial level of success with a new venture, but knowledge and the market itself.

Moreover, there are risks that are fully acceptable in one industry, but not in others where they could be considered risks that you cannot afford to take. Drucker examined the pharmaceutical industry and used it as an example. The goal of pharmaceutical manufacturers is to develop drugs which can cure or alleviate disease. Yet it is not unusual to go through all the tests verifying the safety of these new drugs and still develop a product that is hazardous to use. This happens frequently, unfortunately.

The solution for taking the right risks is to think ahead and to do a thorough analysis. That's what the Doolittle raiders did when the decision was made to launch the raid even though it was known before launch that there was insufficient fuel to assure reaching their post-strike recovery bases in China.

I once witnessed top decision makers at a major aerospace company make the decision to commit huge economic and human resources to a product and business of which the company knew nothing. This was based on an almost offhand comment from a salesman present at the meeting. The salesman thought that there was a demand for such a product based on a recent trip to one of their government customers. Little additional serious investigation was planned. Much to my amazement under these circumstances there were a lot of announcements and a flurry of activity and assignments plus a great deal of money spent and other resources committed. Then eight months later after money was spent and resources wasted, the project was quietly abandoned. That's not the way to do it.

The basic concept that Drucker recognized is to think through what is the worst thing that can happen before committing to taking the risk. If you can recognize and accept this worst-case scenario and have completed the analysis this requires, you are ready to proceed despite the risks involved.

THERE IS ALWAYS FEAR IN ANY RISK

With the analysis of any new venture or new opportunity, there is not only risk, but possibly fear which may have little basis in fact, as until a full analysis is completed, we don't know all the facts or what is true or accurate and what is not. Tony Robbins says that FEAR should stand for "False Evidence Appearing Real". There is much truth in this, for usually the more we know and understand a situation, whether it has to do with a business opportunity or anything else, the less fearful we are about the engagement because there is less false evidence. So reducing the fear associated with any opportunity can be achieved by getting all the facts at an early part of the analysis.

AN ANALYSIS NEEDN'T
TAKE A LONG TIME

An acquaintance of mine by the name of Lou Lenart passed away in 2015. He was in his nineties. He was a Hungarian Jew and had left Hungary at the age of ten with his parents to escape the Nazis. As soon as he finished high school he volunteered for the Marine Corps when the US entered World War II. The Marine recruiting sergeant had looked at the skinny young kid with the Hungarian accent and said "The Marine Corps is a pretty tough outfit. And basic training isn't easy. Are you sure you can make it through basic training?" Lenart had immediately replied, "If you can make it, so can I." He did make it and immediately volunteered for flight training and became a Marine fighter pilot. He flew combat missions against the Japanese and finished the war as a captain.

Because of his war experience, Lenart was made a flight commander in the fledging Israeli Air Force. In 1948, seven Arab countries invaded Israel, and on 29 May 1948 an Egyptian armoured column was slowly approaching Tel Aviv. This is the story that Lenart told me and why he was invited to speak at Air War College in Montgomery, Alabama that year.

The only force that the Israelis had to oppose the Egyptian column were four surplus Messerschmidt 109 airframes flown in parts from Czechoslovakia. However, these were not the same as the famous German aircraft flown during World War II. It was the same ME-109 airframe, but the only engines available were underpowered and unreliable. The Czechs designated the plane the S-199 and it was all Israel had to defend their new country, so the Israelis were grateful for them. Four of these aircraft had been flown in from Czechoslovakia and reassembled in Israel, but they hadn't even been test-flown yet to see if they were safe to fly. Lenart was called to the Israeli Air Force Headquarters in Tel Aviv and asked to lead the flight of these four aircraft against the Egyptian column. Lenart agreed to do so but asked for a one-day delay in order to flight-test them before combat. He knew he was taking an additional risk flying them in combat without flight-testing them first. He was told that he couldn't even have a one-day delay to do this. The armoured column was too close. If he delayed one day, there might not be any Tel Aviv to defend by the next day. On the positive side attacking the enemy column immediately with un-flight-tested aircraft would be a complete surprise to the Egyptians as they had been told that the Jews had no aircraft. They would therefore be unexpected. The pay-off would be greater than the expenditure and the risk.

Lenart understood the risk that he and the three other pilots would be taking. They all agreed that it was worth it and took off immediately. Under these circumstances, just getting the four aircraft off the ground and into the air was an accomplishment. The risks that Lenart and the other three pilots faced in combat were not only loss of their lives, that was a normal risk of the activity they were engaged in. Nor was it the loss of the aircraft. The biggest risk was that they would not succeed in turning the Egyptian column, or at least stopping it from penetrating to the commercial and population centre of Tel Aviv. They could not destroy the enemy column – the four fighter planes were not armed with enough ordnance to do that, and they knew it. In any case, Lenart and his comrades did succeed in halting the Egyptian advance, proba-bly because of the considerable psychological effect that the air attack had on the Egyptians, who did not expect the Israelis to have combat aircraft. However, the attack was not without its price: one aircraft was lost, and its pilot killed. Another of the pilots was Ezer Weizman who 10 years later became Commander of the Israeli Air Force, after that Secretary of Defence and later yet, President of Israel.

Lenart's analysis of his risks didn't take long to determine what should be done and to take the appropriate risk based on the opportu-nity. He took the risk that needed to be taken. A review of his action reinforces an important central fact about risk taking. Risks should always be taken because of an opportunity that presents itself. Some-one with a life-threatening illness agrees to a risky operation because the operation can save his or her life and that is the only option. That is an opportunity for this individual as powerful as the opportunity presented to Lenart to save Tel Aviv from capture.

RISKS ARE BASED ON DEVELOPING OPPORTUNITIES

If there were no opportunities, there would be no risks. However, failing to take any action involves the greatest risk of all and one can see this in a host of human endeavours from personal life decisions, business decisions, or on the international stage and a country not taking actions because they are unpopular or undesirable. Once you start looking at reasons not to do anything considered risky, you will find them. Yet one good reason for taking a risk may outweigh many reasons for not doing so.

In assessing risks on your way to the top, you must decide what opportunities you want to pursue and what associated risks you are willing to accept and which you are not.

Drucker recommended:

- Focus on maximizing opportunities and not minimizing or eliminating risk
- Looking at major opportunities jointly not individually and in isolation
- Analysing whether an opportunity fits what you want to do
- Striking a balance between easier short-term improvement opportunities and longer range, more difficult ones.

In summary, you can't eliminate risk if you want to reach the top, but you can manage it and take the risks that are right and appropriate for the opportunities that are going to help you to reach success.

---

1. "Peter Drucker Biography". *The Famous People*, last updated 29 May 2017, https://bit.ly/2KCyqEg, accessed 27 July 2018.
2. Drucker, Peter F. *Management: Tasks, Responsibilities, Practices* (New York: Harper & Row, 1973, 1974), 512.
3. Drucker, Peter F. *Managing for Results* (New York: Harper and Row, 1964), 206.
4. Ibid., 207

CHAPTER 19

THE IMPORTANCE OF A POSITIVE ATTITUDE

Results are gained by exploiting opportunities, not by solving problems. Those who perform love what they are doing.

– Peter F. Drucker

Drucker was a management thinker who focused on the positive. He knew that in many situations the attitude of an individual can be more important than ability, resources, past success, or sometimes anything else. Moreover, he saw that those who loved what they were doing, did well. This can be extremely important for one's self-development and self-management, overcoming adversity, and success in anything that you do. This clearly implies that if you are not in a career or job that you enjoy, or you have come not to enjoy it, you should quit and do something else or do it elsewhere.

DRUCKER'S MANY CAREERS

Drucker left his ongoing careers several times. Some reasons for staying in his career, as well as for changing his career, were clear. He began with an apprenticeship in cotton trading because he was genuinely interested in working in this business at first, but he got a law degree at the University of Hamburg simultaneously probably to satisfy his parents' desires and he read extensively on many topics at the same time. The wide reading and exploration of other activities aroused his desire to eventually do research and become a professor. So he left the apprenticeship after a year while he had managed to get his law degree at night school. But he never practised law. Instead he went on to the University of Frankfurt and earned a PhD in international law because, as he told his own PhD students, "It was the easiest PhD to get", risking, I suppose, a mass exodus of his students who were overchallenged or underwhelmed with the field of management in which we were at the time labouring for our PhDs. He worked at the same time in journalism because he liked to write, but abandoned his goal of becoming a professor and researcher at the University of Cologne when Hitler came to power in Germany. Understanding perfectly the likely implications under Hitler's rule forced his decision to emigrate to England. This limited his own abilities to do research and to write immediately until he mastered the language.

Financial demands forced him into roles as an economist while working for a bank and an insurance company in which he may have had little interest: even Peter Drucker had to eat! Although he changed his strategy several times, he never abandoned his goal of becoming a professor, and he left England and immigrated to the US. He believed that there, in the US, he would have better opportunities for securing a teaching position than in the United Kingdom. Then in the US finally, the combinations of writing, temporary duty as a government employee, and an unexpected consulting opportunity landed him a professorship at New York University where in 1969 he was eventually awarded New York University's highest honour, its Presidential Citation[1] and he could indulge himself to think and write about what he called social ecology, a title, if not an entire field he invented which focuses on relationships between people and their environment. This was the umbrella profession Drucker defined as his life's work, whether he was teaching, writing, consulting, speaking, or doing something else. And he loved it.

DID DRUCKER GIVE UP ON CORPORATE MANAGERS?

Drucker loved it all, yet it was rumoured that for the last few decades of his life, he abandoned what he had devoted himself to ever since he had written *Concept of the Corporation* in 1946. Some said that this was because corporate managers had ignored his guidance, ethical and otherwise, and he had abandoned them to devote his genius to non-profits. I doubt that. The study of either profits or non-profits falls under the definition of social ecology. Further, one of his many insights into business was that great advances were possible by bringing ideas from one industry and adapting them to another. Long after he began his study of non-profits, he shared the insight that paid employees must be led and treated as if they were non-paid volunteers, as in a free society knowledge workers can always go elsewhere, and frequently do.

DO YOU HAVE A POSITIVE ATTITUDE?

We all get depressed from time to time, and have bad days as well as good ones, but how is your overall feeling of attitude, and how can you improve it if it is not as good as it might be? Abraham Lincoln said that,

"Most folks are about as happy as they make up their minds to be."[2] Yet Lincoln himself suffered from bouts of depression.

RESEARCH ON HAPPINESS: HOW TO INSTANTLY BECOME HAPPY

What President Lincoln said is not so far-fetched. Modern research in psychological methods and techniques have produced some amazing results. Norman Vincent Peale became world famous when he wrote the bestseller *The Power of Positive Thinking*. It stayed on the *New York Times* bestseller list for almost four years and to date has sold over five million copies. Basically, Peale's method was to stay positive in your beliefs for attainment of any goal in the face of adversity and to press on. It is hard to argue with the success idea. I've seen and experienced many ideas myself that seemed hopeless but succeeded, and it seems to me that while you may ultimately fail in some desired goal, you would most assuredly fail if you did not believe in your ultimate success. Legendary football Coach Vince Lombardi of Green Bay Packers expressed it this way: "We never lose, but sometimes the clock runs out on us."[3]

But can we become instantly happy on demand? Maybe we can, and it is possible that Drucker mastered this ability. Four years after Peale's book, Dr Hornell Hart at Duke University published his own, *Autoconditioning*.[4] Hart's basic methodology was a two-minute self-administered test which he called a "mood meter". You took the test, used some self-hypnosis techniques, and then took it again. It sounds a bit oversimplistic, but it worked. The self-hypnosis caused a notable improvement in mood. Your attitude can indeed change to help you reach success. And Drucker was all for that.

Those who want to try this can create a self-induction into hypnosis by simply relaxing the body completely by parts, focusing first on the hands and fingers and proceeding throughout the body concluding with the toes and feet. Once you are completely relaxed you concentrate on whatever you want whether it's happiness, pain control, or something else. When you are done with your session, you bring yourself to full awareness with a slow mental count from one to ten. I never discussed this technique with Drucker, although now I'm sorry I did not. I've since been amazed at the number of successful people who use this and similar methods, but they rarely reveal it publicly.

There have been hundreds of techniques introduced since Peale from neurolinguistics to fire-walking and Silva mind control. Drucker did not involve himself or recommend these to anyone directly. However, his actions demonstrated that he used specific techniques for development. Take his reading habits. As I explained earlier, his wife reported that he did not read management books. He scanned them. But he did read history. I believe that he used historical results from other fields to develop management theory to test and apply. In this way, he did reveal his theory that the greatest advances in any industry came from something practised first in an entirely different industry.

I was always particularly interested in what I call 'mind stuff'. That's where I came across the technique that one of my sons used to pass the exam which eventually got him into West Point and through their four-year programme successfully. In fact, I used similar techniques myself to get into West Point. You will need to explore these on your own. Different techniques work best for different people. My thinking is that if Drucker noticed a technique in his own self-development, he probably tried it. His personality seemed always upbeat and positive and when I asked my professors prior to taking the exams for my PhD what books to read or where I should concentrate my preparation, he alone told me: "Don't read or study anything additional. You are ready for the comprehensive exams right now." I followed his advice, although I continued to use various techniques for stress reduction.

Some years ago, during one of our reunions at West Point, I got into a discussion with perhaps my most celebrated, best-known and successful West Point classmate, Pete Dawkins, and described some of these techniques. Dawkins was a champion athlete, a football player who had won the national Heisman Trophy and who had earned letters in other sports as well. The Heisman is awarded annually to the single most outstanding player in college football in the US whose performance best exhibits not only excellence as a football player, but integrity as well. He was elected captain of the football team.

He was in the top 10% of our class academically. He was appointed 'first captain', the highest cadet rank attainable as a member of the Corps of Cadets. He was elected class president. He was a member of the West Point Glee Club. There were few honours that he didn't win. I discovered that he had used some of the techniques that I had learned later in life. This study led to many changes and innovations at West Point including the use of meditation for stress reduction and goal attainment and other techniques which I learned on my own over the years. It all depends on how you perceive things. Let me use myself as an example.

WHAT HAPPENED IN MY OWN LIFE

Drucker's comment about exploiting opportunities, giving more results than solving problems was meant to encourage us to be proactive rather than reactive. There are bad situations that arise in everyone's life that require solving problems and being proactive in doing so. Your personal attitude and reaction to these are of major importance as you continually progress in life. All of us encounter challenges and negative events in our lives, but critically it's not what has happened but rather how we react.

Not many know that Drucker encountered severe medical challenges towards the end of his life. Yet he never complained publicly except to once tell an interviewer that he was less focused in old age on hoping for a long life and more interested in an easy death. However, he was still productive and accomplished much despite the disabilities which he could not control.

My own challenge has been less severe, yet it has been a challenge. Almost two years ago I suffered a major stroke. It completely paralysed me on the left side of my body and took away my speech. This was a big issue for one depending on speaking for a living. I practised and although my speech returned within days, at first, I couldn't speak coherently. That took some weeks. I was laid out supine and at first could not move to sit up. I spent several weeks in a hospital in a rehab ward for stroke patients after paramedics took me from home to emergency. I was released from the hospital in a wheelchair. I could do almost nothing for myself. I slept little. With difficulty, I could walk about 15 feet with the walker and I was extremely proud the first time that I did although the 15 feet wore me out completely. For someone who had previously been very active physically, this was a substantial change. I had no stamina at all. My happiest event was when I left the hospital for home. Yes, I was in a wheelchair, but I could also use the walker to a very limited extent.

I was restricted to the first floor of our two-storey home and slept in a spare bedroom which was on the ground floor. I could bathe and use bathroom facilities only with the help of a caregiver. I had a special chair-like device fitting over the side of the bathtub which I could mount with assistance, and then the caregiver would wipe me with a cold, wet, washcloth with soap while with difficulty I manipulated a flexible shower head and showered. Somehow, my wife, Nurit, put up with the many challenges of a stroke victim while maintaining a full schedule and still going to work.

Our new life was not easy. Not only could I do little by myself, but even small medical events could have a big impact. For example, I fell from the walker and scraped my right elbow to the bone. It took almost two months to heal. I had a caregiver from 9am until 1.30pm five days a week. I was in plenty of pain but could take no effective painkillers. That's because of the medications I was already taking to prevent another stroke or a heart attack, so my blood was already thin enough. Even an aspirin made my blood too thin and could cause a major problem if I took it. I could sleep only for about four hours maximum before pain woke me up. Finally, I found that if I watched TV for several hours I might get tired enough to return to sleep for two or three more hours. According to reports on the internet, stroke survivors tended to be depressed and have a high suicide rate. That I could understand. Meanwhile my wife tried to keep things together and worked full-time as a clinical psychologist. To the best I could I tried to take care of myself, so she could sleep at nights.

I was determined to return to work. I had been president of an accredited MBA-granting graduate school. I now restarted the Institute of Leader Arts to conduct international training even before I could speak. Previously I had been in excellent health and prided myself on being stronger than almost anyone I knew. But despite my strength and apparent good health, I had had this major stroke. I don't know what caused it. I do know that both my physical condition and my positive attitude helped with my rehab.

My first big goal was to move back to the first floor where I had my office and could get back to a computer. I knew that I wouldn't be able to do much work, but I could still write. I had three speeches previously scheduled for Mexico City a month after the stroke. Of course, there was no way of making those, and I cancelled them and my flight. I had accepted another in China, in six months' time. I thought that I'd be able to make that one. I was wrong, and I had to cancel that one, too.

My long-range goal, of course, was to fully recover. I was told that a full recovery would probably not be possible and that I should be thankful that I was still alive, but in any case, my first goal was to simply get upstairs and to my computer.

I had a physical therapist twice a week when I got out of the hospital, for several weeks. First, I had to learn to get up out of the wheelchair by myself and get to my walker and to sit down in the wheelchair again afterwards. The therapist showed me how to do this and some exercises to learn how to stand up from the wheelchair and engage the walker. On the days that she didn't come I exercised with the walker on my own with the help of my caregiver an hour a day. After several weeks, I regained enough upper body and leg strength to get upstairs by putting both arms and pulling on the single banister we had as I went up, or eased myself down with both arms on the banister when I went downstairs. I needed a safety belt with someone holding on in case I should fall. My physical therapist at the time was amazed at my ability to do this. She told me that she wouldn't have believed it possible so soon. I knew that you can generally do much more than you think you can and I felt that I was a lot better off than a lot of our wounded troops from Afghanistan or Iraq. After all, I had 'only' a stroke

Falling is one of the major dangers of stroke victims. I have fallen many times, but fortunately only once on the stairs and though sometimes bloodied, I have never broken anything. I have been lucky. I exercised every day strengthening my legs and arms. After some time,

I could use a wide-based cane instead of the walker. The cane had about a 12-inch base, but even walking with that wide-based cane was difficult at first.

Then, I decided I could take a shower by myself in a shower stall using the cane which was nickel-plated and drying it after drying myself. The shower stall was small enough that there was no place to fall, and my caregiver stood outside the shower in case I did fall. Fortunately for me, I never did. Anyway, I got away from that chilly water that my caregiver used to soap me down with.

When I first started working on the computer, I only had the energy to write for about half an hour a day and I learned to build this up over time. In addition, I had a daily workout of about an hour and started going out to restaurants in the evening with my wife acting as caregiver. This helped my morale and we progressed from wheelchair to walker to wide-based cane to regular cane and eventually today, walking without any support from a cane at all.

What kind of work did I do at the computer? First was my writing. I had two projects in mind, one is the book you have in your hands. I had used many of Drucker's techniques that he had taught me regarding his own self-development and which he had used to reach the pinnacle of his management-thinking career. I thought that he would appreciate the fact that his ideas were still helping others.

I knew that he kept busy with useful work even when he was in his nineties and ill with the ailments of age. To deal with the depression and hopelessness that tends to go with strokes, I got busy with my own work as soon as I could. I developed a book proposal and had several of my publishers read it until my editors at LID and I agreed that they, who had previously published my book *Peter Drucker on Consulting*,[5] were the best suited to publishing this new book. I am also a syndicated columnist with seven publications, print and online, for a monthly column on Drucker's ideas which reach an audience of 1,000,000 readers a month in four countries. I had written several months' worth of material in advance, so I didn't miss a single column despite the stroke. The techniques used were the same I've talked about in this book.

In addition to my writing, I disconnected the Institute of Leader Arts from the California Institute of Advanced Management (CIAM), the graduate school of which I had been president and CEO. With two associates both now in Northern California, I planned to introduce new concepts of international training and consulting when my rehab was more complete. And this was happening fast.

During this time, with a lot of hard work one day, miracle upon miracle, I managed to walk for several steps without the cane. I looked like a version of Dr Frankenstein's monster. But I walked! I considered this a major victory at the time. It was great for my morale.

My next goal was to make a live presentation. I learned how to drive again, and I created a one-hour presentation and gave it to an audience of students and faculty from CIAM at the invitation of the current president, Jennie Ta. I was worried that I might get tired standing for an hour and asked for a chair. However, I presented on my feet for an hour and I felt I could have continued if it was necessary. The presentation that I created and gave was entitled "Innovate or Evaporate" and it went over well, and I have now added it to my training repertoire. I also said a few words as guest of a national Korean military veterans group, with about 500 in attendance in Los Angeles at their first annual meeting.

My friends and associates consider me a miracle. My caregiver, who had several previous stroke patients told me that I was different. Her previous stroke patients were partially paralysed but had not made the progress that I had. Though physical therapists tried to work with them they did no additional exercise when the therapist wasn't present. They never thought about returning to any type of work. They apparently accepted their condition as a sentence and that was that.

What did I do differently? I had a different perception and attitude. I set successive goals and continually worked towards achieving them because I had an intense desire and intent to reach my goals. My attitude was different. I hope yours will be when you encounter adversity as well.

They say that an advice-giver should 'walk his talk'. I think that I have done this. How am I doing now you may ask? I have not yet fully recovered. But I am still progressing and getting stronger every day. I work out with weights several days a week. I have not fully recovered my strength and stamina, but my body looks almost the same as before the stroke. Some call me a miracle or an inspiration. I know others that have overcome far more difficult challenges and they are my inspiration.

Recently I had the opportunity to interview for another job as a university president of a much larger accredited school than I had run previously. I decided not to interview, not because I couldn't do the job, but because I was so busy with my other activities that I didn't feel that I had the time.

Everyone recovers at a different rate. I know that I am very lucky, and many people have helped me. However, I've been told that attitude has played a vital role in my case. I was 79 years old when I had the stroke, so age is no excuse not to rehab and continue with your life.

In any case, I have recovered enough to work at almost the same level as before the stroke in both my professional speaking and writing. No, that isn't accurate. I think that I can work at a higher level now. I can only add that if you will adopt Drucker's techniques and maintain a positive attitude you will be amazed at what you can do.

WAYS OF CREATING PERSONAL ATTITUDE CHANGE NOT RECOMMENDED

There are other methods of creating personal attitude change. Drucker neither used nor recommended them. I don't recommend them either. Some are just too temporary or actually can cause harm. Others are addictive and may even be self-destructive. For example, what's wrong with acquisition of things? Feel bad? Buy yourself a piece of expensive jewellery or a new car. Or eat chocolate. Will you feel better? Absolutely. But how long will this good feeling last? Not long. It's very fleeting. Some attempt to change attitude by the acquisition of wealth itself. But this seems to require more and more wealth to maintain the desired change. In addition to leading to the destruction of personal relationships, it frequently leads to poor personal or business decisions.

Drucker avoided these traps by adherence to a personal code. His personal code of ethics was based on thorough investigations followed by analysis and rigid adherence.

This was easy to see in Drucker's personal life. Drucker was wealthy, but he did not attempt to make a public display of it or make the mere accumulation of wealth a life goal. He lived in a modest home in a regular neighbourhood. He did not wear expensive jewellery or thousand-dollar suits. He did not drive an overly expensive car. He did not seek the lifestyle of the rich and famous. His power came from who he was, and though he had accumulated wealth, he did not display it unnecessarily. He was straightforward and honest with all who knew him, including his students.

MAINTAINING YOUR PERSONAL POSITIVE ATTITUDE

Like much else, your personal attitude, once achieved, is addictive. Once you have an image of yourself, you will automatically and routinely attempt to live up to it. If your self-image is one of personal courage, physical or intellectual, or both, you will always attempt to live up to it and it will be much harder to violate these feelings. Moreover, others that you associate with, as well as those that may have contact with you more distantly, will easily recognize your attitude and will recognize and respect you accordingly. It will greatly assist you in continuing your self-development and in reaching your goals in life. This is an important fact which is true of organizations that you may work in and have a rising level of responsibility for as well.

ATTITUDE CAN BE PRIMARY

In watching the 2018 Winter Olympics in South Korea, both what the athletes accomplish and their attitudes as revealed during pre- and post-performance interviews, I cannot escape the conclusion that ability, performance, and other important factors are still significantly affected by personal attitude. As Drucker demonstrated, these are all very much under our control and very important as we seek to reach our goals, whether recovering from a stroke or during our way to the top.

> **THE MOST IMPORTANT BEHAVIOURS DRUCKER USED TO REACH THE TOP:**
> - Personal values and integrity
> - Unrelenting innovation
> - Goal setting
> - Professional competency
> - Commitment
> - Self-confidence
> - Planning
> - Risk management.

No one is going to live forever, and despite my success in meeting my own challenges to date, I – or any of us – can still get hit by a truck unexpectedly or could have a setback. There are no guarantees. But as I write these words and were this to happen, consider, would I have been better off giving up a year and not taking action despite my challenges? I think not. That was Drucker's way to the top and it has been mine as well. I hope that it will be yours, too.

1. Drucker, Peter F. *Management: Tasks, Responsibilities, Practices* (New York: Harper & Row, 1973), 325.
2. Lincoln, Abraham. *Brainy Quotes*, https://bit.ly/2APdqdQ, accessed 28 July 2018.
3. Lombardi, Michael, "New Orleans Saints Never Stood a Chance Without Sean Payton". *NFL Front Office View*, November 30, 2012, https://bit.ly/2AVgNjE, accessed 28 July 2018.
4. Hart, Hornell. *Autoconditioning: The New Way to a Successful Life* (Englewood Cliffs, NJ: Prentice-Hall, 1956).
5. Cohen, William A. *Peter Drucker on Consulting: How to Apply Drucker's Principles for Business Success* (London: LID Publishing, 2016).

INDEX

AN INTRODUCTION TO WILLIAM A. COHEN

Dr William A. Cohen was the first graduate of the doctoral programme that Peter Drucker co-founded. What Drucker taught him changed his life. Shortly after graduating, Cohen was recommissioned in the Air Force and rose to the rank of major general. Eventually he became a full professor, management consultant, and the author of more than 50 books, while maintaining a nearly lifelong friendship with his former professor. In 2009 he was named a Distinguished Alumnus by Drucker's school, Claremont Graduate University, and two years later he co-founded the non-profit California Institute of Advanced Management with the mission of offering affordable graduate degrees based on Drucker's principles. He served as its president from 2010-2016. He now serves as president of the Institute of Leader Arts, an international training and consulting company.

He can be reached at **wcohen@stuffofheroes.com**.